WHAT OTHERS A

JOY

I just finished reading *JoyRide—Life, Death and Forgiveness* by Pamela Koefoed. As the scenes portrayed in the book flow back over me, my heart is stirred to a greater level of hope. I feel I have witnessed the victorious power of love, and the overcoming resilience of the human spirit. This story of triumph over unimaginable difficulty is made all the more poignant by the awareness that it is true.

Lewis Crownover, Oregon, founder of Sound of the Harvest
www.soundoftheharvest.com

A true story about the amazing power of the will to overcome any obstacle and the power of love that sustained two sisters who refused to be overcome with discouragement and hopelessness. You will not want to put this book down until you have finished it. You will come away with the knowledge that you are never alone no matter how big the trial is that you are going through. An exciting read.

RitaAnne Poorman, Arizona
Minister and author of *Prayers from the Proverbs*

How did this young girl escape the relentless onslaught of neglect, abuse, betrayal, and emotional assault, and emerge gloriously to fulfill the purposes for her life? Want hope for a seemingly impossible situation? Read this incredible story. I will recommend it to friends and to clients in my counseling practice.

Joni Zepp, Colorado, MA, RN, LPC
Spiritual director, jonizepp.com

As a general education and special education teacher for 39 years, I have often dealt with children like the two girls in the story. Pamela's captivating story is told from the perspective of a child who must live with the repercussions of an addicted parent. This book holds your attention and often holds your heart.

Dianne Harrison, California, BS Child Development, MA Education
Reading Specialist and board of directors Spirit Driven Band Ministries

What a "ride"—This is a beautiful story of triumph over tragedy; beauty from the ashes. The love and resilience of a child is remarkable. Joy is possible even in the most difficult circumstances. *JoyRide* will touch your heart as it did mine.

Donna Newcombe, Oregon, Pastor

This book entirely captured my heart. Pamela's descriptive writing paints the heartache, fears and also extreme loyalty she possessed at such a young age. In this personal memoir, you will see clearly the value of keeping a soft heart, being strong when necessary and always forgiving.

Lisa Ambrose, Canada
Housewife and mom

Love, love, loved it! JoyRide is a captivating journey of unconditional love, forgiveness, and the profound power of prayer and Jesus in our lives. Joyride is inspirational, honest, thought-provoking. I couldn't put it down. A fill-your-heart-with-joy read that should not be missed. Read it and believe!

Stephen and Kris Brey, Washington
Retired, Environmental Remediation at Hanford Site

JoyRide is a powerful testimony of three children who beat life's odds. With shattered lives of trauma, abandonment and abuse, they could have taken a similar path of destruction. Pamela's life expresses the humble dependence and trust, the unwavering love and forgiving spirit of a little child.

JoAnne Meckstroth, Alaska
Founder of Women of Impact Ministries

JoyRide is Pamela Koefoed's journey. It proves that anyone with a tragic past can see God's great love overcome and always win. I was touched and moved by Pamela's story of grace and joy, and I know you will be as well. It is a privilege to endorse Pamela's work.

Daniel Black, California
Love Fest Global

In this captivating narrative, Pamela Koefoed will touch your heart as she takes you with her on her incredible journey through a most difficult childhood. You will cry with her, as I did, as she shares her well-remembered thoughts and emotions, and rejoice with her in the mercy of God as He rescues her out of seemingly impossible circumstances.

Ben R Peters, Chicago, author
Founder of Kingdom Sending Center and Open Heart Ministries

JOY Ride

LIFE, DEATH & FORGIVENESS

A MEMOIR

PAMELA KOEFOED

JOY*Ride*

Life, Death and Forgiveness
by Pamela Koefoed

www.joyridebook.com

Copyright © 2013 by Pamela Koefoed

All rights reserved.

Page layout by Lee Pierce and cover design by Steve Fryer.

Published by GoldenTree Press
P.O. Box 728, Lakeview, Oregon 97630
Email: Info@joyridebook.com

PROLOGUE

I've often contemplated the final day of my parents' married life and envisioned my father's climactic departure. In my mind, I see his downcast, tear-streaked face. Early one morning, moments before the sun rises, he bends his small frame over a maple wood crib, tenderly kisses my sister, Robin, pausing to look at her one last time. He wipes tears from his eyes and quietly steps across the dimly lit room to a white wicker bassinet in a corner where I lay. He lightly strokes my cheek, kisses the top of my nearly bald head and walks out the door.

He stands outside the apartment with his heart and hopes drowned in a deep-seated grief which only those who have lost their entire family can understand. One last time, he notes the cheap, brass colored "57" attached to the door of the apartment where two years earlier he and my mother welcomed Robin and then me into their lives.

In my mind's eye, I picture Dad hesitating on the apartment balcony torn between emotions of despair and his rational thoughts. *What will become of my daughters?* A foreboding gloom hovers overhead. He mistakes it for his own sorrow. *They'll all be better off without me.* He shakes his head to no one but himself. *I'll spare my girls the ordeal of being caught between two parents and two homes.* With one trembling hand, he wipes tears from his face and rushes down the staircase to his car.

The early August sun has just peeked through the Sacramento city skyline as my dad hurries from the home he and my mother had made for us. Then he simply vanishes from our lives.

CHAPTER ONE

*I*t was always the same: Beauty before breakfast. Dark red smeared over her pale lips, black on her unblinking lashes, a brush loaded with pink powder to her high cheekbones. Then came the back combing of her caramel blond hair into a classic beehive, followed by a misting of Aqua Net and the gluing down of every possible stray to her bumped up "doo." It was 1967, the era when the modern woman selected light, nearly neutral tones of lipstick, but not my mother, she chose deep red, a sign of glamour and sophistication.

Robin and I stood beside her that April morning, peeking up at her like two curious kittens. Robin was four and a half years old and I had just turned three. Mother examined her reflection in the bathroom mirror, tilting her head from side to side, pursing her lips, then smiling. "Hm...not too shabby," she said, in a voice as sunny as the day. She dotted a fake, black eyeliner mole on her right cheek and chuckled. "Just like Marilyn Monroe." She nodded her approval. Then lowering her head, she met our inquisitive stares, and smiled. "Well, girls, there's one thing I'm darned sure of, we may not have much money, but we can look like the upper class." She returned to her reflection in the mirror. "I'm just about done. Bet you're hungry, huh? What sounds good to you? Scrambled eggs? French toast?"

There was a knock at the front door.

"I'll have to get that in a second." Mother grabbed a bottle of perfume and spritzed herself with Jean Nate After Bath Splash. The room filled with a delicious lemon drop fragrance. Someone knocked again. Mother poked her head out into the hall and hollered, "Be right there!" She hastily checked her makeup, dabbing the corners of her lips with a Kleenex, and dropped the tissue in the basket beside the toilet. "Wonder who that could be," she said, pushing past us, her heels clicking on the wood floor.

In addition to the single bathroom, our cozy duplex had a small living room/dining combination, a tiny kitchen and two bedrooms. Out the back door was an unenclosed field of grass that stretched far in the distance to a busy two-lane street, and off the front porch, our green lawn met up with a grove of tall eucalyptus trees.

"Hey, come on. Let's go see who it is," Robin said, scurrying after our mother. I padded down the short hall and stood beside her in the living room as Mother opened the front door.

"Good morning ma'am," said a young policeman wearing black pants, cap, and jacket. "Your neighbor called the station and complained of a strange smell and said his eyes and throat stung. Another officer answered the call and found an open canister of chlorine gas back there," he said, pointing to the large field outside our back door. "Right behind your place."

I wondered what he meant by a "strange smell" and "chlorine gas" and gaped at my sister. Robin glanced at me, her eyes wide and curious. She shrugged her shoulders, smirked, then tilted her head back, and smelled the air. I had no idea chlorine gas could damage our lungs or that a long enough exposure to it could kill a person. Since Robin wasn't worried, I wouldn't worry either. And since she was playing, I'd play, too.

Robin sniffed for odors and I went right along with her, titling my head back and sniffing the air. We made snuffling sounds, eyed one another humorously, and kept up the silliness. In mid-snuffle, Robin stopped for a second and faced me. "I don't smell a thing," she said before resuming the game. I giggled. "I don't smell a thing," I said, mimicking her. I threw a hand over my mouth, stifling my giggles, and made louder sniffing noises, beginning to sound like little snorts, which made my sister and me laugh even more.

"Have you seen anyone back there?" The policeman asked Mother.

"No, officer, I haven't."

He craned his neck around Mother, scanning the room, and grinned at Robin and me playing our smelling game.

"Anything else?" Mother said.

He cleared his throat. "Well, ma'am, your neighborhood here's been evacuated. You'll need to leave for the day."

"Thank you for the warning," Mother said, her voice calm and even.

"The evacuation's immediate."

"Yes, I know. Have a good day, officer," she said, shutting the door.

She whizzed past us, grabbed clothes from our dressers, and a few personal items from the bathroom, including toothbrushes and her makeup.

A short while later, the chlorine vapors reached inside our duplex and made their way to where Robin and I sniffed for smells, and then came the burning. We blinked and rubbed our stinging, watering eyes, pushing the palms of our hands against them.

Mother worked fast. Within minutes of the policeman's visit, she came into the living room holding a travel bag in one hand and washcloths in the other. "Girls, I'm about ready to leave." She dropped her bag near the front door. "Feels like an onion's been peeled." Her heels tapped a rapid beat across the floor on her way to us with washcloths. "Here, press these against your eyes," she said, handing Robin and me the wet cloths, and pressing one over her own watering eyes. "That's better. Let's go see your grandparents."

Leaving our home as we did, urgent and hurried, it all seemed like a fun extension of the sniffing game. I had never feared anything and this emergency didn't scare me. In order to see our way to the car, we alternated our wet washcloths from one eye to the other as we tramped out into the open air. A breeze blew against my face, chilling my damp skin. Mother turned toward us, a washcloth covering the bottom half of her face. "Girls, put them over your nose and mouths," she said and rushed to the car.

Robin and I scurried after her. If there had been passers-by, no doubt they'd have thought us odd—Mother in a powder blue, knee length skirt, knit top, and 2" pumps, and my sister and me in pajamas, with shoeless feet, and unruly hair, nearly running across the walkway to the car, our round, dark eyes peering through the little area above the washcloths.

Mother opened the door of her 1967 red Impala, a gift from her father, and Robin and I bounded into it. She cranked the ignition, revved the engine and backed out of the drive-way. The short road, ending at our place, had two other du-plexes, exactly like our own, and just like us, they also had evacuated their residences. We turned onto a busy two-lane street and I bounced along on my knees with the speeding motion of the car.

We went around the block and Mother slowed her car along the street intersecting with the bottom half of the field behind our duplex. She brought it nearly to a complete stop, coasted along and stared off in the distance at two sheriffs striding across the field, their heads pointed down and eyes searching the windswept grass.

"Girls, I don't know anyone who would put chlorine gas in our field," Mother said. "Maybe it was just a prank. It doesn't make any sense that someone would deliberately try and hurt us."

Uh-oh, I thought.

After we eased past them, Mother white-knuckled the steering wheel, throttled her red car and from there drove madly to our grandparents' home.

The game I had been playing with Robin was over. My eyes and throat still stung. *Why would someone try to hurt us?*

CHAPTER TWO

everal days after the evacuation, Robin knelt on her knees next to me on the soft dirt beside our imaginary lake, near a grove of eucalyptus that grew along our front yard. It was a busy water puddle with plastic boats no bigger than my hand floating on its surface.

A steady breeze blew and the overcast sky splatted a few raindrops around us. We fought against the forces of nature trying to blow over our boats. Robin repositioned her toy in the water. "This way, Pam," she said. "Point yours so the wind can't blow it over."

"Looks like you're having fun," Mother called cheerfully to us from the porch. She put her hands on her hips. "I'm going next door for a few moments. Robin, keep a watchful eye on your sister."

Robin didn't hesitate. "Okay, Mommy, I will," she said. This confidence came from having already babysat me on other occasions, such as whenever Mother ran to the store for a few groceries or visited with the neighbors.

"If you need me, I'll be at John and Sally's," she said, pointing at the duplex next door. "I'll be back in a little bit. Stay in the yard."

John and Sally were what Mother called "good people." They smiled a lot, practically every time I saw them. There were, however, also individuals Mother referred to as "bad people."

Mother's father, known as Poppy, owned a bar called The Green Parrot. Robin and I were babies when Mother began taking us there. Once, while my sister and I sat at a picnic table about seven feet from the "adult only" area, a bad person entered the bar—a scraggly dark haired man, wearing jeans and a t-shirt. He sat near Mother and said something to her about having a good time. "I bet you're real good," he said, smiling a toothless grin. Mother gulped the last of her beer, and left sooner than she had planned. On our way home, she turned to Robin and me seated beside her. She lowered her voice and spoke in a near whisper. "That was a bad man."

"Why was he bad?" Robin said.

Mother crinkled her nose and pursed her lips. She spoke as if she had something distasteful in her mouth. "He's a creep."

I understood that there were good people. They smiled and I liked smiles. Then there were creeps. I didn't like creeps. They were bad.

As my sister and I played with our boats on our pretend lake, the sprinkles turned to a light rain, but the weather wouldn't keep Mother from visiting the neighbors or leaving Robin and me outside in it. She had let us play in much worse weather, in downpours with lightning, and in ferocious wind that tousled my long hair wildly about my face. She said she loved a good storm and a little rain wouldn't hurt anything but a flea, and since we weren't fleas, we'd be fine.

One evening that spring, Mother answered a strange phone call. "Hello. This is Joy." A second later, she thrust down the receiver. "What a creep!" At least once a day for weeks, Mother had phone calls like that.

Mother's parents Nana and Poppy lived ten minutes from us in a newly built home. Since infancy, Nana had babysat Robin and me at their house each weekday while Mother worked part time for the phone company, filing, operating a Dictaphone, answering phones, and typing.

My grandparents' house was no fun at all. It had planters all around the front filled with giant, prickly cacti and white pebbles, and a backyard with more of the same. There weren't any cool trees or low places where water collected. And when we stayed with them, we could only play outside with adult supervision, and never in the rain.

To celebrate the New Year, Mother, Robin, and I enjoyed dinner at Nana and Poppy's. The menu included ham, gratin potatoes made with cheddar cheese and diced onion, peas, green salad tossed with Italian dressing, and buttered rolls. Nana had also prepared a celery tray with dip, and my favorite vegetable, green olives with red pimento centers.

Mother wiped her chin with a cloth napkin, placed it in her lap, and leaned toward Poppy who was seated at her left. "Daddy, I'm still getting those calls," she said, her voice low and tense. Her forehead creased with worry. "I guess I'll have to change my number."

Poppy cut a piece from the slice of ham on his plate. He bit into it, chewed, and spoke with his mouth half full. "Any idea who it is?"

"Not a clue." Mother gripped a glass of ice water. "Daddy, he's following me."

"Huh." Poppy's face looked grave. "That's a bad one."

I sat on a plastic booster seat at the table and stared at the detestable peas on my plate and considered Mother's words. I hadn't known being followed wasn't good. Sometimes, I trailed Robin around our duplex and in the yard. Was this bad?

Nana, sitting across the table from Poppy, reached a hand toward Mother. "Joy, pass the rolls, please."

"Would you like anything else?" Mother said, handing her the basket covered with a linen hand towel. "Some more salad?"

"This'll do. Thank you." She took a buttered roll from the basket. "About that fellow, he follows you?"

Mother nodded.

"Do you know for sure he does?"

Mother put an elbow on the table and rested her chin against the back of her hand. "That's what he said."

Nana shook her head. "Why even bother listening to him? He's not worth two seconds of your time. When you hear his voice, just hang up."

"I can't. Uncle Bud's trying to trace the call."

Uncle Bud was a special agent with the FBI and had nabbed the notorious ringleader of a murderous criminal gang on America's Most Wanted List. This made him famous. Well, at least in our family. All his close relations venerated him like he was the president of the United States.

"That prank caller's only trying to frighten you, dear," Nana said.

"Well, he's doing a pretty darn good job of it. That creep called last week right when I walked in the door from work. Oh!" She grit her teeth. "He makes me furious. Said he followed me from the phone company." Mother shuddered. "How does he know where I work?" Her eyes narrowed. "Now, I keep searching for him on my way to the phone company, and watching the rearview mirror on my way home. Of course, I don't know what *he* looks like." She gestured with her hands and snorted. "Geez. I'm getting paranoid."

Poppy shook his head. "Tis bad, real bad."

Mother tapped her slender index finger against her temple. "Any guy alone in a car behind mine is suspect." She lifted her chin and looked indignant. "Well, he better watch out. He doesn't know who he's messing with," she said, raising her glass of ice water to Poppy, the pinky of her hand dangling. "I'm my father's daughter and Bud's niece."

Poppy's cheeks flushed red. "Now, now, me daughter's embarrassing me."

Mother chuckled. "Daddy, when you and Bud get ahold of him, he'll be sorry."

Nana's eyes darted from Poppy to Mother. "Well, Bud can run his investigation. But you'd better park close to the entrance at work." Her voice rose. "And for goodness sakes, Joy, lock your doors!"

"I know!" Mother said, rolling her eyes. "I am!"

I tensed at the sound of Mother's irritation and hoped she wasn't mad.

Nana pursed her lips. "Joy Lynn, I didn't mean to upset you. I just worry some."

Several minutes later, while we ate homemade pumpkin pie, Poppy questioned Mother about the "creep." He spoke in low tones, used half words, and incomplete sentences. "The bad caller. The chlorine canister. What does Bud think? Could be the same guy."

"I'm not sure," Mother said. "But I'm darned sure of one thing." She held a piece of dessert on her fork and slid it in her mouth. "This pie's delicious." Then she turned serious again and shuddered. "Geez, Daddy, the things he says he'll do to me. At first when he called he just breathed into the phone and I thought it was a prank, but lately he uses vulgarity and threatens rape. It's giving me..." Suddenly, she stopped and eyed Robin and me listening intently to the conversation. "I've said too much, already."

CHAPTER THREE

A short while later, one Saturday morning, Poppy and Uncle Bud came to our home with a load of empty boxes. As was told to me, the police never learned who put the canister of chlorine gas in our field, and Uncle Bud's investigation failed to produce the stalker. Fearing for Mother's safety, he advised her to move in with her parents.

All day, they packed every item in our possession and hauled the boxes to Nana and Poppy's garage. I'm certain they did so as covertly as possible, scanning the streets of Sacramento as they went, on the lookout for a suspicious looking man.

I was sad. We had left the home I loved more than any other place and I moped around my grandparents' home for days. "Pammy, look," Mother said one evening before bed. "I'm not thrilled about having to leave the duplex either, and living at Poppy's isn't my top choice, but it's only temporary. Besides, everything happens for a reason."

The less obvious reason for my unhappiness had to do with our sleeping arrangements. My strong-willed, German Nana split up Robin and me. As soon as we arrived, she directed Robin to the room where she and I had napped on many occasions. And then she led me by the hand across the hall. "You'll sleep here," she said, pulling me into the second spare room.

I glanced at a crib against one wall and a pile of toys against the other, and threw down my bottom lip at the whole lousy idea—the room, the crib, sleeping without my sister. "Can't I sleep with Robin?"

Nana shook her head. "You'll be fine right here. You're a big girl."

I was almost four and had never slept without my sister. And a big girl? I knew that big girls didn't sleep in cribs. Tears trickled down my face. I sure didn't feel very big. In fact, from my perspective everyone in our household towered above me, made all the decisions, and I obviously had no rights. I folded my arms and planted my feet. "Please, Nana?"

"Pammie." A concerned look appeared in her dark eyes. "I don't want you leaving the house and getting hit by a car." She went to the crib and lowered the sidebar. "Here. Let me help you in."

"But I won't go outside."

Nana scooped me up, still with my arms folded—I weighed no more than forty pounds—and placed me inside the bed for babies. "I'll feel much better knowing you are here." She pulled the blankets up to my chin and bent over me. "Ready to say your prayers?"

"No."

"No?" Her eyes widened. "Don't tell me no." She stroked my head, brushing my bangs from my eyes. "Fold your hands."

I kept them under the blankets.

She frowned at me. "You're so stubborn. Why don't you say your prayers with your grandmother?"

"I want my sister."

Her eyes softened and she placed a cool hand against my warm cheek. "You'll see her in the morning. This time I'll pray."

Now I lay me down to sleep.
I pray the Lord Thy child to keep.
If I should die before I wake,
I pray the Lord Thy soul to take.
Amen.

"Maybe tomorrow night, you'll pray with me." There was displeasure in her voice.

I loved Nana and didn't mean to disappoint her.

"You'll stay put until your mother or I come for you," Nana said while tucking the blankets under the mattress. "Sleep well," she said, flicking off the light switch on the wall near the door and leaving the room.

Really? A crib could keep me in my room? Not much chance of that. In the morning, as the first rays of light filtered in through the solitary window beside me, I waited all of fifteen minutes for Mother or Nana to come for me before pulling myself to the top of the guard rail, throwing one leg over the side, and breaking out of jail. "I'm not a baby," I mumbled on the way from my bedroom to Robin's room across the hall.

Nana didn't only worry about me being hit by a car. She had delusional fears of someone kidnapping Robin and me. In those days, entrepreneurs went throughout the neighborhood selling encyclopedias, dishware, and insurance, and Nana eyed them all with suspicion and distrust.

"The news said some bad men have disguised themselves as door to door salesmen. They're going around neighborhoods stealing little children," Nana warned. This disclosure and her intense stare and eyebrows scrunched together frightened me. "They snatch them up right from their homes and their parents never see them again."

The benign world in which I lived no longer seemed safe. Later, when Robin and I were alone in her room, I told her I didn't like the way Nana treated me.

"Someone could steal us?" I said.

Robin's eyes grew wide. "If someone knocks at the door, I'm never answering it."

We had been living with Nana and Poppy for a few months when, while Nana drank beer and watched her favorite soap opera on a small television in the kitchen, sometime after lunch, our doorbell rang. She peeked through the yellow and white checkered kitchen curtain. "Girls! Quick! Come here!"

My sister and I went to Nana and stared up at her peering through the kitchen curtain. "There's a salesman at the door."

Oh, no ... It's a bad person, a creep. My heart was in my throat. I'm certain my eyes were wide with fear. "What'll we do?" I said.

"I'll not let him in and I won't answer the door until you're both out of sight." Nana motioned down the hall toward our rooms. "Go hide and don't come out until I say so."

Robin and I bolted down the hall, hid in her closet, and waited several minutes until Nana retrieved us.

Then there was the ice cream man. Nana made me believe he used his playful music to lure little children to his van so he could kidnap them, of course. Thanks to Nana, that first year living with her, all my fearlessness disappeared and I became afraid of the people she warned us about, strangers who sold things from house to house and ice cream men who rode around with their alluring music.

Summer arrived with the heat and with it came Nana's unpleasant mood. From across the room, I studied her stern face, devoid of any warmth. "Play a game of Hide-and-Seek with your grandmother," she said without a trace of joy. "You hide. I'll count to ten and find you."

Nana had never played this sort of game with Robin and me. Sometimes, she would flutter her eyelashes at us, purr, and tell us she was a butterfly. We'd try fluttering our eyelashes, too, while making the sound of a butterfly's wings flapping, and we'd all laugh.

Nana's frown lines around her mouth deepened. "Don't you like Hide-and-Seek? You've played it before, haven't you?"

"Sure we have," Robin answered.

"Well, then, what *are* you waiting for?"

Mother wasn't home much. She worked a nine to five shift and dated the men who called on her. By default, Nana did everything a mother should do for her children. She washed our hair and rinsed it with a can of cold beer, right from the refrigerator. She cooked meals, did all the laundry, and sewed beautiful dresses for Robin and me. But play games? Never.

That's weird. Why does Nana want to play? And why is she mad? For a couple seconds, I tried catching Robin's eye, hoping she would speak up and convince our grandmother to let us do something else.

"I really don't—" Robin began to say in protest.

Nana leaned forward on the sofa and picked up a glass of Ripple, a cheap wine, and sipped it. She held it in one hand and waved us away with the other. "Just don't stand there. Get going."

Robin padded down the hall with me in tow. "Do you wanna play with Nana?" she whispered outside her bedroom.

"No, but we have to," I said.

"She's counting. Pam, hurry. Go hide in your room. I'll hide in mine."

I crossed the hall to my bedroom and searched for a hiding place. From the living room, Nana hollered. "Ready or not, here I come!" Scrambling for the closet, I hid inside it with the door left open. The back of my head brushed against the clothes suspended from hangers and my legs pressed against a box of Nana's shoes.

Several minutes later, I heard Nana coming up the hallway. "Pam?" she called from right outside my bedroom door. "Are you in here?" I peered at her from within the closet, anticipating the moment she'd find me and call out, "Found you!"

She entered my room and headed straight for me, stopped four feet from where I hid, and stretched my name into two syllables. "Pam...mie!" Nana couldn't have missed my large, round eyes peering at her from within the shadows. She stepped forward two more feet. I smelled the Ben Gay she always slathered on her hands and the wine on her breath. She glowered. "Pammie!"

What did I do to make her mad? A creepy feeling crawled up my neck and my head swam. *I wish Mommy'd come home and stop the game.*

"Pam, are you in here?"

The fury in her eyes and the ire in her voice frightened me. I recoiled further into the closet and stood pressed between the row of clothes, the box, and the wall. *All I have to do is call out, "You found me," and the game will end.* The contents of my stomach crept up my throat.

She peered inside the dimly lit space. "I said, are you in here?"

For a second, our eyes locked. Hers were hard and angry, and my chin trembled like I might cry.

Nana slammed the door and suddenly all light vanished. The pitch black space smelled musty, of old things, and I couldn't see my hands against the door. I didn't mind the dark, but my grandmother closing me in the closet distressed me. I pushed, but the door didn't move. *Why is Nana doing this? I did something bad.* "Let me out," I said, my words were thin, weak wisps.

For a few moments, I listened to my own respiration, the inhaling whoosh of air entering my nostrils and the exhaling of breath. As if something weighty were on my chest, breathing required effort. I heard nothing else, just my breath, and wondered if Nana had gone. Again, I pushed against the door.

Nana spoke loudly from the other side of the door. "This'll teach you to hide from me! Don't ever hide from your grandmother again!"

I want Mommy. Mommy, come home. Where's Robin? Robin can let me out. For several moments more it was so quiet I heard only my puffs of air—inhale, exhale, inhale, exhale—and I figured Nana, standing on the other side of the door, heard my breathing, and if Robin were still in her room, even she could hear my labored breaths.

The handle turned and the door slowly opened. My heart pounded against my chest. Nana stared down at me, a menacing smirk across her face. "Don't you *ever* hide from me again!" A blast of stale wine odor hit my nostrils. She shook her head. "Never, never hide from me," she said, turning on her heels and stomping from my room.

Robin stood near the crib, with the end of a ponytail in her mouth. Just seeing her filled my eyes with tears of relief. "It's okay," she said. "You can come out now."

At that moment, I realized how much I needed my sister. I took a deep breath, went to her and moved as close to her as possible without being in her arms.

"That was weird," she said, holding my hand.

"Uh huh," I answered.

"You okay?"

I nodded.

"I didn't like Nana doing that to you." She bit her bottom lip and rubbed her forehead. "She locked me in my closet, too, and told me to never hide, and said a little boy died because he hid where there wasn't any air."

The concept of death was foreign to me. My heart was still pounding against my chest, and I didn't answer.

"She was trying to scare us," Robin said.

Nana had shattered my faith in her, and I felt in my heart that she could never be completely trusted. "She's mean. Why is she mean?"

"I don't know."

"Maybe she'll lock us up again."

"She better not," Robin said with fierce determination.

CHAPTER FOUR

I stared up at Nana, drinking a sour smelling concoction. Her drink smelled awful and I crinkled my nose. Nana smiled down at me. "Oh, really, Pammie. It's not that bad." She sipped from her glass, half filled with buttermilk, the other with beer, and smacked her lips. "Yum! Yum!"

Every morning, Nana always drank a glass of Coors mixed with sour buttermilk. Then she'd clean the kitchen, do a little laundry, or work on a project. This time, it was sewing. "Girls, come in here," she called from her room, "and try these on." She gave us the dresses she had finished sewing and after we slipped them on, she turned Robin before her, checking for loose threads and a correct fit. Then she did the same with me. Turning me around, she scrutinized the hem of the red, velvety material. "Robin, now you'll have a new dress for school when it starts next week and Pammie has one, too."

"Robin, I'm going to school with you," I said, smiling up at my six-year-old sister.

"Not this year," Nana said. "You're too little for school. Wait another year then you can go." She trimmed a loose thread along the hem of my dress. "That should do it. Now, why don't you girls go let your granddad see how pretty you look?"

Robin and I spotted Poppy at the kitchen table reading the Sunday paper and sipping a steaming cup of coffee. We stopped where the hall met up with the dining room. Watching him, Robin leaned over and whispered in my ear, "Pam, you tell Poppy."

Poppy had sold The Green Parrot to a lady named Edith and went into the swimming pool building business. He worked most every day of the week and socialized at the bar on his off time. We so seldom saw him, I felt as I did around people I barely knew, apprehensive and shy.

I poked Robin's shoulder and whispered back, "No. You."

"You," she whispered.

"You," I said.

Poppy must've heard us whispering back and forth. He sat up and glanced over his newspaper at us standing against the far wall. A warm smile filled his face. "Look at me pretty granddaughters."

His manner of speaking fascinated me. On the rare occasions when he was home, I'd hover near him, studying his face, and waiting for him to talk so I could hear his inflection and the unusual use of words. If he had come from Ireland, I would've expected a brogue, but he was born in Portland, Maine. I knew he should've sounded like everyone else, but he didn't, and this amused me.

I wanted my granddad's attention, and hoped he'd say some more funny sounding words, and maybe he'd even perform a trick. When Mother was home she'd say, "All right girls, leave your granddad alone." But she wasn't home now, and I stepped from the shadows along the wall, Robin coming with me, and went to him.

"Poppy play the coin game," I said.

At first, he acted like he wouldn't. "No. No. Yer old granddad's reading the paper," he said in his Irish voice.

Robin pleaded with her large, sky blue eyes. "Please? Poppy, please play."

He laughed a deep, throaty rumble. "I don't know if yer old granddad has any." He set down the newspaper, the cup of coffee, and stood up. He wore the same outfit every day. A freshly washed and pressed short sleeved, white shirt and navy blue work pants. He patted the single chest pocket where he kept a little black record book. "Yer granddad's broke," he said with a mischievous smile.

"Please, Poppy," Robin and I said.

"Well," he said and scratched his head, "let me check me other spot." He shoved both hands into his pants' pockets and jingled the change. "This'll be the one." He showed us a special penny and pushed it in his right ear. "Where'd it go?"

"It's in your ear," Robin answered.

He bent down, and we examined the ear where we last saw the penny. Robin frowned and stared at Poppy's closed hand. "Oh, I know where it is. It's in there," she said, pointing at his fist.

Years before, while working with machinery, three of the fingers on Poppy's right hand were wacked off at the knuckle. We began prying back each undersized appendage, but the penny wasn't under his knobby thumb, the short index, or the stumpy third. We pulled open his whole hand.

"It's not there," Robin said and giggled. "It's in your hair."

Poppy stooped down and my sister and I explored his short, brown hair and peered into one enormous earlobe, then the other. All the while, he was chuckling in that deep, throaty rumble.

We ran out of the obvious places a penny might hide. I giggled. "Poppy, where'd it go?"

The smile lines at the corner of his mouth spread across the jaw of his tanned face. His eyes sparkled and he laughed. "Aye, me granddaughters, it's gone. But maybe yer old grand-dad can find it." His right hand enclosed his left earlobe. He tugged, pulled, and contorted his face. "Well, lookie here! I feel it coming out me ear."

My granddad's special powers amazed me, and I hurried onto the empty chair beside him to get a better look. He tugged his lobe twice more, rubbed his short index finger inside his ear, and pulled out the coin. Robin and I gasped. "How'd the penny go from that ear," Robin said, pointing at his right, "to that ear?" She pointed at his left.

Poppy's interactions with us were the tricks he played, like making the coin disappear, but other than these rare, playful times, he never engaged us on any level, and I figured grand-dads were just like that.

As far as I knew, Poppy was my dad, but not any sort of regular dad—he was grand. All the kids I knew just had the ordinary, non-grand, type, but not Robin and me. We lived with a regular mom, grand-mom, and grand-dad. It never crossed my mind that I should have the plain variety of dad, too, like the other kids in the neighborhood.

A full year had passed and Mother had mentioned no plans of moving. She took advantage of Nana and Poppy, coming and going from their home as she pleased without any apparent desire to take care of my sister or me.

One evening in early summer around dinnertime, I sat on my knees on a dining room chair and played on the kitchen table with my Aunt Cindy's childhood doll, Baby. A radio beside me was tuned to the news and Mother listened to the weather forecast while stirring a pan of sizzling hamburger and onions seasoned with garlic salt and pepper. The delicious aroma filled the house.

Robin entered the kitchen. "Where'd you get that?" she said, marching over to me.

I danced the doll across the table. "Somewhere."

She grabbed for it. "You got it from my room. Can I have it?"

I whisked Baby away and clutched her against my chest. "No, I'm playing with her."

"But you took her from my room and you're supposed to ask. Let me have her back," she said.

Mother came over to the table, the stainless steel spatula glistening with grease in one hand. "Girls, that's enough of that." She turned up the radio's volume. "I'm trying to hear the news."

The local radio station featured weather forecasts, sports updates, traffic reports, and regional information. Just then, the dramatic voice of a reporter came over the airwaves. "During this evening's rush hour commute, Keith McKern of Sacramento was involved in a near fatal, head-on, collision."

The spatula slipped from Mother's fingers and fell to the floor. She gasped and shuddered. "Oh, no!" The color drained from her face. "Girls, that's your father!"

We hadn't seen or heard from him in four years, not since he left when I was a few months old, and Mother had never mentioned his name or her marriage to him. "My father?" I said in total surprise and confusion. "Who's my father?"

"Shh! Pam, not now."

I hadn't even known that I had a father. "Mommy, who's my father?"

"I said be quiet."

The news reporter continued speaking. "He was rushed by ambulance to UC Davis Medical Center and is in critical condition."

CHAPTER FIVE

*W*eeks after Dad's car accident, Mother, Robin and I entered Van's Market, rounded a corner, and then suddenly stopped. I followed Mother's gaze across the row of checkstands to a man heading straight for us.

Strangers and their questions intimidated me. Inquirers often asked me to repeat myself and my face would go hot. I spoke with an impediment, leaving off vital letters, such as "R", and people outside our immediate family couldn't understand me very well. As the man approached, I ducked around Mother and hid behind the folds of her knee length skirt.

He was staring at us from a couple of feet away, and for half a second, no one said a word. I stole a peek of him from between Mother's stocking covered legs. The stranger stood only about five and a half feet tall. Built like a pole, he had a black buzz top hairdo.

The man smiled timidly at Mother. "Hello, Joy."

"Keith," she said, her voice full of concern. "How are you? Are you all right?"

I'd heard that name, but I didn't recall from where, and I stared curiously at him as he nudged his black, horn-rimmed glasses against his brow. "I'm fine. And you?"

"I'm all right." Mother reached behind her and found my hand. Grabbing it, she pulled me to her right side. Robin was on her left. "Girls," she said, "this is your father."

My father? I glanced up at Mother. Her gaze was fixed on Father's moist eyes. I flashed a puzzled look at my sister gawking at him with her mouth half open and I knew she was as surprised as I.

"I learned from the radio about your accident," Mother said. "Weren't you badly injured?"

"A woman crossed the divider and slammed head on into me. My spleen was ruptured and I had surgery, but I'm feeling fine," he said.

My father's eyes, brimming with tears, looked at me, and then at Robin, and then back to me. His probing stare worsened my feelings of bewilderment and anxiety. I ignored the impulse to hide my face inside the folds of Mother's skirt or turn away, and stayed there with my eyes on his. *He's my father. What does that mean?* Looking at him was like seeing my own deep brown, almost black, eyes in a mirror. I had his dark hair color, too. My mind whirled questions around so fast I could barely hear my own thoughts. *Why's he crying? Where's he been? Will he come home with us? Other fathers live with their kids. Why doesn't he live with us?*

He pushed his hands into the pockets of his black slacks. "Joy, it's good seeing you, Pammie, and Robin." He sounded choked up, like at any moment he might burst into tears and I wondered what sadness had come over him. "Would it be all right to visit the girls sometime?" he said, clearing his throat. "I'm off work Saturday. How about this weekend?"

Mother concentrated on her former husband. The creases along her forehead deepened, her eyes narrowed, and she was silent for a few seconds. She glanced at my sister and me. Then she stared at our father. "Keith," she finally said. "I think that'll be fine. We're living with my parents over on Foster. You can find their number in the phone book."

On the way back to Nana and Poppy's house, Mother looked over at Robin and me seated beside her. "Well, that wasn't what I expected, meeting your dad in Vans. Girls, I think I'm in shock."

"My tummy was shaking," Robin said.

"There's nothing for you to be frightened of," Mother said.

"I don't think I'm scared, just excited and, Mommy, I don't know what's wrong. My tummy hurts."

"It hurts? Is it a pain or is it queasy?"

"It feels funny."

"Maybe you're overwhelmed. You haven't seen your daddy since you were in a crib. I think you were two and Pammie, you were a few months old. Robin, do you remember him?"

She shook her head. "Not really."

I shut my eyes tightly. Ten seconds later, I opened them. "I do," I said.

"You do?" Mother said, laughing. "Pammie, you're so funny." She laughed some more until tears streamed down her cheeks. "You remember your daddy?" She gripped the steering wheel with one hand and dabbed her eyes with the other. "I think you're pulling my leg."

"I'm serious," I said.

Mother giggled. "That's right you are." She tried gaining control of her emotions and stifled her giggles. "Your mother's not nuts, girls. Promise." She breathed deeply and smirked. "Darling, tell me what you remember about your dad. Do you remember him changing you? Or giving you a bottle?"

"Mommy," I said, feeling frustrated. "But I do. Really I do. I remember a dad feeling. I felt it at the store and I felt the same thing a long, long time ago."

"You felt something?"

"In here," I said, pointing at my heart.

Three weeks after Robin and I met our father, Mother took one of Nana's homemade dresses from my closet. "Your daddy's coming by to see you and your sister in a little while. You'll be spending a whole day together," she said, slipping the dress over my head and smoothing the wrinkles from the full skirt.

Dad had already been by Nana's house a couple of times, and Robin and I were getting to know him. I liked being near him, especially with Mother in the same room, but Robin and I hadn't ever gone anywhere with him. "Mommy, are you coming too?" I said.

"Not this time."

I thought about other parents in the neighborhood, the Lawrences across the street and the Pullyahs around the corner. They lived together in the same house with their children. Why couldn't we? "But he's Daddy and you're Mommy, and you're supposed to be with each other."

Mother placed both hands on my shoulders. "Darling, it's not that simple." She studied my face, pressing together her lips. "How can I help you understand? You see, a long time ago I stopped loving him."

My mouth fell open. "You don't love Dad?"

"Goodness, Pammie." She giggled. "Of course, I love your dad, but I'm not *in love* with him and that's why I divorced him." She walked over to the dresser. Opening the second drawer, she took out a pair of white socks. "Your dad's a good man, but he and I are two uniquely different people. I outgrew him, I suppose."

I felt my face scrunch up.

"Darling, it wasn't anything he did. I got bored staying home all the time. All he did was work, and come home, and watch T.V. He's not interested in the things I like doing. I wanted to go out dancing and to elegant dinners, but your daddy doesn't like to dance. It was my wish for him to leave. I thought it best we live in two houses. His leaving was my decision."

*Divorced. That's what it's called. Mommy doesn't want to be with him because...*My bottom lip trembled, but before the tears surfaced, Mother quickly changed subjects. "Here," she said, sounding bright and happy. "Sit on the floor and put these on." She gave me the socks. "You and Robin will have a nice day with him. He's taking you to meet your aunts, uncles, and your other grandfather. Your grandmother Perlita died last year of an aneurism. You would've liked her. I did. Your dad's family will be there, everyone except his youngest sister, Gay, and, for some reason, none of your cousins."

"I have cousins?"

"You do," she answered. "Two of your daddy's sisters have boys. Merle has four and Kathleen has one." She smiled and her eyes sparkled. "You know what?"

I shrugged my shoulders.

"Your Aunt Kathleen and I were pregnant together, me with you and she with Allen." A far away look came over her face. "Kathleen's a kick in the pants. She and I had more fun being pregnant together..."

Later when Dad, Robin, and I entered his brother and sister-in-law's home, my aunts, uncles, and grandfather greeted us at the door. Someone offered Robin and me a soda pop and Dad a beer, and we convened in the living room where all the adults talked at once, joked in loud voices, laughed, and drank.

My grandfather, seated on a kitchen chair across from us, took a long swallow from his glass of brown fluid. The ice tinkled. "Carolyn," he said to our hostess, "I'll have another, please."

"Who's driving?" she said.

"Oh, I'll be all right. Another drink won't impair me." He smiled up at her worried eyes. "Gosh darn it! Carolyn, I've had more and done fine."

Dad chuckled. "Carolyn, I'm ready for another beer, please."

"Anyone else?"

Her husband Ross held out his empty beer can.

"Don't you think you've had enough already?" Aunt Carolyn said.

It wasn't a joke, but all the men laughed, including Dad.

"I don't know what to do with you." She tsked and shook her head, disapprovingly. "You can have one more, but that's all."

After everyone had refills of booze and beer, the talking continued with louder voices and longer laughter. Robin and I sat on the sofa next to Dad, taking it all in, observing the men getting drunker by the minute, and the sober women slowly sipping on soda and wine.

A couple of hours later, Dad got up from the living room sofa, and the conversations in the room stopped. All eyes turned to him. "Time to get the girls back to their mother," he said, motioning to us and grinning. "Don't just sit there."

Robin and I stood and headed for the front door.

"Wait a minute. Where do you think you're going?" Dad said. "Robin and Pammie, aren't you forgetting something?"

"I don't know," I said.

He put a hand on my shoulder and directed me toward my three aunts, three uncles, and grandfather seated in chairs. "Yes, you are. Shouldn't you say good bye?"

Robin and I waved. "Bye, bye."

"Not so fast." Dad chuckled. "Go give them all hugs."

Dad went over to our waiting relatives. He grinned at his sister Merle, leaned down, embraced her, and they kissed on the lips.

Their affection shocked me and I stared with wide, unblinking eyes. No one in Poppy and Nana's house behaved in this manner. Robin tailed Dad down the line and then my turn came. One aunt embraced me and kissed my cheek, another smacked my lips, but I rubbed away the germs with the back of my hand. Dad and Robin were lovingly manhandled by relatives in front of me.

Uncle Ross lifted me onto his lap. "Pammie, how'd you get so pretty?"

I bit my bottom lip and stared at his brown eyes. They were warm as the summer day and when he grinned, they twinkled.

"You can't leave yet. You just got here. But it looks like your old man's set on going." He put me back on my feet, hugged me, and kissed my forehead.

Saying goodbye was like having my face spit washed. Next I went to Aunt Carolyn and got off easy with her. She hugged me. "Oh, I sure love you, honey," she said. Uncle Ronnie, seated beside her, squeezed me so hard I let out a little puff of air. He chuckled. "Isn't she cute?" he said, still hugging me.

I stepped over to Uncle Nick and didn't see his kiss coming. Before I could duck, he smacked my lips. "Yuck!" I said, wiping the slobber off my mouth.

The last person in line was my grandfather. I went to him, and my eyes fell upon the forest of light brown and grey chest hairs poking through his open V-neck collar. This characteristic worried me. *Is that fur?* He wrapped his hairy arms around me and brought me in close. *What kind of people have fur?*

"It was good seeing you," he said, pressing me against his hairy chest and patting my back so hard it shook my shoulders. His warm breath, brushing against my face, smelled of whiskey, and I stared up at his deeply wrinkled face and his fat lips glistening with saliva. I hoped he'd be satisfied with a hug.

Grandfather puckered up, aimed his massive, gaping smacker for my mouth, and made his move. From my perspective, it looked like he would swallow my face through his gargantuan lips. I turned my head and felt the impact, then the moisture of his kiss. Wiping his saliva off the side of my face, I followed Dad and Robin out the door.

CHAPTER SIX

*R*obin's seventh birthday arrived the following June. That afternoon, Mother brought from the oven a delicious smelling Duncan Hines cake and put it on a cooling rack on the counter. The whole kitchen smelled of chocolate. "Can I have some?" I said.

"Not now, we'll have this after Poppy gets home from work tonight," she said. "Before we do anything else, I need to speak with your Aunt Cindy." She got her purse and car keys. "Come on, girls."

The three of us climbed into the hot interior of the red Impala. Mother turned on the air conditioner and drove a short distance to a two-story apartment complex with tan stucco exterior walls. On the downstairs level, large evergreen shrubs grew between each picture window and apartment door.

"Your grandmother's here," she said, pointing at Nana's parked car two spaces over from where we had stopped. "Girls, I need to speak with her and your aunt about something." She turned off the engine and cranked down her window. "Roll your window down and wait right here. I'll be back in a few minutes."

Robin and I cranked down all the windows. The seats and dashboard dwarfed us and we sat on our knees for a better view of our surroundings. We watched our mother as she ascended the stairs and entered one of several apartments on the second floor. A scrub jay squawked from somewhere overhead and a light breeze swirled warm air around us. The minutes trickled into what seemed to be an hour. Sweat beaded up on my forehead under my bangs, and my shorts clung to the back of my damp thighs.

Finally, after what seemed like a long time, Aunt Cindy's door opened. Nana came outside, slammed the door and hurried down the steps. Her short, mousy brown hair bounced with each long stride. She rushed across the parking lot to our car and opened the back door.

"Girls, get out and get in my car," she said in a way that allowed no argument.

I was confused by Nana's command, but I promptly obeyed. She had as much right to order us around as Mother. Robin and I slid out onto the hot pavement. The heat radiated to my feet through my thin-soled sandals.

Nana, her eyes were bloodshot and she staggered toward her car, opened the passenger door and motioned to us. "Pammie, Robin." Her voice and words sounded strange. "Come on, hurry up. Get in."

Robin got in first, but I hesitated. Nana wasn't acting right and I was suddenly afraid to go with her. "Pammie," she slurred, "why are you still standing there?"

Just then, Aunt Cindy's apartment door flew open and Mother bolted through it. She slammed it shut, leaned over the rail, saw Nana putting us into her car, and raced down the flight of stairs.

"Pammie, climb in beside your sister," Nana said.

Finally, I pulled myself up onto the seat, which seemed to be such a long ways up, and I sat next to Robin, and I exchanged worried glances with her as Nana shut the door. She was running around to the other side when Mother began yelling. "Stop! No! Don't take them!"

"Will you wait a minute?" Mother, breathless, said before Nana got in the driver's seat. An arms length was between them. "Wait," she said again and paused to catch her breath. Nana gripped the open door. "Joy Lynn!"

"I won't let you take the girls. They came with me and they'll leave with me. You're not leaving with them." Mother said in a voice full of panic.

"Don't you tell me."

"No, don't get behind the wheel."

Why are they fighting? I didn't like the sound of their raised voices or the sight of Nana's face, twisted in rage, or her eyes, red and swollen. *What's wrong with Nana?* My heart pounded in my chest and I wanted to go home with Mother.

For a second, during an interlude in their quarrel, birds in the nearby trees twittered and chirped, a motorist whizzed by, and it looked like their fight had ended. Relief washed over me, but it evaporated as rapidly as it had come. Suddenly, Mother left Nana, made a dash around the car for us, the heels of her sandals clicking on the pavement, and threw open the door.

"Get out," she said, sounding panicked. "Quickly!" With a hand on my back, she steered me across the hot pavement to her waiting car. "Girls, get in and stay right here." She lowered her voice and met my eyes. "And don't leave the Impala."

I felt something pressing against my windpipe and I nearly burst into tears. Black mascara ran from Mother's bloodshot eyes down her ruddy face, and several strands of hair clung to her sweaty forehead and cheeks. She didn't look like my mother who always had everything under control, her makeup neatly applied, her hair perfectly done. I had never before seen her in this condition.

Nana ran up the flight of stairs and Mother followed. When they entered Aunt Cindy's apartment I wondered why.

There we sat, my sister and I, both scared into silence, in the identical position of powerlessness, and at the total mercy of two irrational women. I met my sister's forlorn look of dismay and I suppose my expression mirrored her own sad, down-turned mouth and shocked wide eyes.

Soon, all three women raced out the apartment door and down the flight of stairs on the other side of the green lawn that separated us from them. Nana ran inches ahead of Mother and Aunt Cindy. Mother yelled. Nana yelled. And Aunt Cindy yelled.

It all seemed like plain and simple madness. They had lost their minds. I slunkered down into the seat and wished to go home. Through the open car windows, I heard their shouts coming closer. *Make them stop. Someone make them stop.* I thought of the times when Robin and I had bickered. *We say sorry and are nice again. That's what Mommy, Nana, and Aunt Cindy need to do.*

My grandmother sounded indignant. "My girls *will* go with me!"

Mother cried. "Your girls?" She came beside the Impala. "Robin and Pammie aren't *your* children!"

It dawned on me then. *It's about Robin and me. They're fighting over us.* And I thought my mother's and grandmother's fight had to do with who would get to drive us home, but then I decided that couldn't be it.

An abrupt quiet seemed to spring up out of nowhere. I sat on my knees and peeked out the open window. My mind raced and I looked from face to face, scanning them for signs of a ceasefire. Aunt Cindy stepped in front of Nana, blocking her from going further. She spoke calmly. "Mother, don't get in the car. Please don't. You're too upset and you're not thinking clearly. Come back inside and we'll talk about this."

They stood near the Impala for another minute, staring at each other and then, all at once, they rushed for the driver's door. Mother reached it first, jumped in, and slammed her hand down on the lock. *Click.* Nana jumped into her car, floored the gas, and sped out of the parking lot in a fury with Mother in pursuit.

During the car chase, I sat beside Robin on the back seat. The hot wind blew in through the four open windows and whipped our hair. Loose strands of Mother's hair stuck to her reddened cheeks. She seethed, and the monster-sized anger coming from her frightened me. I felt her palpable tension as easily as I felt the speeding motion of the car. My breathing had become labored and my head was dizzy, and I assumed my equally silent sister had come under the power of the same paralyzing fear.

Moments later, Mother brought us to a screeching halt outside our grandparent's home. "This way girls," she said, leading us to the front door.

I stuck to my sister for comfort and went with her into the kitchen. From there, I heard Mother and Nana yelling, shouting words I couldn't understand. Their raised, angry voices came from Nana's bedroom down the hall.

The whole dismal affair, Mother and Nana running, shouting, raging, speeding, pulling Robin and me from one person's car to the other and back again, upset me greatly, yet, I couldn't cry, or speak, and even breathing had become difficult. Stomach acids crept up my throat, and I couldn't react to the crisis that was intensifying by the moment. After a long while, Mother and Nana came into the kitchen.

"Would you calm down?" Mother said, raising her hands in exasperation. "Would you just listen?"

Something large was clutched against Nana's chest. Her arms were wrapped around it, concealing it from my view.

She hurried over to Robin and me at the table. Mother's face was white with fear and her eyes grew wide. She stepped toward Nana, pleading with her hands. "Please, don't. Wait until Daddy gets home. Why are you doing this?"

Nana opened her arms and poured a mound of jewelry onto the table. There were gold necklaces, rings with precious stones, fashion pins, and gaudy clip-on earrings. "Joy, these are for Robin and Pammie..." Her voice shook. She lifted her trembling hands, pulled a ring off her finger and added it to the cache. "I want the girls to have this. I'm leaving all my jewelry to them."

Her actions made no sense at all. I knew her gift, given in a state of rage, had nothing to do with Robin's birthday and I wanted her to take it back. She bent her tear-stained face forward, breathed heavily as if exhausted, and for a second it seemed like she wanted to say something else. I glanced over at Mother and swallowed the lump in my throat. Robin said nothing but looked as if she were about to cry.

Without another word, Nana turned from us and went to the living room. Then she let out a huge sob. "Joy, I'm really going to do it. I'm going to kill myself."

I looked to Mother for help, but she stood absolutely still near Robin and me.

Nana went into the living room and wailed. "Today!" She ran across the carpeted floor. The screen door banged shut. The sound of Nana's pounding footfalls on the walkway faded. Her car door slammed, the tires screeched, and she sped away.

CHAPTER SEVEN

The morning after the big fight, I sat up in bed as the sun rose and admired the shaft of golden light bursting in through the window and splashing onto the carpeted floor. By this time, I was five years old, and a couple weeks earlier, after Nana had realized I wouldn't leave the house in the black of night and become a grease spot on the road, she moved me from the crib to one of two twin beds in Robin's room.

A pan clattered in the kitchen. "Nana's home," I said under my breath, so as not to awaken Robin. The night before, Nana hadn't come home in time to tuck Robin and me in bed, and I had missed the prayers we always said together, and her tender bedtime care. I grinned and bounded from the room.

Mother poured oatmeal into a pan on the stove. I looked around the room for my grandmother. She always made breakfast. "Mommy, where's Nana?" I said with a sleepy yawn.

"Pammie, be ladylike and cover your mouth," she said, stirring the oats. "Your grandmother's in the hospital."

I hadn't forgotten the previous day's events—Nana's running from the house, the phone calls that came long after she fled, or the visitors with their sad, swollen eyes who came by to see us.

"Why's she there?" I said, now alert and worried.

"She attempted suicide."

The word "suicide" meant nothing to me and I waited for further insight. Mother kept her eyes on the bubbling pan of oats. "Go, get dressed," she said, dismissing me.

A little while later, the phone rang. Mother nervously lifted up the receiver. "Good morning." Her eyes filled with tears and her mouth trembled. She choked out the words, "Where's Daddy?" After hanging up the phone, she went straight to her room.

The way I'd heard it told, the attending police officer noted Nana's skid marks turning sharply away from the cliff's edge. He explained the meaning of the black streaks and said they showed us that she hadn't really meant to kill herself.

A few days later, Poppy and Mother attended Nana's funeral, but Robin and I stayed home with a babysitter. Shortly before sunset, they returned, followed by Uncle Bud's wife, Aunt Marylou. "Robin and Pammie, come in here for a minute," she said. Her voice trembled. "Here, have a seat with me on the sofa." We climbed up and sat there with her. "I told your mother I'd visit with you about your grandmother." Her eyes filled with tears. "Nana's gone to Heaven."

For a moment, I considered this. Heaven might as well have been Africa; they were both distant places of which I knew nothing about and since Nana had gone away, I expected she'd return just as people do when they travel across the sea. "When's she coming home?" I said.

"She's not."

"But why?"

"She can't, and I don't think she'd even want to if she could. Heaven's a very pretty place."

Death was unfamiliar. I had never known who died and I didn't know that Nana's body had ceased functioning or that pallbearers had lowered her lifeless body into the cold ground.

Tears fell down Robin's cheeks. "I don't want her to be gone. I don't want her to be gone," she said again. "I want her back. It was my birthday. Why'd she die on my birthday?" She sobbed into her hands.

"Robin Lynn," Aunt Marylou said gently. "I don't know why she left us. But your Nana has gone to be with Jesus. And she has a mansion and maybe a beautiful flower garden. She loves roses. Maybe she has a rose garden. And the streets are pure gold there. Someday, we'll go be with her."

Then, I realized the big fight had been about Nana leaving us. *Maybe Nana told Aunt Cindy and Mommy that she was going to take us with her to Heaven. Maybe they were trying to stop her. Mommy wouldn't want us to leave her.* I thought about my sister's tears and Mother's depressed face and Aunt Marylou's sadness, and I decided that I wouldn't want to go somewhere faraway because it would make the people I love cry.

The changes came so suddenly and still I didn't understand why my grandmother never came home. After her funeral, Poppy spent more time than ever at work and the bar, often stumbling into the house in the middle of the night. Aunt Cindy moved without leaving a forwarding address and we didn't see her for a long time. Mother pretended Nana had never existed, and since she hadn't, grieving had no place in her life. It was the same as when Dad had vanished—she never spoke of Nana.

Slowly, I learned the meaning of death. It meant Nana didn't tuck Robin and me in each night or recite prayers with us. It meant she wouldn't make us breakfast, or wash our hair, rinsing it with beer, or sew us new dresses. There was a vacant place at the dining table. Sometimes, Poppy joined Mother, Robin, and me there for dinner, but death had left Nana's spot empty.

One night while Mother washed dinner dishes and handed the plastic ware to me for drying, I asked about my grandmother. "Why isn't Nana back?"

Mother's brilliant blue eyes hardened. "Pammie, she's not coming back!"

Another time, when I particularly missed Nana, I reached out to Mother for reassurance. "Mommy, I miss Nana," I said.

There was no comfort for me. Mother just gritted her teeth and glowered, and I withdrew in fear. To avoid being hit with sharp, bitter words, and stinging stares, I silently vowed never to speak of my grandmother in Mother's presence.

Mother still had her secretarial job at the phone company and now that Nana wasn't home to care for us, Robin and I were stuck with a babysitter, a woman near the school Robin and I would soon attend. In September, Mother enrolled Robin in second grade and me in kindergarten. After school one day, I walked to the sitter's house and told the woman just what I thought of her. "Mrs. Smith, I don't like you." I folded my arms into a pout and scolded her. "You're not nice."

Mrs. Smith never smiled. The frown she always wore grew into a scowl and I could tell that she was fighting for control of her emotions. She looked mad. "Pam, be mindful of your elders! Go stand in the corner." She pointed to a particular spot near the family room. "You can stay right there until your mother comes for you. Then you can explain your poor behavior to her."

I dropped my eyes to the floor and went to the corner where I stood for an hour and stewed over all the reasons I didn't like my babysitter.

On the ride home, Mother asked me to explain why Mrs. Smith was upset. "What did you say to her?"

"I didn't lie," I said.

Earlier in the week, I told my teacher a made up story about Mother being pregnant because I wanted some positive adult attention and, later when my teacher asked Mother about her due date, she told her that there wasn't a baby coming to our family. That night, after we were home, Mother had explained to me the importance of always being truthful.

Mother eyed me suspiciously. "What did you say?"

"The truth."

"Pammie, you are never to tell your babysitter or anyone you don't like them. Why did you say that to Mrs. Smith?"

"She's mean."

"Yeah, I don't like her either," Robin said. "She doesn't let us talk in the house and she yells at Pam all the time for nothing. We have to stay on that plastic thing on the floor. She says we'll make her carpet dirty."

Weeks later, one Saturday evening at the sitter's, Mother walked into the room after a date. She wore a skirt that ended just above her knees and a blouse with a rounded collar. Her dark blond hair was in a classic, late Sixties bouffant style and her lips were glossy red. The babysitter, elsewhere in the house, didn't meet her at the door. Robin and I stood side-by-side in our fuzzy, footed pajamas and welcomed Mother's arrival.

Mother ushered us into the guest room where we kept our coats. "Girls, I need your advice on something." Her voice was high and girlish.

"Okay," Robin said.

"Todd asked me to be his wife." Todd was one of two boyfriends.

She glanced from me to Robin and sighed. "But I have a teeny, tiny, problem. Last week, Max also proposed."

Neither Robin nor I said a word. I don't know what went on in my sister's head, but absolutely zilch went on in mine.

"I like them both, but I really don't know who to choose." She sounded troubled. For a couple of seconds, Mother seemed to be waiting for our reply, but Robin and I were silent.

"You know, this means you'll have a new daddy?"

Mother intertwined her fingers and folded her hands in front of her skirt. She gazed at Robin's blank face. "Well, girls, who do you think I should marry?"

She tried picking apples from a tree that had never grown fruit. Robin was seven. I was five. And Mother was twenty-six. How were we to know what a grown woman should do?

Max had never been by to meet Robin and me. However, on another occasion, before Mother departed on one of her dates, Todd came into the house and met us. As soon as they had left for their evening out, Robin told me she didn't like Todd and I agreed. He seemed like he'd be no fun at all. I didn't want Mother marrying a total bore.

We lacked maturity and experience to play matchmaker, but we had all we needed to know about which dock to steer this boat toward. Robin and I whispered in each others' ears and came to an agreement. She stepped forward. "Mommy, marry Max."

"Yeah. Marry Max," I said, beaming.

CHAPTER EIGHT

$\mathcal{M}$ ax Williams had brown hair with bangs swept to one side. He wore plastic framed glasses and was three or four inches taller than Mother, slender, and quiet, seldom ever speaking. Mother said he was the "silent type" and encouraged me to "respect" that part of his nature.

After a week-long honeymoon, he and Mother moved us into a three-bedroom rental on one of Sacramento's major arteries, Watt Avenue. Vehicles of all types rushed along the street outside the front door, but out the back door we had a haven with a grassy yard surrounded by a tall privacy fence. In that special place behind our home, there were purple flowers the size of luncheon plates that grew on six-foot tall bushes and a solitary tree loaded with tart, fuzzy-skinned fruit.

Mother put me in a room across the hall from Robin's. With both our doors wide open, we could see each other. Seeing Robin was almost the same as sharing a room, I decided. The Monday after our move, she enrolled Robin in second grade and me in kindergarten at the new school, Thomas Edison Elementary, a couple of blocks from our home.

Mrs. Browley, my kindergarten teacher reprimanded me lots of times every day. My speech impediment had me mispronouncing many words and she repeatedly corrected me. I faced other challenges, too. I couldn't tie my shoes, tell time, write numbers or letters—not even those in my name.

Mother hadn't prepared me for kindergarten. She didn't see the value for children's books and had never read to Robin or me. In fact, there weren't any books for kids in our house. Mother didn't show us how to do anything academic. She didn't teach us the spelling of our names, or how to hold a pencil, or how to recite the alphabet, or how to count.

Sometime during the first week at Thomas Edison, just after the morning bell rang, I picked up the fat, black pencil and obeyed Mrs. Browley's name writing instructions.

"That's not the correct hand," she said from across the room.

She could've been speaking to any one of the twenty-eight kids in my class. I knew how many kids there were because Mother had said that in my class of twenty-eight, another boy and I were the only students who wrote with our left hands. Mother thought left-handedness was a sign of intelligence. She said Einstein was a genius and he was left-handed, but perhaps Mrs. Browley didn't see it that way.

"Pam!" Mrs. Browley snapped. She hurried across the room with a ruler pointed in my direction, ignoring the curious and startled stares of her class of students, and she leaned over me, smelling of Vicks VaporRub, with black-framed glasses balancing on her nose, and her eyes looking ten times larger than they really were. "Hold your pencil with your right hand."

I dropped my pencil like it had stung me and grabbed it with my other hand.

"That's more like it. Now, keep it there," she said sternly.

All throughout winter, bug-eyed Mrs. Browley tried re-forming me into a right-handed person without success. Shortly before recess one afternoon, she confronted me with a ruler held high in the air, and she slapped the knuckles of the hand in which I grasped the fat pencil. "You will not"—Her jaw trembled and her pale complexion turned a deep red—"write with your left hand!"

No one had ever struck me, not even Mother, and I dropped the pencil, swallowed hard to stop the tears forming in my eyes, and stared down at the worksheet on my desk. I knew I was bad. "I don't know what hand to use. Which one's right?"

"What did you say?"

My lips trembled and my voice had little strength. "Which one's right?"

"Right, not white. Pam, pick up your pencil with your right hand."

By natural inclination, I picked it up with my left.

"Not that one!"

I switched hands and clutched the fat pencil clumsily.

"Left handedness is a sign of retardation. Just look at your letters." She continued her scolding in a voice loud enough for everyone in the room to hear. "Pam, your letters are backwards." Her ruler pointed to the place at the top of the page. "Just look at this P in your name."

A lump formed in my throat and I kept my eyes on the worksheet in front of me. Her voice softened. "Are you watching?"

I nodded.

"You write P like this." Holding my right hand clutched around the fat pencil, she directed my hand and wrote P in the correct direction. "As it stands, your name is backwards. You read from left to right and you write from left to right," she said, still guiding my hand. "Your name's not Map," she said, shaking her head in disgust. "Do you want to be called Map? Map is not a name. It's a thing."

I wanted to tell her she was wrong, tell her what Mother had said about Einstein, but that meant I'd have to speak again and she wouldn't understand, and who wanted to speak when they had to repeat themselves? So I just shook my head.

Two important events occurred in June. One day after Max arrived home from his civilian job with the military, he took us all to the pet store and Mother selected a couple of poodle puppies, a girl she named Suzette and a boy she named Pierre. And my kindergarten report card arrived in the mail.

"That Mrs. Browley!" Mother leaned across the sofa, stretching her arm around Pierre and Suzette lying there with her, and handed it to Max. "Why doesn't she just retire? She's obviously been in the classroom too many years. Honey, look at this. She flunked Pammie."

I thought the school was punishing me for using my left hand. Spending a second year in kindergarten was the ultimate penalty, especially if I had to return to Mrs. Browley's classroom. "I don't get to go to first grade?" I said.

Throughout my first year in school, I let Mother know about some of Mrs. Browley's teaching methods. Once after I had told her about Mrs. Browley striking my hand with a ruler, she called the school office, putting an end to the corporal punishment, and letting the school administration know exactly what she thought of my kindergarten teacher.

Mother stroked the back of my head, running her fingers through my long hair, in an unusual sign of compassion. "That's what this letter says. But, let's not trouble our heads over it. I'll take care of everything Monday morning when I call your principal to file another complaint against that witch."

Max lowered the newspaper in his hands, glanced up over his reading glasses, and gave her a disapproving look.

"I mean that teacher of yours," Mother said, correcting herself and smiling smugly. "Maybe she'll get fired."

My frown faded to a wide grin as I agreed with Mother, hoping the principal would be mad enough at Mrs. Browley to fire her.

"Pammie, I have great news for you," Mother said not long after. "Your principal's placing you in the classroom with the other kindergarten teacher. He assured me that she *will* let you use whichever hand you want."

Summer unfolded into a better season for all of us. Robin and I began spending two or three Saturdays a month with Dad. He took us roller-skating, miniature golfing, and visiting our relatives on his side of the family. Mother quit her secretarial job, saying that she didn't have to work with Max's good paycheck. And since Mother wasn't working, she canceled Mrs. Smith's babysitting service.

While we were out of school, Mother kept Robin and me with her, taking us to The Green Parrot where we sat at a picnic table, ten feet from where she relaxed at the bar, and to the grocery store where she offered Robin and me shopping cart rides. We'd climb onto the metal basket and she'd race down the aisles, giggling, while my sister and I clung onto the sides, laughing and coaxing her, "go faster, faster."

When we were home, Robin and I played unsupervised in our backyard, running through the sprinkler, splashing in a plastic kiddie pool, and eating bucket loads of the fuzzy-skinned fruit. We brushed Pierre and Suzette's thick, curly coats and tumbled with them on the soft grass.

Nearly every night, the delta breezes from nearby San Francisco kicked up their heels and lowered the hot Sacramento temperatures. It could be a hundred during the day, but at night the cooling, ocean breezes arrived, dropping the thermostat to the comfortable sixties. The evenings at the end of summer are famously called Hot August Nights because the coastal breezes don't arrive. The heat is sweltering and everything but the hose water seems warm and sticky. "Girls, how would you like to sleep in the backyard tonight with Pierre and Suzette?" Mother said one August night. "Max put a mattress on the patio for you." We didn't have an air conditioner and the house was especially hot.

Robin and I hurried into our rooms and threw on our pajamas. We raced out the door to the back patio and lay with our puppies on the firm mattress. It was much cooler outside. The air smelled of freshly cut grass. Soft light from the living room filtered through the sliding glass door between our outdoor bed, the living room, and Mother and Max sitting there watching television.

A million twinkling stars covered the night sky. A frog croaked nearby. Robin and I agreed the end of summer left us feeling a little sad.

"Twelve days to go 'til third grade," Robin said.

"Oh, I was trying not to remember."

"Not remember school?"

"Yeah."

"I like school."

"Not with Mrs. Browley."

"Next time will be better. You'll have a different teacher."

"Will it? Robin, don't leave me, okay?"

"I can't go to class with you."

"Yes, you can. Just say you're a kindergartener."

Robin giggled. "Do I look five?"

"I'm not five. I'm six. You can look six."

"Besides, Pam, you remember what happened last year when I tried being with you at school. I looked everywhere until I found you sitting by yourself on the little kid playground. Remember?"

"Yeah."

"Remember what happened?"

Robin's question reminded me of another reason why I hadn't liked school and I didn't answer.

"I climbed under the fence and walked over to you and then your mean teacher said I couldn't even talk to you. She made me leave. Well, I tricked her," she said, giggling. "I'll let you in on my secret. But you have to promise not to tell."

"I promise," I said.

"That's the *real* reason I sang the Peter Rabbit song to your class. I was checking on you. I wanted to make sure you were all right." She giggled again like she had gotten away with something really sneaky.

The aforementioned event had occurred during the previous school year. One morning, Robin unexpectedly entered my classroom. She went over to Mrs. Browley, standing near the back of the room, and she spoke quietly to her. A second later, Mrs. Browley told her to come with her to the front of the room.

"We have a very special visitor this morning. A student from second grade is here to sing for us. Robin," Mrs. Browley motioned for my sister standing beside her. "You may begin."

Robin scanned the room until she spotted me sitting at a table with another girl. "Little Peter Rabbit has a fly upon his nose," she began and sang all the way through to the final verse. "And he swished it and he swashed it and it flew away!" I thought she sang beautifully and applauded with my class as Mrs. Browley ushered Robin out the door.

The memory of my sister's act of unusual kindness warmed my heart. "I like you," I said, "and I love you."

"I like you and I love you, too." Robin said. "Maybe we should say our prayers now."

Putting my hands together, I scrunched my eyes shut. I peaked at Robin. Her head was bowed. Then we began together, "Now I lay me down to sleep. I pray the Lord thy child to keep. If I die before I wake..."

It struck me then. Why at this moment? I had no idea. But, suddenly, it hit me. "Robin?"

"Why'd you stop?" she said.

"The words are icky. What if I die? Nana died and she's not here anymore. What if you die?"

"We won't."

"But the words say we might, when we're sleeping. What if we do?"

"You aren't dying in your sleep. Besides, if you did, you'd go to Nana. But it won't happen. You won't die and I won't die. Okay?"

"How do you know?"

"Just don't worry about it."

"But the words..."

Robin put her arm around me, lying there. "Don't worry. I won't leave you and we won't die."

CHAPTER NINE

*M*iss Sylva, my new kindergarten teacher never scolded me for using my left hand. Once after math, Clarence—chubby cheeked, toy grabbing, always in trouble, smarty pants Clarence looked at my worksheet and my name written across the top. "Map?" He laughed. "What kind of name's that?" It was recess and Miss Sylva called the class out onto the black-top for a game of kick ball. Clarence playfully chanted my backwards name, "Map, Map, Map," while marching outside with the other kids.

I reluctantly left the room to join the others standing in a circle, waiting for Miss Sylva's signal for the game to begin.

Three kids stood between Clarence and me. Clarence waved and smiled, "Hello Map." Then turning to another boy, he pointed at me. "That there's Map."

My head dropped and I stared at the smooth black pavement and wondered what to do. *I could call him a dork or I could hit him or I could stomp on his foot, but Mommy would be mad. Maybe I'll tell Miss Sylva.*

"Hey you," Clarence said, interrupting my thoughts, "Map."

I looked up at him.

"What kind of a name's that?"

Clarence laughed and the other boy stared at me with an expression of concern on his face. I wanted to run back to the classroom and hide from all the kids now looking at me. "My name's not Map," I said, meekly. "It's Pam."

Although I had two years in kindergarten, my classmates progressed in their scholastic skills much more rapidly than I. Everything I wrote was backwards, letters, numbers, and my name.

On the final day of school, the kids in my class spoke excitedly among themselves about graduating to first grade and I sat quietly in my seat, chewed my fingernail until it bled, and then sat on my hand to hide the blood from Miss Sylva.

"Pam, don't look so glum," Miss Sylva said, coming to me with a note in her hand. "You're bright enough to catch up with all the other kids. Is that what's worrying you? Do you think you might have to spend another year with me?"

I nodded.

She smiled and hugged me. "Can you give this to your mother for me? It's a letter telling her and your stepdad that you passed."

My jaw dropped. "I did?"

"Yes, you really did."

I sat up in bed the first Monday of the long summer holiday, freshly wakened, and gazed out the window at the verdant lawn. A wren sang nearby and farther away was the sound of a lawnmower. The air, warm and still, had that particular touch of a new time of year.

The entire summer lay ahead of me. "Gosh," I mumbled. "I'm not going back to school for a long time and boy am I glad." I thought of all the fun things I'd do, climb our tree, play with Robin, and teach our dogs tricks, how to sit and roll over.

Aunt Marylou and Uncle Bud had four kids the same ages as Robin and me. The previous summer, Poppy built our aunt and her family a cement pool. After that, Mother often took us to their house for hours of swimming. "Maybe we'll go to Aunt Marylou's and swim," I whispered. "That would be fun."

Near the end of the week, Max and Mother moved us off the frenzied thoroughfare to a house with a brand new, fresh paint smell on quiet Wyant Way. Our home had a snug kitchen and a dining area. Three bedrooms and a single bathroom were down the only hall, and a glass door off the living room opened to the back patio and yard.

The day we moved in, Mother showed Robin and me the floor plan. "You get your own rooms again," she was saying over her shoulder as she led the way to the first bedroom on the right. "We shouldn't have to move again for a long time. Girls, this will be your home for many years. After all, your stepdad's buying it." With a wave of her hand, she gestured toward my twin bed against one wall and a three-drawer dresser against the other. "Pam, how do you like it?"

It was late afternoon and ambient light filtered through sheer white curtains covering a single pane window behind the two posts of my bedframe. My eyes roamed the room, landing on the collection of dolls arranged side by side on the twin bed. "It's so nice. Mommy, thank you." I lifted a doll to my shoulder and cradled her before giving Mother a fast hug and following her and Robin down the hall.

"Robin, your room's this way," she said, entering the bedroom at the end of the hall. She stepped aside and let Robin and me enter.

Next to a neatly made bed was a closet with a double door cabinet over it, and across the room, a three-drawer dresser with a few toys on it, an Etch-a-Sketch and a wire Slinky. A window with lined drapes overlooked the front yard.

"When your Poppy bought the house on Foster Way," Mother said, "I met some of the kids in the neighborhood. Let's see, there was Shirley, Dee Dee, Brother Bob—We all attended high school together. Gee, we had lots of fun. All these years, we've remained close, like family."

Mother went to the window and opened the drapes. Sunlight streamed in, brightening the room. "Ah. That's much better." She leaned against the doorway and placed a hand on one hip. "Two girls from down the road stopped by to meet you this morning. I think they're your ages."

"Will they be back today?" Robin said.

"I don't think so. They said they'd come by tomorrow. Well, it looks like you'll have no trouble making new friends."

Later that month, Max's voice outside my bedroom woke me when the yellow glow of morning had just crested the horizon. "We had a little problem last night." His voice was so low that it was barely audible.

I rubbed tiny, "sleepy seeds" from my eyes, and stared across the length of my bed at Mother who was standing in the hall. "Well, good morning to you, too," she teased before replying to Max's statement. "Honey, what did you have trouble with?"

"It's probably nothing worth worrying over," he said.

"You were up late again." Mother said and tied the belt around her full length terry robe. "I'm surprised to see you so early." She scratched her head, tousling her uncombed, short hair. "What did you have trouble with?"

"The drapes were on fire."

Mother's eyes grew wide. "What? Where?"

"In the living room."

"But how?"

"Joy, I don't know. Come on. I'll show you."

A fire in our house? While we were sleeping? Max doesn't know how it started. Mommy doesn't know why.

As if there weren't anything to worry about, somewhere outside my window, a sparrow sang and another began singing in response, their voices rising, happily chirping. The birds seemed happy enough, but I was scared. *How come there was a fire in the living room? What would make the curtain catch fire?* I pulled the covers up to my chin. *What if there's another fire when we're asleep?*

CHAPTER TEN

*T*he weeks passed and I forgot about the curtain fire. Mother plunged into family life, keeping house, making meals, and teaching Robin and me various non-scholastic lessons. The kitchen, my favorite room in the whole house, became our classroom. Here she taught us how to set the table, wash dishes, mash potatoes, batter fry chicken, and in this very kitchen Mother lectured us on the facts of life.

Days before the sex talk, one fall afternoon in first grade, I rushed through the front door and announced the latest news. "Mommy! Henry wants me to be his girlfriend." Henry, in the same grade with me, lived a few houses down from us.

"That's nice dear," she said. "Go play now."

An obvious no big deal, I let it go. But Henry didn't. During school recess and lunchtime, like a lovesick puppy, he trailed after me. The idea of being his or anyone's girlfriend repulsed me, and I hid from him. He found me. I ran from him. He chased me. Sunday mornings, he waited for me on the front lawn of our house and took off his shoes and left them there. I put smelly dog doo in them. Even this deterrent didn't hamper his efforts. Finally, I flat out told him, "Henry, leave me alone!" But he acted as if he hadn't heard.

Many afternoons, after the school dismissal bell rang, Henry trailed behind me on the eighteen-minute walk home. Henry's maniacal pursuit vexed me, but I didn't hate him. As

I walked toward my house one afternoon, I heard Pierre and Suzette barking. They must've anticipated my homecoming and the moment I'd enter the house, hurry through the living room to the back door, and go outside and pet them. That's the first thing I did each day after school. And there was something else. Henry was lying prostrate on my front lawn. *He's not moving. What's wrong with him? Maybe he died.*

Mortified, I ran to him. "Henry! Henry!"

He rolled over onto his back. Little yellow leaves, carried by the wind into our yard from our neighbor's tree, clung to his striped red and blue shirt and grey corduroy pants.

"What're you doing?" I said.

He jumped up and looked embarrassed. "Waitin' for you." He rubbed his eyes and brushed the leaves off his clothes. "Guess I fell asleep. Hey, I wanna show you somethin'." He crossed the lawn to the side of my house where no one could see us and I followed. "Come over here." He raised his voice. "And look in my hair."

"Well, okay," I said reluctantly.

Pierre and Suzette, our only witnesses, peered longingly at us through the spaces between the slats in the redwood fence. Henry bent his head forward and parted his greasy, blond hair with his grimy fingers.

I stepped closer and took a peek.

"Do ya see 'em?" he said.

"See what?" I said.

"Don't ya see somethin' movin?"

I stared at his scalp. "Those little brown things?"

"Yeah. Those things. I think I have lice." He sounded positively disturbed. "Can ya pick 'em out?"

I'd heard about lice and knew they were contagious. I jumped back and shook my head.

His face turned bright red with embarrassment. "Come on," he whined. "Can't ya get 'em off me. Please." He scratched his head. "They itch."

This must be what girlfriends do for their boyfriends. I'm not getting lice. Touching head lice was out of the question. I couldn't bring myself to do it. I crossed my arms and glared at him. "Henry, stop trying to make me be your girl." I marched into the house and left him standing there.

One Saturday morning, when the last of the pink and red roses that grew along the side of our front lawn had bloomed, Mother told Robin and me to sit on the kitchen table. I stood on a chair and climbed up beside my big sister. Across the room, a cool breeze blew through the open kitchen window rippling Mother's plum colored blouse and whipping short strands of hair along her face. She closed the window, patted the loose strands back into place along the sides of her bouffant, and came over to us.

"Girls, it's time you learned about the facts of life," she said. "When I was a girl, your grandmother never talked to me about dating, or romance, or what happens to a girl at puberty."

Ignorant of the entire subject, I didn't understand. *What does she mean the facts of life? And what's puberty?* But I was an eager learner and concentrated hard on her presentation.

"When a man meets a woman and they fall in love..." She looked at us with unusual misty-eyed warmth. She covered menstruation, dating, boys and girls holding hands, kissing, and other activities which could lead to "conception"—That was a big word. Mother explained its meaning. She held back little, including a minuscule amount of information about the very act of sex which leads to conception. And just like the inquiry of who we thought she should marry, I didn't have the wherewithal to grasp the full meaning of this information, mind boggling as it was. Most of her talk zipped right over my seven-year-old brain.

I glanced at my nine-year-old sister's strained expression, her furrowed brow and squinting eyes. As far as I was concerned, I would never hold hands with a boy or do those other things. Mother grinned and her eyes twinkled, and I wished she'd stop talking about boys and girls, men and women. *There will be none of that kissing stuff for me. Yuck!*

Twelve minutes later, Mother concluded her facts of life speech. "Your daddy and I fell in love, and from that love..." she smiled affectionately, "we had you girls." She placed a warm hand against each of our cheeks, adoring us with her eyes. This is different, I decided. *Mother never smiles into my eyes and she almost never touches me.* Her weird behavior made me feel good and I hoped she would have more talks with us but on a different subject. "Do you have any questions?" she said.

I didn't know what to say and apparently, neither did Robin. A confused expression flitted across her face, and we both shook our heads and shrugged our shoulders.

Mother's eyes had lost their sparkle. "Well, okay. Then get down from the table and go play until lunch." Her voice was no longer warm, signaling the end of our special moment.

As I hurried from the kitchen, a sinking feeling came over me. I wasn't sure why but I thought it might have to do with the bleeding and pain Mommy said I'd have someday. A chill ran up my spine, and I was afraid.

CHAPTER ELEVEN

I didn't have eyes for Henry, but I sure as anything had them for Dad and Max. I wanted to be a daddy's princess and ached for a close relationship with both my father figures. Dad was fond of Robin and me. Every couple weeks, he came by and took us on fun outings. But I had doubts about Max. He and I hardly ever spoke. To my way of thinking, if he liked me, we'd have conversations.

Once, Max took us all camping. The whole time, he said few words, except for the afternoon I napped in our green canvas, army tent and a little animal, inside the sleeping bag with me, ran across my bare feet tucked within the heavy cotton bag. I shrieked.

"Kid, what is it?" Max had said from outside the tent door.

I trembled. "Something's in my sleeping bag." Just then it scampered up my body, its tiny claws scratching my bare legs. When it reached my torso, two tiny, beady eyes stared into my face. I froze in fear. The little brown thing was no bigger than my hand. It now ran across my torso, and out the open tent door.

Max laughed. "Kid, it was just a chipmunk. He was more afraid of you than you are of him. Go back to sleep."

Sometimes when Dad took Robin and me with him, we'd stay the night in sleeping bags on his living room floor. Spending the weekend with him this way reminded me of the camping trip with Max. It was almost the same thing, except at Dad's there weren't chipmunks, and we had a toilet that didn't stink, and a television that stayed on until the Native American chief with the beautiful full headdress, came on at midnight, speaking with hand signals and saying the "Our Father Who Art in Heaven" prayer. Then the set emitted a high-pitched buzz, the screen went grey, and that's when Dad would get up from his chair. "Time to turn off the boob tube," he'd say before clicking off the knob.

When he wasn't working, Max tinkered around the house, messed with his new silver Corvette, and watched sports programs. I'd trail behind him, smile, and pop the question. "What are you doin'?"

He'd always tell me the same thing. "Nothing," or he'd say, "Going crazy."

Then I'd reply, "No sir!" and he'd chuckle.

One evening as the sun began to set, I tailed him to the front yard and watched him wash the Corvette parked in the driveway. He sprayed it with water, lathered it with soap, and rinsed off the bubbles.

I asked him the obvious. "What are you doin'?"

"Going crazy, kid." He pulled the hose around and I followed close behind him. "Kid, your mother's calling you," he said, spraying the passenger side.

"No sir," I said.

Max hosed the bubbles off his fancy car and a light mist showered down on me so I stepped out of the way. "Really, she is." He smiled playfully. "Well? Didn't you hear her?"

"Nope."

"Go on, kid. Go play in the freeway."

I knew I wasn't supposed to be in the street, and I put on my stubborn face with folded arms and refused to leave.

"Kid, can you give me a hand?"

He had actually conceded and I couldn't believe my ears. Max needed my help. I felt a smile spread across my face. "Can I spray your car?" I said, reaching for the hose.

He handed me a towel. "Dry the hubcaps, kid."

That evening, I hugged Mother goodnight and then, forgetting that Max didn't hug, I hurried over to where he was seated in front of the television and wrapped my arms around as much of him as possible. Max stiffened and kept his arms at his sides. *Why doesn't he love me?* I would've been satisfied knowing he just liked me. I watched his face for signs of liking me. There weren't any. "Goodnight," I said.

He cleared his throat. "Night, kid."

Two months later, I looked at the miracle in our living room. Santa Claus had visited our home, while we all slept, and left dozens of presents around the Christmas tree. Robin and I received "Baby Tenderlove" dolls, a miniature pool table, games, bathrobes with fuzzy slippers, and new bikes. Mine was a blue Huffy with a white banana seat, a sissy bar, and a set of training wheels.

It was a chilly, winter day and I was riding my bike, balanced by two extra wheels attached to the back tire, in the street outside our home. The sun was out and Max was trimming the dormant rose bushes in the front yard. "Kid!" he called to me. "Come over here and let me see your bike for a minute."

I dismounted on the lawn and watched him remove the training wheels. "Why are you doing that?" I said.

He steadied my bike for me. "Here, get on."

My heart beat fast and my mouth felt dry as a potato chip. "I can't. I'll fall."

"Kid, it's easy. Get on and pedal. I'll hold onto your bike."

He bent over me and I looked up into his grin. Max's

brown bangs fell across his forehead practically covering his smiling brown eyes. I could do this, I realized. I could ignore the fear pounding in my chest. "Promise not to let me fall," I said, climbing onto my bike. "Promise," I said again.

He gripped the back of my seat. "Kid, you won't fall."

"You have to promise."

He gave me a little push, holding me up, and trotting alongside me. "Go on, pedal as fast as you can."

I pedaled with Max hanging on, running, and panting. I pushed harder against the pedals, gaining speed, while Max ran faster. A rhythm had formed, down stroke with one foot followed by the other, down with one, then the other. Near the end of our road, from somewhere far away, Max hollered, "Kid! You're doing it! That's the way!"

Suddenly, it dawned on me and I smiled to myself. *Max isn't holding onto my bike and I'm riding without training wheels.* I went up Wyant Way, elated, like I'd escaped confinement and broken into freedom. My feet couldn't pump fast enough and I soared past Max, watching me from the driveway.

I wanted Alicia and Bonnie, two of my friends who lived across the street from us, to see me riding my ultra neat bike without training wheels. My bike with me on it flew past their house. They weren't outside, but I waved just in case they were watching out the window.

That night as Max watched television, Mother came into the bathroom while I was brushing my teeth. "Do you think you should thank Daddy Max for helping you with your bike?"

I rinsed my mouth and put my toothbrush in its place on the stand near the sink. "Daddy Max?" I called, galloping down the hall and across the living room.

He turned from the television with a look of surprise on his face. This was the first time I'd called him "Daddy."

"Yeah, kid."

"Thanks for helping with my bike."

"Sure, kid."

I wrapped my arms around him and squeezed. He stiffened, reached one arm around me, and patted my back. A surge of affection came over me. "I love you," I said, holding onto him.

"Me too," he said.

When I went to bed, I sought for sleep curled up in my white blanket, the one that had been Robin's when she was a baby, and considered Max's small sign of affection. *He said he loves me.*

CHAPTER TWELVE

"*A*licia and Bonnie said they're taking swimming lessons. They have swimming passes and they asked Pam and me to swim with them," Robin said as Mother spooned out scrambled eggs onto our breakfast plates. "Can we go with them? Please. I mean, may we?"

School was out again for the summer and most of the neighborhood kids would be at the community pool, just a few blocks from our home. I wanted to swim with them more than anything and, along with Robin, I raised my eyebrows, frowned, and pleaded with my eyes.

Mother shook her head. "Geez! You'd think someone was dying. We'll be visiting Uncle Bud's and Marylou's soon. Cross my heart. And you can swim then, with your cousins, and since there's a pool in the family, you're both good swimmers already. You don't need lessons." She smiled broadly. "I swear! You girls are a couple of fishes. You could teach your girlfriends to swim. Besides, who do you know who gets to have coke and pizza, and select songs from a jukebox?"

"We're going to The Green Parrot?" Robin said.

"That's right."

Going to the bar with Mother was all about getting things we'd never get if we went to the community pool–soda pop and pizza, for instance. Swimming with Alicia and Bonnie sounded like fun until Mother pointed out the ordinariness of it.

Practically every day, we made the twenty-minute drive to The Green Parrot. Immediately upon entering the bar, Mother took her usual seat with her three closest drinking buddies. The large room, like a lot of California bars in the early seventies, stank of beer and cigarette smoke. Poppy sat to her left near the double swinging doors, separating the pizza order area from the barroom, and Brother Bob and Uncle Ernie—neither were relatives—sat to her right. Robin and I were at a picnic table, sipping cups of 7-Up through red plastic straws. Often, Mother and the bartender, Edie, were the only women present. Since we saw our uncle, who wasn't really our uncle, and Mother's brother, who wasn't really her brother, and Poppy here, she called it "a family place."

After lunchtime during the first week of summer vacation, Robin and I kept our eyes on the scene at the bar and waited for Mother. I thought she was more beautiful than any person I'd ever seen, and powerful, and incapable of making a mistake. I noticed the attentiveness paid to her by our "uncle," her "brother," and various other men who came in for drinks. I figured they felt about her as I did.

Mother alternated her activity at the bar between talking, laughing, smoking filter-less cigarettes, and sipping beer. I watched her puff a cigarette to the half way mark. Here she squished it inside of a brown, plastic ashtray, and extinguished the orange glowing end. She straightened the compressed remains, rubbed it between her two slender fingers, and set the remaining un-smoked half beside her drink for later use.

Poppy drank more than ever since Nana's death. Seeing him made me miss Nana even more. I wanted Mother and Poppy to talk about her and about our lives before her death. It had been three years since her suicide, but Aunt Marylou was the only adult who ever mentioned her name.

Mother joked with Poppy. He clenched his lips around a black pipe, and used his body more than words, nodding, shaking his jowls, widening his eyes, and gesturing with the three short fingers of his right hand.

All day long, Robin and I sat at the picnic table, only getting up to use the bathroom at the back of the "family place" or to drop a quarter into the jukebox.

"This is *really* boring," I said to Robin, seated across from me.

"I know, Pam. Maybe Mommy will take us home soon."

I watched the smoke from a dozen lit cigarettes and our granddad's pipe spiral upwards where it hung like a thick cloud over the beer and wine drinkers.

Robin and I sipped our sodas and, every now and then, glanced up at Mother and checked the level of fluid in her stein. We'd comment to one another about the quantity in her mug and talk about the fun we'd have when we went home. As soon as Mother swallowed the last foamy drop, we'd get to go home. Unless she ordered another one.

The sun began setting when Mother finally got up from her stool and staggered toward us. "Girls, time to leave," she said, her words sounding funny, as though she had a mouth full of cotton.

One late afternoon around the first of July, Robin and I were elated to arrive home from The Green Parrot before dark so we could play outside for a while. Mother put the finishing touches on dinner when Max got home from work and we all sat at the beautifully arranged table. Four glasses were filled to the brim with water and ice cubes. There were matching plates loaded with delicious smelling pot roast, potatoes, and carrots, and saucers for dinner rolls, a crystal covered butter dish, and a bottle of salad dressing—the kind made with vinegar, oil, water, and a packet of seasoning.

Mother had on a pretty dress nearly as blue as her eyes. She sat next to Max and handed him the crystal salt and pepper shakers, but he didn't meet her steady gaze and he didn't say a word. Lately, a tangible hostility had existed between them. I couldn't remember the last time Mother and he went on a date or watched television together. Many nights after Robin and I went to bed, they spoke sharply to each other. The atmosphere around them felt tight, like a balloon the millisecond before it bursts.

Mother studied Max's expressionless face. "Honey, don't you like your dinner?"

His eyes were on his plate. "It's fine."

Several minutes later, Mother looked at him as tears slid down her cheeks. "Are you sure it's okay?"

Max shifted his focus from his plate to her questioning stare. "I *said* it's fine," he snapped.

I fidgeted in my chair and Mother gave my leg a swift kick. It wasn't the first time she had done so. Kicking Robin and me under the table was her way of telling us to sit still and be quiet. I stiffened and bit my bottom lip and saw Robin out of the corner of my eye picking at the roasted potatoes on her plate.

"What is it? Another woman?" Mother's face reddened. "Why don't you just tell me if it is?"

Max flashed her a bitter look. "*You* tell me, Joy," he said with his mouth half full of food.

"Tell you what? About *your* new friend?" Mother dabbed the corners of her eyes with her cloth napkin. She stood and tossed it onto the table.

Max rose from the table without replying and left the room.

When Mother returned to the table, Robin held up her empty glass. "Mommy, may I have more milk?"

She gritted her teeth, picked up a serving spoon from the platter with the roast on it, and struck Robin's face. I gasped and choked back sobs. Blood began pouring from my sister's nose. She ran to the bathroom crying. Afraid I'd be next, I ate every last bit of food on my plate and kept all my troubling thoughts to myself.

The quarrel escalated into angry shouts. Robin and I, not knowing what to do, went to my room and hoped for the best. We sat on my bed and stared at the hall outside my door. Heavy footfalls drew near—Max was hurrying up the hall toward the room he shared with Mother.

"That's right, walk away from me," Mother said from behind him. "You can tell me. What's *her* name?"

Max stopped suddenly and spun around. Facing her, he raised his hands in frustration. "Look, you've had too much to drink and you don't even know what you're talking about. Do you really want to know her name? It's Joy Williams."

"Fann-tastic!" she said with her hands on her hips and an angry grin on her face.

He raised his voice. "I'm telling you, there isn't anyone else."

Mother wagged a slender finger at him. "Max, you think I'm a fool. Don't you? Well, I'm no fool."

"I don't think that at all. Would you like to know what I think?" He gave her no time to respond. "What I think is that your drinking's out of control and why don't you stay home sometime? That would be different, now, wouldn't it?"

Mother rolled her eyes. "Tell me, is she pretty?"

"All right, I've had enough of this. Why don't you tell me something," he said, boring holes into her with his piercing eyes. "Joy, I've got your number. Who've you been meeting up with?"

"I'm not."

"Liar."

Mother doubled up her fist and punched Max in the eye. He slapped her face.

She gasped in pain as she threw her hand over her cheek and rushed to their bedroom.

He stormed from the house.

I'd never been so afraid. I scooted closer to Robin and, touching arms, felt her slight trembling. Her eyes filled with tears, "Pam," she said weakly, "are you all right?"

"I don't know," I said. For the first time since dinner, I noticed Robin's nose. It was bright red and swollen. "Does it hurt bad? Your nose, I mean."

She touched it with a finger and winced. "A little. I think it might be broken."

The house had grown quiet and Robin and I stayed in my room, not knowing what to do, not having anyone but each other to turn to for help and comfort. "I'm not ever going to ask Mommy for milk," Robin said. "Mommy hit me." She shuddered and her eyes filled with more tears. "She doesn't even spank us, but she kicks us under the table and she hit my nose."

An hour or so earlier, my trust in Mother was solid, but that was before I witnessed her assault Robin and then Max. Sure, he had slapped her, but I understood why. He had reacted in self defense. Mother's moods were unpredictable and explosive. I was the only one in our household who she hadn't hit. Tears rolled down my face. "Robin, Mommy might come in here and punch me next. Huh?"

"No, she's not going to do that. Besides, you haven't done anything to make her mad. Mommy's mad at me and Max."

That night in bed, I couldn't sleep. Someone came to the foot of my bed and peered down at me, and I was gripped with a paralyzing fear. I wanted to scream, but I was too frightened. I wanted to pound on my bedroom wall, alerting Mother and Max of the intruder in my room, but my arms had lost their strength and all I could do was claw the surface of the wall beside me with my fingers. The figure moved closer to me and, in the semi-dark room, I began making out her features. It was Mother. Then, without speaking to me, she left my room. A few moments later, she returned with a glass of water. After drinking it, I fell asleep.

CHAPTER THIRTEEN

$\mathcal{T}$he first Saturday after the fight, Max went to his parents' house to help them with something and Mother took Robin and me with her to The Green Parrot. We arrived a half hour before opening and waited in the parked Impala between a large trash bin belonging to a nearby grocery store and a stack of empty cardboard boxes. Edie arrived at noon and unlocked the back door.

"Girls, come on," Mother said, leading the way. She turned into the ladies room. "Wait here," she said. The lavatory, the non-fancy kind, had a white porcelain sink, cloth hand towel dispenser, and a single toilet stall all within a few feet of the door.

The room, confining and cold, smelled of mothballs. "It stinks in here," I said. A spring-loaded mousetrap sitting in the corner had a shriveled piece of cheese in it. "Mommy, do we have to wait here?"

Mother opened the bathroom door. "Pammie, you and your sister will be fine," she said and left us there.

"Robin, she's not making us stay in here all day, is she?"

"Beats me. How would I know?" She folded and unfolded her arms. Several minutes later, she grinned. "Hey, let's think of a game. It'll make the time go faster. Let's see..." Robin went over to the towel dispenser beside the sink. "We could play...umm." She tapped a finger against her lips. "I know, the towel pulling game."

The white, metal box attached to the wall had an opening for a spool of continuous feed, cotton hand towels. Robin pulled down on the cloth. "This is how you play. We each take turns pulling the towel and the first one to reach the end of the roll wins."

"Wins what?" I said, "a get out of jail free card."

"No, silly. A stick of gum. Of course, we'll have to get a pack. We'll do that later."

After ten minutes of continual pulling, we realized the crinkled cloth coming from the metal box was wet and well used. "This is gross," Robin said, releasing her hand full of damp towel. "We'll do something else."

"Come on," I said, and I opened the door and peered out at a row of adults around the bar, seated with their backs toward us. "Let's sneak out and see how far we can get before Mommy catches us."

"She'll be mad," Robin said. "Really, really mad. I don't want to get hit again."

Her mention of the incident from the previous week changed my mind and I shut the door and went to her. "Mommy really scared me."

She flipped up the back of my hair playfully. "Scared you?" She smiled. "It was my nose she hit." Robin shifted her attention to the empty mousetrap. "Do you think there are mice in here?"

"Yes," I said. "If a cute little mouse comes out of hiding, let's catch it and keep it as a pet."

There wasn't any place to sit and Robin leaned against the wall. Soon, she began talking about the night of Mother and Max's quarrel. "I can't believe Mommy did that to me, and for what? All I did was ask for a glass of milk." She raised her brows and her eyes widened. "She's been acting really weird.

Have you noticed? Something's wrong. Did she kick you under the table last night?"

"Uh-huh." I stared at the trap in the corner and thought how happy for the mouse that he had escaped. "I talk too much."

"No you don't." She leaned closer to me, standing beside her, and tapped my arm. "Look at me."

My eyes met hers. There was a look of compassion in them. "You didn't do anything to deserve getting kicked. Talking's not bad. Asking Mommy to take us to Aunt Marylou's isn't a crime."

An hour or so later, long after we had become antsy, Mother poked her head into the bathroom.

"Mommy, I don't feel good," Robin said.

Mother frowned, rolled her eyes, and shook her head as if Robin had bothered her. "Are you sick?"

"I don't know. My tummy feels weird."

She tsked and sighed. "Girls, this way." We followed her out of the bathroom and to the serving area where she pointed a slender, polished fingernail at a picnic table, motioning for us to sit there.

Mother took her usual seat between Uncle Ernie and Brother Bob. Other men sat along the bar at the end farthest from us, near a television set with a baseball game playing on it, the volume turned down low. Mother smoothed the wrinkles out of her skirt, crossed her legs and balanced on the stool by hooking one two-inch heel over the barstool's footrest. She held a smoldering cigarette in her one hand and a mug of beer in the other. Her red nails glistened under the overhead lights.

I kept my eyes on that Budweiser, gauged our release from the stuffy, smoke-filled room by the quantity of beer in the clear mug, and hoped the one in her hand would be her parting drink. Mother chugged down the bottom half of her beer and ordered another. Robin met my eyes and we both released a long, breathy puff of disappointment.

Uncle Ernie turned to Mother. "Joy, your dad was by yesterday. Gosh, he looks real good. Says he's just finished tuning up Marylou's pool. It's such a beautiful day. Real hot, though, just right for swimming. Too bad you and the girls are stuck in here on such a fine day." Ernie's black bushy eyebrows rose as he smiled sheepishly, and snickered. "The girls might enjoy a swim."

I loved the sound of his suggestion and stared hopefully at Mother. When summer first began, she had promised us a day of swimming with our cousins. I crossed the fingers of both my hands and showed them to Robin.

She laid her head on her folded arms on the table. "Uh-huh."

I began thinking hard. *Say yes, yes, yes. Mommy, take us swimming. Take us swimming. Take us swimming.* I closed my eyes and squeezed my crossed fingers. *Please, please. Say yes.*

"Not today, Ernie," she said.

"Well, maybe some other time," Ernie said quickly, too quickly.

I uncrossed my fingers and laid my head on the picnic table with my sister.

Brother Bob shot the bull as usual, but Mother sulked.

"Joy? Is everything okay?" Uncle Ernie said.

"I'm fine," she said.

He lifted his full stein of beer to Mother. "Well, anyways, here's to better days ahead." He sipped the foam off the top.

Mother, the social queen of The Parrot, lifted her mug without a word.

Brother Bob studied her for a long moment, his eyes un-blinking as he scrutinized her facial expression and slumped shoulders. Then he playfully shook her arm. "Joy, do I smell bad or something?"

They'd all been friends for years and she often confided in them. "Look guys," she said and tapped the long, red tip of her manicured nail against the bar-top, "Max and I had an argument. That's all." She picked up the lit cigarette on the edge of the ashtray and took a long drag. "Would you just lay off for a while?" she said, blowing thick white smoke from her mouth.

Several minutes later, Robin told me she felt hot. We both had on shorts and cotton tops. An overhead air conditioner rattled against the ceiling and blew out cold air. Robin sat up, clutched her blond ponytails in her hands, and pressed them against the sides of her head. Ten minutes later, she looked at Mother who was a short distance from us. "Mommy, I don't feel good. I think we should go home," she said.

"Are you sick?" I said.

She glanced at me. "I feel weird. Maybe I am sick." Then, with her hands pressed against her stomach, she looked over at Mother. "I think I'm sick," she called, "my tummy doesn't feel good."

Mother ignored her, but Ernie waved his fingers up and down at us and smiled. He threw out his lower lip to make an especially sad and ridiculous face, a definite demonstration of support for Robin's plight. "It's a shame she's not feeling well, Joy. Oh, the poor, poor dear," he whined and shook his head.

"Yes, okay," Mother said before sipping the white foam off the top of her newly ordered mug of beer. She cast a steely stare at my sister and smashed her cigarette against the side of the plastic ashtray.

Several more minutes went by. "Mommy, I think I'm sick." Robin spoke a little louder. "Mommy!" Her bottom lip quivered.

We had known Ernie just about as long as we knew anyone. He and Mother had attended the same high school and grew up in this neighborhood. Usually, when Ernie came into The Green Parrot, he stopped at our table and greeted us, patted the tops of our heads, or gave us hugs. Mother said he was weird, but I didn't think so. Sometimes he offered us a soda pop or gave us quarters for the jukebox. I liked Ernie.

"Joy, I hope Robin's not getting sick," he said.

"I know, Ernie," she said with a look of exasperation. "I'll take care of it." She picked up her black purse and flicked her finger at Robin and me to follow her to our car.

I sat beside Robin in the front seat and felt Mother's glowering disapproval. The black asphalt in front of us seemed to stretch on forever. The hot weather played tricks on my eyes. The heat caused phantom lakes to appear and ripple in the distance. Once we drove over a particular spot, they vanished and popped up again a little further down the road.

At home, Mother motioned for us to follow her. "Robin, a hot bath will lower your fever," she said and turned into the bathroom where she filled the enamel tub with warm water. "Get in." She said little else. Her hard slate expression, her tense jaw line, and piercing eyes spoke volumes.

Robin got into the tub and Mother went to the living room where Max was watching a baseball game on television. Mother's irritation boiled over. She loaded her slingshot and aimed her word stones, again accusing Max of infidelity. They hit their mark and he reacted with icy replies. The tension between them frightened me and I sucked in my breath and prayed they'd stop before someone threw a punch.

I didn't want to leave my sister's side, but something caught my attention in the hall, and I went to the doorway to check it out, and peered at Robin's room. White and grey smoke trailed in thick puffs out of the cracks surrounding the upper cabinet doors of her closet. That cabinet was far too high for any of us to reach.

I screamed for Mother, and she rushed down the hall, saw the smoke, and yelled for Max.

"Max, Robin's closet's on fire. Hurry!"

He responded immediately, rounded the hall corner, saw the smoke, spun on his heels, and ran to the kitchen. In half a minute, he stood on a chair and reached up for one of two upper cabinets in Robin's room.

"I'm done," Robin said, getting out the bathtub, the water dripping from her. She pulled her clothes on over her wet skin while I turned my attention back to her room and the smoke billowing from the cracks along the cabinet doors. Max grabbed the doorknob, pulled, and large amounts of inky black smoke and intense, orange flames rushed at him. I thought he would be burned alive.

Right then and there, I had the sensation of all the blood rushing out of my face. My head felt light and somehow disengaged from the rest of my body. Instantly, I found myself outside on the doorstep, but I had no idea how I arrived there. I began screaming in terror. I caught my breath, inhaled deeply, and yelled, "Fire! Fire! Call the fire trucks! Fire! Fire! Fire!"

Someone reached out through the open front door, tightly gripped my thin arm, yanked me inside the house, and slapped my face. Pain shot through my cheek. It was Mother. I didn't understand why she struck me or what I had done to deserve her wrath. She glared down at me. "Now, be quiet!" she scolded.

That very second, Max hollered from Robin's room, "Joy, better take the girls outside and hurry, call the fire department!"

Soon, the sound of sirens brought the entire neighborhood to life. Ours was a fairly new subdivision with young families and a few retirees. All up and down the block, our neighbors stood in little groups on their front lawns, the sidewalk, and even in the road. There was a great deal of pointing toward our house and worried whispers as two fire engines pulled up to our curb. Alicia, Bonnie, and Henry joined Robin and me on the lawn near the rose bushes that separated our place from our neighbor next door.

Firemen worked inside our house, shouting directions, their axes chopping and water spraying. The commotion overwhelmed me. After they extinguished the blaze, a fireman approached Mother and Max. He removed his sooty hat. Beads of sweat glistened on his brow and ran down his sideburns. Patches of soot covered his face. "We got it out before it had a chance to spread. That's the good news." His face remained grave. "Unfortunately, there's extensive smoke and water damage to that bedroom."

Mother stood with both hands on her hips. Her jaw jutted out and pink blotches covered her face.

Max shook his head in disbelief.

"Do you have any idea what started it?" the fireman said.

Max's bangs hung over his eyes. "No, sir, I don't," he said, pushing them back into place.

"Were there flammable liquids in the closet?"

"No. Nothing like that's kept in the house."

"There'll be an investigation," the fireman said. "We'll go back in there later and have a better look at it."

That evening, Max said we would stay with Aunt Marylou and Uncle Bud for a while. On the way there, Mother looked over her shoulder at Robin and me in the back seat. "Everything's going to be okay," she said. I wondered how anything could ever be like it had been, but I chose not to respond. Neither did Robin, nor Max. Mother went on to tell Max that she had slapped me because I had been hysterical and that's how you wake children from their hysteria. She sounded arrogant like she had saved the day by stopping my screams.

"It's a good thing the slap worked. Pammie may have gone on like that for a long time." She looked back at me again. "I've never slapped you until today," she said.

The next day Robin and I were in the swimming pool for hours with our cousins, Kat, David, Dwayne, and Cindy. We swam until dark. Practically every day that week we swam until our teeth chattered and our lips turned blue. By the time Mother and Max took us home, my fair-headed cousins and sister had a ghastly, greenish glow to their blond hair.

We went home without knowing what caused the curtain and closet fires and the investigators hadn't contacted Mother or Max with their findings. At least, this was Mother's reply to Aunt Marylou's inquiry about it.

The smoke had destroyed Robin's bedroom furniture, clothes, and toys. A board was nailed over her closet and her door was kept shut. She slept on a twin bed across from me in my room. With her there, fire and the unknown didn't frighten me. She'd watch out for me, lay awake listening to the steady rhythm of my breath, keep her ears attuned to the sounds in our home, sniff the air for evidence of a new, yet to be discovered, fire. If the curtain or my closet caught fire, she'd alert me and the rest of our household. She'd hold these vigils, as I later learned, every night, well into our teen years.

CHAPTER FOURTEEN

*I*n August, Mother called cheerfully from the bathroom, "Girls, get your shoes on. We're going to see your grand-dad."

Mother's happy mood was always welcome—it meant smiles and giggles and nice things said to Robin and me. We climbed into the Impala's front seat, and Mother slipped on a huge pair of Van Ray sunglasses, cranked up the volume on the radio, and sang.

Years before while she was in high school, she was on the school choir and in the glee club. Near the end of her high school career, she tried out for the San Francisco Opera and was accepted, but for some reason she decided against it. I admired my mother's singing. Her beautiful soprano voice complemented Barbra Streisand's coming over the radio.

It was hot and Mother slid the shiny, silver lever on the console, switching on the air conditioner and blasting us with frigid air. We always went straight through the first stoplight on the way to The Parrot. However, this time Mother turned left at the four-way intersection and headed toward downtown.

"Mommy? Where are we going?" Robin said.

"To see if Poppy's visiting his friend Luke at a bar across town."

We hadn't seen Poppy at The Parrot in over a week. For some reason unknown to me, he wasn't coming in as much as he used to.

Robin furrowed her brow. "Luke?"

Mother giggled. "You've never heard of him? Hmm. Well, he and Poppy are best friends. They go way back." Luke tends bar, she told us, and Poppy visits him every day, except Sunday. Just like The Parrot, it's closed Sundays, she explained.

Near our destination, we merged into slow moving traffic and trudged along in brownish exhaust haze. We arrived at an old business district where rows of automobile dealerships had their hundreds of vehicles lined up on the pavement. Mother pulled in behind a bar called The Vagabond. She stopped on the chipped and broken asphalt parking lot, turned off the motor, and checked her appearance in the mirror, patting a few loose strands of hair, and touching up her lipstick. "I'd take you in if I could, but minors aren't allowed inside," she said. "Stay right here and roll down the windows. I'll be back in a few minutes."

Thin clouds gathered overhead. Within the first hour of waiting for Mother, the sky became a dense, white ceiling and our car, a hothouse. Gradually, the sun moved toward the west. Heat and humidity increased inside the Impala. The interior temperature soared and we steamed in our sauna. Sweat dripped from my brow. My t-shirt clung to my stomach and my shorts stuck to the back of my thighs. Robin complained of a heat-induced stomachache.

I climbed through the open window on the passenger door, and sat on the window ledge. Robin joined me on the other side. We sat there, our legs dangling inside the car, our torsos, shoulders, arms, and heads outside in the fresh air. We talked to each other across the Impala's roof.

Pretty soon, Poppy came out, and elated to see him, we waved and shouted his name. I thought he'd come over and visit with us, but he just chuckled, ducked into his Ford truck and drove away. Robin shook her head and frowned. "Why didn't he come and talk to us?" I didn't have an answer.

Our perches made for a great way to watch the traffic on the busy street, the automobile dealerships across from us, and the rough looking bar. For several hours, we entertained one another with challenges. We each tried spotting the most Volkswagen Bugs when they appeared on the roadway, we counted customers entering and leaving The Vagabond, and we dared one another to yell "hello" to them.

"Hey! Daddy!" I shouted to a grey haired fella leaving the bar. "Dad-dy!" I hollered while waving wildly at the befuddled looking stranger. After staring at me for a second with his mouth hanging open and his eyes staring blankly, he got into his car and left. Robin and I melted into laughter.

School would begin in September. Robin did well academically and said she'd be happy to be anywhere but here and said she looked forward to fourth grade. Our stomachs gurgled and we shared our common worry: would we ever have something to eat? The craving for something to wet our thirst was harder to take than the ache of hunger, and we hoped Mother would return for us and take us home.

"That busybody!" Mother said one morning in August. She stormed through the house, opening and slamming kitchen cabinets, and stomping around as she put bowls of Frosted Flakes on the table for Robin and me. "Girls, time to eat," she said, abruptly.

The memory of the spoon incident motivated me to remain silent whenever Mother sounded or even looked angry. Robin and I, sitting across from each other, ate without saying a word. Mother rushed through the kitchen with a smoldering cigarette between her fingers. She opened the refrigerator, across from where we sat, took out a beer, and came to the table with her drink. "Did either of you tell Marylou I leave you all day in the hot car?"

Her angry voice and squinting, hard glare terrified me. I shook my head. Most everyday for a solid month, Mother had left Robin and me in the scorching hot Impala during her visits with Poppy inside her new, favorite bar.

"No, promise, we didn't," Robin said.

Mother stared into Robin's wide, apprehensive gaze, and I swear she could read her thoughts and already knew the truth. Her facial features relaxed. "You've never lied to me before," Mother stated factually.

Robin poked her finger into her chest and drew a big X. "Cross my heart, hope to die. Stick a needle in my eye. We didn't tell."

The next Saturday, when Max began mowing the front lawn, Mother took us to The Vagabond to *see* Poppy. Robin and I knew what she really meant. She'd have a great time with Poppy and, if we were lucky, when he left the bar, Robin and I would *see* him get into his pickup.

Mother parked and checked her hair in the mirror. "Girls, you get to come inside today." She grabbed her handbag and called for us to follow.

I couldn't believe my ears. "Can we really?"

"It's 'may I'. And yes. Come on."

I knew a California law forbade children from being in bars that served liquor. "But I'm only seven."

Mother laughed. "Really? Is that so?" Her eyes sparkled mischievously. "I know how old you are. Pammie, you and your sister get to hide," she said in a voice implying that hiding would be fun.

The Vagabond fascinated me. It had been off limits for weeks, and it was a mysterious, forbidden place. Often, I wondered what transpired within its windowless walls. At the back entrance of the long, dirty beige building Mother opened the door. "Remember you aren't permitted inside here." She put a finger to her lips. "Sh! This way, girls."

As soon as we entered, we were assaulted by a frigid blast of air, loud music, raucous talking, the stinging odors of cigarette smoke, and booze. It was chaos and I didn't know which to plug, my nose or my ears.

I plugged my ears and trailed behind Mother and Robin. They appeared before me as shadow figures in the poorly lit environment. I stuck close to their dark forms entering a large room. A minute later, my eyes adjusted to the dimness.

On the right, twenty to twenty-five men and women sat and stood with their backs to us along a massive countertop. We crept passed them without their knowledge and went by a jukebox and several empty tables in the rear of the building.

We turned down a short hall. When Mother stopped and then Robin, I almost ran into them, distracted as I was checking out our surroundings, eyeing the people at the bar, and scanning the row of drinkers for Poppy. Mother opened a door and led us inside a little room with a vanity sink and wall sized, gold framed mirror, cloth towel dispenser, and single toilet behind a stall.

A second ago, hiding in a place forbidden to children was a mysterious adventure, but this bar wasn't that much different than The Green Parrot and the secret place Mother had found for us was no more than a private room where women urinated and fixed their makeup. *How boring. It's just a bathroom.* There wasn't anything exciting about hiding near a toilet.

"Really? We're hiding here?" Robin said.

"Just for a little bit," Mother said. She applied red lipstick and patted her lips with a Kleenex. "Would you like a 7-Up?"

"With a cherry?" I said.

Mother turned from the mirror and lifted a disapproving eyebrow at me. "Pamela Jean Marie, I'm surprised at your manners. You know how to be ladylike. Say, 'yes please'."

"Yes, please," I said, embarrassed I'd forgotten.

She looked at her hair in the mirror. "Robin, 7-Up?" she said while patting the stray ends into place.

"Yes, please," Robin said.

Mother opened the door and pointed a long finger at us. "Girls, you stay put. I'll be back with your orders."

At least, the room was larger than The Parrot's bathroom, but there wasn't any place to sit and I wondered how we'd occupy ourselves during our time of hiding. I had on a cheap pair of sandals with barely a sole and the plush white carpet felt like a cushy layer of foam under my feet. A heavy, flowery fragrance was in the air. It reminded me of some of Mother's barroom girlfriends, women who plastered their faces with a heavy layer of makeup and their hair with spray. They also wore strong perfume.

Twenty minutes later, Mother returned to the bathroom with our drinks. "They're topped off with cherries," she said pleasantly. "Luke gave you each an extra." She grinned and gave them to us. "I'll be back in a few minutes. Wait right here."

The way my mother saw it, putting us in the bar's bathroom was good parenting. She wasn't leaving us alone at home or making us stay outside in the hot sun. I was supposed to be grateful to be in an air-conditioned room. I wasn't. I didn't like being near a toilet, not getting to play, and being away from Mother.

We stood in the bathroom and waited for hours. In that amount of time, a few barroom ladies entered, reacted with surprise to our presence, and used the toilet, or touched up their hair and makeup. However, nothing else of interest happened here.

Robin and I agonized with boredom. "Do you like hiding?" I said.

"You can't really call this hiding," she said. "But if you mean, being here, then no. I hate it."

"When we go home, I'm playing outside with Pierre and Suzette. I'm training them for the circus."

Robin said that she thought that sounded fun. "Hey, do you think Max cares that we're in here?"

"Yeah. If he knows. He wouldn't like it. I know he would tell Mommy to stay home with us." I breathed on the mirror and drew hearts in the fog. "I wish he did know. He'd stop it for sure. Then, Mommy would take us to The Parrot. Any where's better than being stuck here."

"Hmm," she said like Mother often does when she's considering something. Without a window or clock we had no idea of the time, but we knew we had waited for most of the day. We laughed at our stomachs making gurgling noises. Each time they growled, we made light of it and giggled.

Then, after hours of waiting, Robin huffed. "Oh, this is maddening! I can't believe this." She went to the door and opened it. "Let's go see Mommy. It's gotta be dinner time."

I stepped right behind her, and we peeked our heads out the door and glanced down the hall toward the long bar, filled with customers.

Robin pointed. "She's over there." She led the way to our mother seated at the furthest end near the entrance. "We'll tell her we need to eat," she said over her shoulder.

We eased ourselves out of the bathroom and headed for the dark wood counter surrounded on one side by rows of booze and on the other by mostly grey haired, talking, laughing, yelling people. The music from the jukebox combined with raucous voices produced an ear splitting noise. Robin and I tiptoed up to Mother. She was seated beside Poppy and a man I didn't know. Cigarette smoke from dozens of patrons produced a heavy, fog like haze that hung in the air.

Luke, the bartender had bushy chest hair, and a gold serpentine chain showed through the open collar of his polo shirt. He leaned over his side of the bar in front of Mother and laughed at something she said. Poppy and the other man joined in the friendly bantering, laughing loud enough to be heard throughout the room, even above the noise of the crowd.

Robin and I were beside Mother now, watching her, and waiting for the conversation to end before revealing our needs.

Mother's eyes, fastened on Luke, sparkled. She told him something and laughed in a way that sounded like happy cackling.

"Me daughter's a genius," Poppy said, slamming his drink onto the counter top. The white foam slopped over the edge and ran down the side of his glass mug. "Brilliant, a genius."

Mother laughed and put her arm around Poppy's shoulders. "Dad, I got it from you."

I reflected on the adoring way she smiled at, laughed with, spoke to, and gently touched Poppy, and I contrasted her affection for him with how she treated Robin and me. *How come she doesn't do that with us? We're her children. Why doesn't she put her arm around us?*

"Mommy," I said and tugged on her pant leg.

She looked down in surprise at my sister and me standing there. "Go back..."

Robin interrupted. "We're hungry."

"Now, now, now." Poppy removed the pipe from his mouth and shook his red jowls. "Here's me granddaughters," he said to those around him. He raised his beer stein to his wet lips and smiled at Robin and me, staring up at him.

Mother reached into a black handbag sitting on the counter beside her. "You and your sister aren't supposed to be in here." She sounded panicked and I thought she might get her car keys and take us home. But instead of her keys, she retrieved her wallet. "Go next door to the burger stand. Here's five dollars to buy something to eat." She gave Robin the money. "Then go to the car. I'll be out in a few minutes."

I was disappointed that we weren't going home, and I looked hopefully at my grandfather for help. *Why doesn't Poppy tell her to take us home?* I examined his smiling face for traces of benevolence, and searched his glassy eyes for understanding. He lifted his mug to me and chortled. "There's me granddaughters, fellas," he said to the men seated further down from him. "There's me granddaughters," he repeated.

Mother winced and giggled. "Daddy, you shouldn't."

Forget it. He's just like her. He doesn't care if we're stuck in this place. All he wants to do is drink and laugh with these people.

Mother's "minutes" were much longer than mine. In my sense of time, they were as days. Hours later, long after Robin and I had hamburgers and milkshakes, the summer moon rose in the west and slowly disappeared to wherever moons go late at night. It was finally time for us to leave. Mother exited The Vagabond. She weaved across the gravel parking lot and stumbled to our beautiful red Impala. She opened the door, slid into the front seat as though she were made of putty, her head bouncing from side to side, her eyes rolling around, her arms flopping onto the steering wheel, her hands squeezing it. My heart fluttered, my stomach muscles tightened, and I exchanged worried glances with Robin.

As if the key hole were moving, Mother tried for it first in one place and then another. I hoped we wouldn't stay in the parking lot all night. After several failed attempts to put her key through the slot, she fit the puzzle pieces together, cranked the ignition, pulled onto the road, wove in and out of the lane, and, by some miracle, we arrived home without wrecking into something.

After we were in bed, Max and Mother spoke to each other out in the living room. The walls were thin, without a bit of insulation, and over the past year I overheard lots of conversations. Now I heard Max telling Mother something about the mail.

"A letter came for us," he said, his voice hard and cool.

Mother's answer was too slurred for recognition.

"We're being questioned."

"Questioned?" she said.

"The fire investigation, Joy. Hell, we've had two fires and you're off at the bars. Get a hold of yourself! Why don't you just go to bed? We'll talk about this in the morning."

CHAPTER FIFTEEN

A big sixth grade girl entered my class one morning with a note from the principal's office. She handed it to my second grade teacher, Mrs. Carlisle, who read it quickly and then pointed toward me. "Pam," she said. "Your mother's waiting for you in the front office. Gina will take you there."

I went with Gina, her golden blond ringlets springing against the base of her neck with every step. "So, I guess you're having your teeth worked on," she said. "It won't hurt much. Gosh, my dentist adjusts my braces every month." She showed me her choppers, rubbing a finger across the stainless steel wires and brackets.

Mother hadn't said a word to me about a dentist since my last and only appointment, the one in which I bit the man in the long, white lab coat for trying to jab a needle through my gums. He yelped and hollered loud enough for everyone in the waiting room to hear, including Mother. "Pam, don't ever bite someone," she scolded on our way out the door. "And certainly, not a dentist. He needed to numb your tooth so he could drill your cavity."

"A dentist?" I said to Gina.

"Yep. That's why your mother's here."

I gulped hard, entered the office behind her, and walked over to Mother standing near the front desk, talking to the secretary. She faced me and grinned. "Pammie, you and your sister have checkups this afternoon."

Suddenly, I was dizzy.

"Your sister's on her way. As soon as she's here," Mother said, "we'll leave for your dental appointments."

A few minutes later when my sister entered the office, Mother abruptly ended her conversation with the school secretary. "Girls, I know you're nervous about seeing the dentist," she said, overemphasizing the word dentist. She looked back at the secretary, "Gee, Robin and Pammie are afraid of a little dental appointment." And then back at Robin and me, "There's absolutely nothing to worry about. Going to the dentist isn't a big deal."

As soon as we were in the car, Mother stifled a laugh and snorted. "Pulled one over on them. Girls, don't look so worried. We're not going anywhere near a dentist's office. Let's head over to the bar. How about pizza at The Parrot? I think your granddad's there. If he's not, after some lunch, we'll head across town to The Vagabond."

Mother got us out of school early, because she wanted to be at the bar nonstop without an intermission and she didn't appreciate the interruption occurring when at twenty minutes before two, she had to leave her drink, her buddies, her warm seat and go home to await my arrival from school, followed by Robin's an hour later.

A week after our first "dental appointment," Mother came to the school again. "Your follow-up appointment with the dentist is today." She frowned sympathetically at Robin and me, signaling us into a performance of sad and worried faces. "I know just how you feel. No one likes having their teeth drilled." She directed us to the door and opened it. "Darlings, there's nothing to fear. It won't hurt, promise."

Most every day after school and Saturdays, when we weren't with Dad, Robin and I hid inside barroom latrines, near the toilet stalls, or waited in the Impala for Mother, or sat at The Green Parrot's picnic table, occasionally remaining until closing.

I lay in bed shivering one grey morning in November. The wind howled outside and rain splatted against the window. I bundled blankets around myself and drew Baby Tenderlove closer to me.

Mother and Max were arguing in their bedroom beside mine. "And, so?" Mother said from the other side of the wall.

"You tell me!" Max yelled.

I tried to silence the angry exchange between Mother and Max by folding my pillow around my head, but their voices, now louder than before, came through the cushiony material.

Mother and Max stormed out of their room naked as jaybirds and stomped through the hall, to the bathroom. "You tell me." Mother mocked Max's words with thick and acrid sarcasm. "Well, I already told you. It's Daddy I meet up with at The Vagabond."

"Whatever, Joy."

Mother's blue eyes narrowed. "Max! What do you mean, whatever?" She thrust her hands to her hips. "What's your point?"

Max flushed the toilet and faced her. "Who are you seeing?"

"Don't tell me you're jealous of Daddy."

I tugged the blankets, pulling them to my nose, and peering over the edge of the soft fabric. The feel of it against my face comforted me somehow.

"Nice try!" Max yelled. "I asked you who you're seeing."

Mother and Max stared at each other for a couple seconds without saying a word.

"Joy," Max said in a calmer tone. "I know the truth."

"Really?" She laughed bitterly. "Then you know that Daddy and I meet up at the Vagabond."

The color of fury began rising up Max's neck and spreading into his face. "Come on Joy."

She didn't answer.

"How about the bartender?" Max leaned toward her, "Luke."

"How dare you accuse me of having an affair with my father's best friend."

I didn't know the meaning of the word "affair," but I sure knew rage when I heard it. Nana had raged and left us for Heaven. "Mommy, stop," I mumbled, too quietly for anyone to hear. "Don't fight." Tears stung my eyes.

"Hey, I'm just going on my observations and what I've heard. You're never home any more. You're at The Vagabond all the time, Joy, and I've known about that guy for a while. Don't lie."

"I don't give a rip what you think you know!" She pointed her finger in his face and waved it a half inch from his eyes. "Why don't you tell me who your new girlfriend is?"

What happened next transpired in a split second. Max raised his hand as if to strike her and I gasped. Mother doubled up her fist, swung at him, and clobbered his beak. He threw his hand to his face and bent over the sink. Blood gushed from his nose.

Four or five months after the fire in the cabinet above Robin's closet, early in the New Year, my sister and I resumed our usual places in The Green Parrot and Mother took hers. There was always a stein of beer in one hand and a smoldering cigarette in the other. Brother Bob, Uncle Ernie, and some others shot the bull with her. When the cigarette burned to its halfway mark, she smashed it against the ashtray, unfolded the remains, and laid it near her drink.

All day, rain soaked clouds had blocked the sun. A man with cinnamon red hair entered the bar and a blast of cold wind came in with him. I wrapped my arms around my torso and shivered.

Edie wiped off the bar counter with a wet cloth. "Storm's moving in."

The man, a stranger, removed his cap and coat. "Yes ma'am, I think it's here," he said, taking a seat at the end of the bar farthest from Mother.

Mother finished her first drink and ordered another. She and her buddies were jabbering away, their sarcastic humor provoking one another into chuckles and laughter. Twenty minutes later, Mother swallowed the last foamy drops of her second beer and ordered a third. I pointed at the clock on the wall above Robin and me. "Is it six?"

Robin glanced up at it. "Just about."

"How long have we been here?"

"One hour and five minutes."

"Is that all?"

She yawned. "I know. Seems like forever. I'm bored, too." She lifted her nose in the air. "Hey! Do you smell that?"

I inhaled the delicious aroma of tangy, tomato sauce and pepperoni. "Pizza!" My head was faint with hunger. I grinned and rubbed my belly. "Is it for us?"

"Wouldn't that be nice?"

I went over to Mother. "May we get some?"

"Get some?" she giggled. "You mean, have some." She almost whispered. "Darling, the pizza isn't ours. Go back to the table with your sister."

"Ma'am, help yourself." The pizza's owner, the man with the cinnamon red hair, overheard us and brought the pan of steaming hot pizza to Mother. "I can't eat all this." He put it on the bar beside her. "Here, please, you and your daughters help yourselves."

We ate the delicious slices of pizza and waited for three more hours. I shut my eyes, heavy with sleep, and laid my head on my folded arms on the table. Soon the din of voices faded and I slept.

"Pammie. Robin." Mother called from behind a faraway gulf. "Pammie. Robin." Her voice drew nearer. "We're going home."

I sat up, and through the slits of my drowsy eyes, I noticed that Uncle Ernie and Brother Bob were no longer beside her. The redheaded man, and most everyone else had left, and all but two seats were empty now.

Another outsider sat beside Mother. "How about a nightcap?" the man said.

"Geez." Mother cackled. "I guess that's just what I need, a cap on my head." Her voice sounded funny, like her words were warped, misshapen. "I need a rain cap." She cackled again.

"Ah, come on, Joy. Let your girls sleep," the stranger said.

Mother stood and weaved toward my sister and me at the table. "Robin. Pammie. Let's go home."

We pulled on our coats and went out into the chilly night. A light rain splatted against me and I stumbled, only half awake to the Impala. We got in and Mother turned on the heater. Warm air blew on the back seat floor. I shivered with cold and curled into a ball on the floor, under the warm stream. On the ride home, I closed my eyes. Water slushed on the roadway and lulled me asleep.

"Girls, we're here," Mother said in that funny voice. She opened the car door and shook me. "Get up, sleepy head," she giggled. "Wake up and go to bed."

My eyes were barely open when I pulled my nightgown over my head and climbed under the warm blankets.

Several minutes later, Mother stumbled in and kissed Robin's forehead. "Love you," she said.

"I love you," Robin said.

Next she kissed me, her breath warm and smelling of beer. "Love you."

"Mommy, I love you, too," I said.

She clicked off the light switch on the wall and left the room.

The rain had stopped. Crickets chirped outside my window. I turned on my side, pulled Baby Tenderlove against me, and prayed. "Now I lay me down to sleep. I pray the Lord Thy child to keep...Jesus," I said, "will you please keep Mommy, Daddy Max, Robin, me, Pierre and Suzette safe? And my room and dolls? Don't let us be hurt by fire. Amen."

Mother and Max didn't attend church, or provide Robin and me with spiritual training, and I had no idea if they prayed, but mysteriously I had learned about Jesus. My interest in Him extended beyond the childhood prayer that Nana taught me. Robin felt about Him as I did, that He was really with us. Sometimes she and I walked down the street and attended the Good Shepherd Lutheran Church. No one invited us to the Sunday morning services, but we went anyways, sitting on a wood bench, singing hymns, and attending Sunday school.

Only a half hour before, during the car ride, I couldn't stay awake, but here in bed, all desire for sleep vanished. After a while, as I lay there wide awake, it seemed someone entered the room and I felt something I'd only felt a few other times, the feeling of being cherished by someone who thinks I'm special. The feeling that came upon me was greater than the soul caresses I received through Mother's few embraces, or through Dad's tender kisses on my face. If love were a person, he had entered my room and enfolded me in himself. I lay there in my bed nearly enraptured by the experience.

All this time, Mother and Max were in the living room speaking to one another in casual tones. A cupboard banged shut in the kitchen. Someone turned the lock on the front door. Mother accompanied Max to their bedroom. The light switch on the nightstand beside their bed clicked off. Through the wall, I heard their muffled voices before our home became totally quiet.

Then I realized something had changed. The crickets had stopped chirping and suddenly, there was no sound. *Why have the crickets stopped? Why?*

A second feeling came upon me, a feeling of terrific anticipation and expectancy. *What's going to happen? Something. I know it. I feel it.* I wasn't afraid, because love surrounded and held me in complete peace. *Something's wrong. What is it?*

I listened for sounds, but there were none. The house and yard were silent. And still I waited. Approximately twenty minutes later, a loud, incessant, banging came from the front door.

My eyes darted around the dark room, landing first on the soft glow from the bathroom's nightlight across the hall, then on Robin laying motionless on the twin bed across from mine. Pierre and Suzette were barking outside on the back patio.

"I wonder who that could be at this hour?" Mother asked Max.

"I don't know, Joy," he answered with a ring of annoyance in his voice.

Bang! Bang! Bang! Bang! Bang!

"I'll get it," Mother said.

Bang! Bang! Bang! Bang! Bang!

Her light switch clicked. Her door opened and the hall light outside my room came on. I looked down the end of my bed to the hall. Mother zipped past my room in her long robe, the bottom hem of it trailing behind her.

Bang! Bang! Bang! Bang! Bang!

"I'm coming!" she hollered.

Robin and I simultaneously rose from our beds. She, too, had been lying awake, listening as I had and waiting as I had. We stood beside our beds when Mother turned the front door's lock. We slipped on our matching robes and our fuzzy slippers.

The front door creaked open. "I'm glad you answered!" a man said, his voice filled with panic. "Your house is on fire! There's sure a lot of smoke coming from your garage."

CHAPTER SIXTEEN

I grabbed Baby Tenderlove and my baby blanket and walked over to Robin standing beside her bed.

"Pam, ready? Got your slippers on?"

"Yeah."

"Good. Let's go," Robin said without a trace of fear.

We left my room, walked out the front door into the windless, night air. Clouds covered the moon and I strained to see my sister in the dark. I reached forward and grabbed her hand, didn't stop to find Mother, didn't even think of looking back at the garage. There was the smell of smoke and the sound of burning, crackling, the house heaving, and Robin's reassurance. "Pam, you okay?"

I said nothing, because I didn't know how to respond, but I squeezed her hand. The squeeze says, "I'm here with you."

We headed across our damp lawn for Sue's, and this time, by a sheer gift of grace, there were no screams.

A washer, dryer, miscellaneous items, Max's tools, and his beloved Corvette were in the garage. As was later told to me, someone threw open the garage door, Max entered the burning structure, jumped into the driver's seat, backed it through the flames, and parked it a safe distance from our home.

The garage fire burned hot. In a matter of minutes, the blaze spread through the garage wall into the kitchen. The fire crews arrived, blasted the flames with water, and extinguished the fire before it spread throughout our home.

While we waited for the fire to end, Sue offered Robin and me seats at the kitchen table. She brought out a package of Oreo cookies and served us glasses of milk. I ate those cookies slowly, savoring the sweet, creamy middle. Then Mother arrived. "Girls, you scared me to death," she said, her voice trembling. "I didn't know where to find you. Why didn't you tell me you were going to Sue's? You should have told me."

"Joy, you didn't tell them to come here? You poor, poor dear. I had no idea you didn't know. Robin and Pam have been here the whole time."

My only concern had been escaping our burning home and I never once thought about letting Mother or Max know we had left.

When the last fire engine departed, Max came over to Sue's and told us goodbye. "I'll be at my parents," he said as he started out the door, stopped and turned back toward us. He rubbed the back of his neck. "This is unbelievable." He shook his head and stared up at the ceiling. Then he turned to Robin and me. "Girls, are you all right?" He said with eyes soft and tearful.

Robin frowned and nodded.

I shrugged my shoulders.

"Joy, are you going to Bud and Marylou's?"

"I'll call them and let them know," she said.

"Are you okay? Maybe I should drive you? You're pale."

Mother exhaled deeply and blinked several times. "We'll get through this somehow."

"I guess we need to talk in the morning. Call me when you're up," Max said as he left.

The last time we all stayed in Aunt Marylou and Uncle Bud's home, there weren't enough comfortable beds for all of us. Robin slept with Kat. I slept with Cindy. Mother and Max had slept on an uncomfortable hide-a-bed in the game room. "I'm not spending another night on that hide-a-bed," Mother said, referring to the one at Uncle Bud's. "I'll drop the girls off with Marylou and Bud and head over to Gwen and Ted's." Gwen and Ted were friends from The Green Parrot.

I had always enjoyed myself when we stayed with Aunt Marylou and her family, but I needed the reassurance of Mother's nearness and I didn't want her miles away from me. "Mommy, may we go with you? Please?"

"Pammie, I'll be by early in the morning. You and your sister will be fine at Marylou's."

Aunt Marylou and Uncle Bud had a fairly new, three bedroom house and that swimming pool that Robin and I loved. Their home came with all sorts of accessories, including a red and black Japanese teahouse and rock garden with flowering cactus plants, a miniature golf course, and near the back patio, a large cage housing Uncle Bud's special pet, a chimpanzee type monkey named Kong.

After the garage fire, our cousins, Robin, and I played all day and late into the night. We sank golf balls into one of several holes on the artificial turf and competed in staring contests with Kong. Uncle Bud's monkey could out stare any of us kids. We also played flag football and Frisbee. We shot pool in the game room, the former garage, and talked and giggled for hours.

Everything related to living here with my uncle and aunt and cousins appealed to me. Their life was so happy. So normal. Cindy and I were inseparable, spending every waking moment together. Just before lunch one afternoon, I reached for a book at the top of a stack of games in the hall cabinet. "Hey, Cindy. Let's look at one of these," I said.

Cindy pulled a box of Chinese Checkers from the closet and invited me to play it with her.

I opened the book's cover and pointed at a field of wheat, a brown Holstein cow, and a red barn. "We'll do this first and play that later. Okay?"

She brought the game with her as she followed me to the living room sofa. Aunt Marylou reclined on a chair beside us. She was crocheting a blanket for her friend's baby. "Pammie, what do you have?"

I held up the book and grinned.

"Let me hear you read it."

There were four, big, bold words beneath the cow.

"The cow says moo," Cindy read, flipping the page. On pages two and three, mallards stood on green grass beside a pond.

"What about that page?" Aunt Marylou said. "Cindy, let Pammie have a turn."

The letters formed meaningless words and I shook my head. "I can't."

"Try. What's the first letter of the first word?"

I pointed at a large D.

"What sound does it make?"

"The duck says quack," Cindy said, smiling proudly.

My face felt suddenly warm.

Aunt Marylou chuckled. "Cindy, you stinker." She chuckled again. "Pammie, she got this book for Christmas and we've read it many times. Did Santa get you a book?"

"No," I said. "We don't have any books."

Aunt Marylou set her ball of yarn, the crotchet hook, and the blue and yellow blanket on the end table between us. "You must be teasing your Aunt Marylou. Are you sure you and your sister don't have *any* books at home?"

Mother read novels in bed at night, but she didn't read or play games with my sister or me. Aunt Marylou played with her kids, I knew this because Cindy had said she did, and now I realized she also read to them. I wished Mother would be more like Aunt Marylou. "Promise we don't," I said.

"Maybe Joy's too busy. Let's see the next page."

I turned to a horse with his mouth in a tall pile of yellow hay.

"Pammie, try reading that for me. Sound it out."

I had no idea what the big, bold letters said, but I had noticed a pattern and guessed. "The horse says neigh and eats straw."

"You speak like you're from New York." She chuckled, and smiled warmly at me. "What happened to the R's in all your words? The horse says neigh is correct."

Aunt Marylou made childhood fun and Uncle Bud made it special, too. Saturday morning, he cooked breakfast and the delicious aromas of pancakes, bacon, sausage, and eggs woke me. Then at ten o'clock sharp, he summoned us kids to the hall and we lined up outside his bedroom in birth order: Kat, first, then Dave, Robin, Dwayne, me, and lastly, the cutest and youngest of all, little Cindy with her two yellow pigtails.

"Okay," he said.

We entered and stood before him, quiet as ants.

"Did your chores this week?" he said.

We all nodded. Cindy and I lied. Actually, we hadn't done any chores. We were supposed to have helped Robin and Kat wash dishes, but every time Aunt Marylou told us girls to clean the kitchen, my youngest cousin and I busied ourselves with other activities, like exploring the neighborhood and digging through the red dirt at the side of their house, escaping to China from what we thought was horrible servitude.

Uncle Bud tensed his square jaw and scrutinized us with dark, stern eyes. "Did you clean your rooms? Did you do everything asked of you?" After we each said we had, he passed out rewards in the form of sticks of beef jerky and a dollar twenty-five. The three oldest cousins and Robin thanked him and left.

As soon as we were alone with Uncle Bud, Cindy flashed a sweet, innocent smile at her daddy, and his eyes softened. "Dad, can I have another?" she said, pointing at the jerky jar. He unscrewed the lid, and grinning, held it out for us both. All we had to do was ask, I learned. It was that easy. Not asking was always a definite "No," but asking worked really well.

The next Saturday, it rained. Aunt Marylou didn't believe in letting her kids run around in downpours, like Mother did, and my cousins, Robin, and I were stuck inside all day.

After dinner, Uncle Bud called from the living room, "Kids, come in here."

We came from all directions and lined up in front of him.

He sat in a chair near the red brick fireplace where several logs created a warm glow. "Everyone have a seat," he said, waving at the floor.

Cindy and I giggled about nothing in particular and the other kids spoke excitedly to one another. Uncle Bud's eyes were kind and his smile playful. He passed out Bingo cards and stacks of pennies. "Sh! Quiet down and take a board. I'll call out the letters." He reached into a soft, cloth, bag and felt inside it. "If you have the letter and number, cover it with a penny. The first one of you who covers every square wins all the pennies on your board." He held up a little tile and called the first letter-digit combination.

Gusts of wind thrust rain against the south facing windows. Uncle Bud called a succession of numbers, B-9, N-7, G-3, I-5, and so on. Twenty minutes later, near the end of the game, he stretched out the calls, keeping us in suspense. "Oooh-5," he said real slow. "Oooh-4. Oooh-8." Dwayne shouted. "Bingo!"

"Oooh-no!" Cindy said.

Everyone laughed, including Aunt Marylou seated in her chair near the sofa. "Cindy," she said, chuckling. "You're a stinker."

The next weekend, the clouds were gone and the bright sun warmed the late winter day. Uncle Bud gave us rides around the rectangular perimeter of his backyard on a gas powered, orange sand buggy called the Dune Cat. He also brought out a pellet gun and gave his sons, and Kat, and Robin target shooting practice. Cindy and I were too little, he said, but someday we'd be big enough to shoot it.

Every couple of days, Mother came by for a visit. One morning, near the end of the third week, she and Aunt Marylou chatted over cups of coffee at the dining table.

"The house is ready, and I'll take the girls with me today. Marylou, thank you for letting them stay here."

"Joy, this is your home. You and the girls are always welcome. I promised their grandmother I'd always be here for you."

I cupped my hands over Cindy's ear and whispered. "Ask your mother to ask my mother to let me and Robin stay one more night."

She giggled, nodded, and we hovered nearby, waiting for a break in their conversation, and a chance for Cindy to pop the question.

"Any more news from the investigation?" Aunt Marylou said.

Mother shook her head slightly. "I think all our neighbors have been questioned and Max and I met with the investigator.

At this point, their information is inconclusive." She waved her hand. "They haven't found a thing."

"Well, they'll get to the bottom of it. Try not to worry. You know where we are if you need us."

My eyes met Cindy's and we crossed our fingers behind our backs, and showed them to each other. If anything would help, the crossed fingers trick would do it.

"How's Max?" Aunt Marylou said.

Mother sipped her steaming cup of coffee, then said casually, "We're splitting up."

"Joy, I'm sorry." Aunt Marylou's kind eyes smiled. "Every marriage has its problems. Bud and I've had our share. If you both work at it, you can resolve your differences."

Mother's eyes narrowed. She cast Aunt Marylou a look, a mind your own business look, and stood. "We need to get going."

"Please, may we stay," I asked Mother, squeezing my crossed fingers really tight and using my best manners.

"You've stayed long enough. Get your sister." Her voice was cold and unyielding.

On the drive home, Mother rolled down the Impala's window and puffed on the last half of a cigarette. "Pierre and Suzette will be so happy to see you girls. Sue's been feeding them, but I'm sure they've been lonesome for you."

I had missed our dogs and smiled. "When we get home, I'll let them in the house."

"Pammie!"

"They want to come in my room."

"You know better. Max doesn't want them in the house."

A few second later, Mother cranked the chrome radio knob until she found a song she liked. "The garage is redone. Robin, you'll still have to sleep with your sister, in her room."

Robin and I were in the front seat with Mother. I leaned my arm against the door, rested my forehead on my hand, and pouted.

"Pamela Jean Marie!" Mother snapped.

I sat up straight.

"Don't ever lean against the door. It could swing open."

I scooted closer to Robin. "Can't we stay with Aunt Marylou?"

"My no is a no." We stopped at a red light. Mother extinguished her cigarette in the ashtray and waited for the green light. A minute later, she hit the gas and accelerated into the fast moving traffic. "Someone's been complaining again to Marylou about you girls being at The Parrot."

She glanced over at Robin and me for a fraction of a second and slammed on the brakes and threw an arm across our chests. The cars ahead of us had suddenly stopped. We never wore seatbelts and her arm kept us from cracking our heads wide open on the dashboard, she had said.

When we turned at the intersection, Mother explained that since Robin and I couldn't continue going with her to The Parrot, we would be home after school by ourselves.

Robin and I were on different attendance schedules. She arrived home an hour after me. I pressed my fist against my eyes, filling with tears, and fought against the ocean of emotions rising with the tide of events I couldn't control.

"It'll only be for an hour," Mother said. We came to another stoplight. She looked over at me. "Darling, you'll get to watch T.V. You always like watching T.V."

"No, I don't," I answered harshly, because Mother's words and the look in her eyes upset me and I didn't want to cry. A tear dropped onto my shirt. Something about Mother's expression reminded me of a visit she and Aunt Marylou had a few days ago.

"The police questioned Max," Mother had said.

"Joy, they think it's arson?" Aunt Marylou had said.

And I remembered that Mother's olive complexioned face had turned to a pasty white and her eyes had turned dark. Seeing her like that made me feel strange, like I might throw up.

I wrapped my arms around myself. "Please let us go with you to The Parrot," I said.

Robin chewed her lip while fiddling with her shirt hem. "Mommy, we'll wait in the restroom again," she promised.

Mother pressed her bright red lips together and shook her head. "We can sure as heck cross that option off our list."

I thought of the last time I was in our home, of my sister and me fleeing from the house, of the fire in the garage. "I'm scared. What if our house catches on fire?"

Mother stopped at another light. "Slim chance that'll ever happen again. Pammie, when you get home from school, go inside, turn on the T.V., and wait on the sofa until your sister comes home."

"What if we go to Sue's?" Robin said. "She really doesn't mind. I think she likes having us over."

"Geez, girls, it'll be okay. Stop worrying."

I swallowed hard and fought an urge to cry. *Jesus, don't let us die.* I prayed, silently. Then I tried to convince myself it doesn't matter. Another fire won't occur. *I'll be safe inside waiting for Robin. Mother's right. It's only an hour. What could happen in an hour?*

CHAPTER SEVENTEEN

A school fire alarm buzzed incessantly one day. All the kids in my second grade class stood beside their desks, and followed Mrs. Carlisle outside where we lined up on the playground. Standing there, hearing that sound, started the trembling. It began in my legs and moved up into my abdomen.

Any reminder of the house fires brought my family and me back to those terrifying experiences. The screaming of an emergency vehicle's siren or the sight of flashing lights thrust Mother, Robin, and me into near catatonic states. Once a police car in the traffic beside us threw on its lights and blaring siren. We had been speaking and instantly, fell silent. Mother shuddered. Robin's rosy complexion turned grey, her eyes grew wide and staring, and I threw my hands over my ears and trembled.

Second grade challenged me. I lagged behind my peers in reading, writing, mathematics, and practically anything requiring memorization of facts, such as spelling and history. However, I wasn't a total failure.

Every recess, I fought boys for the dominant position of Monkey Bar Champ. The bars were hoops that easily swung, and the kids took turns hanging onto the bars and fighting one another with their legs.

I'd swing out and meet a boy in the middle, our legs flying, tugging, and yanking. I fought it out, squeezing my legs tight around his waist, pulling long and hard. After a while, the boy's face would turn beet red, his hands would slip, and he'd fall, landing on the ground. Then, the next boy in line would fight me. I had a secret weapon that worked most of the time—never quit.

Before the close of the first semester, Mrs. Carlisle told me I had tested positive as a student with special learning needs. "You need the help of a gifted teacher," she said. "I spoke on the phone with your mother about it. Did she discuss this with you?"

Mother hadn't said anything to me about being special, and I shook my head.

"She didn't? Well, that's okay. Like I told her, you'll begin tomorrow morning in a new class where you'll receive the help you need." There was not a word of further explanation.

The next day, I began Special Ed. My new teacher had short brown hair, wore gold-rimmed glasses, and had a pleasant face. She gave me a seat near the back of the room. I glanced around from student to student and studied the various children. *Why am I here?* My classmates included a cross-eyed boy who wore thick, coke bottle glasses that made his eyes look round and huge, like white pool balls with black centers. There were kids with metal braces strapped to their legs and others in wheelchairs. A girl sat at a desk with drool running from her mouth, another kid made strange whining sounds while rocking in his seat.

I plopped down into my chair with a lump in my throat. *Gosh, what's wrong with me? I don't have crossed eyes or a problem walking.* I was waiting for my first assignment when the revelation hit me. *I use my left hand.*

The teacher came by and handed me a reader with a grey cover and a title in bold, yellow letters. "Why don't you look at the first chapter?" she suggested, turning the pages for me. "I'm helping some other students, but I'll be back in a little while and see how you're doing."

My shoulders slumped as I dropped my eyes on the words in the book. *Everyone else can read.* An image came to mind of my kindergarten teacher scolding me. *Mrs. Browley's right. I'm a retard.*

"Pam, I mailed a note to your mother letting her know that we've signed you up for speaking lessons," my teacher said brightly. "You start today."

This was the first time I'd heard of it.

"Every Friday you'll go to the office at one-thirty for a half-hour speech therapy session. Okay? There's something else we'll be working on. The way most other kids learn doesn't work for you. You have something called dyslexia and we have something called DISTAR that helps dyslexic learners. I bet you'd like to learn to read, huh?"

I really did and nodded my head.

She began that day, teaching me the phonetic sounds of each letter and how they blend into words. My former teachers had taught reading through the memorization of lists of words, and I had failed. But through the phonics method, I progressed and eventually read the book she gave me the first day of class, *Fun with Dick and Jane.*

Sometime in early February when the dismissal bell rang, I meandered along the sidewalk leading me home from Edison Elementary. Every now and then, I glanced over my shoulder, looking for Henry. Sometimes, he charged ahead of me and waited on my lawn. Then, as soon as I arrived, he'd say, "Where ya been?" And I'd tell him. And he'd say. "I've been waitin' here all day," and then before going inside the house, he'd show me something neat like his Hot Wheels.

In another hour, the school bell would ring again and Robin would start on her way home. I always had to come straight home from school, otherwise, my mother would know where I was. I believed that she possessed an internal crystal ball, revealing my every move. Once I snuck outside with one of Mother's cigarettes and a pack of matches. At the side of our house, I lit it, held it between my fingers, as I had seen her do, and inhaled on the filterless cigarette. Then I gagged and threw it on the ground.

Later that evening, Mother asked if I had smoked and I confessed the whole stinking truth. She stared into my eyes. "If you ever want to smoke again, I'll light up with you." I couldn't believe my ears. Smoke with my mother? That seemed wrong and I shook my head, "No way," I said. "I don't want to do that."

I kicked a pebble along the sidewalk, rounded the corner, and saw Bonnie, my sometimes friend, talking to another little girl. Bonnie played with me at home only when other kids were unavailable, but ignored me in social situations, such as school.

A girl in my class gave out party invitations to all our classmates and I was the only one who wasn't invited. That same morning, I overheard her telling Bonnie that I was dirty, and wore clothes from Goodwill, and never brushed my hair, and that's why she wasn't inviting me to her party. She said, "Goodwill," like it was something shameful. After that, Bonnie avoided me, and, although we lived four houses from each other, she never wanted to walk with me.

When I arrived home that mild afternoon, Pierre and Suzette barked loudly, welcoming me home. Henry wasn't waiting for me on the lawn and I was disappointed. I reached the front door, grasped the handle, and heard a man's voice, quieter than a whisper saying, "Run! Get away! Run!" Suddenly, a light feeling came over me, my heart hammered in my chest, and I jerked back my hand. Someone who I couldn't see spoke to me, urging me to run. I forgot about Mother's wrath and headed for my neighbor's house.

"Pam! Pam!" Bonnie shouted from across the street.

"What?" I yelled back, stopping on Sue's driveway and staring at her.

She pointed at my house. "Don't you see it?"

I scanned everything along the front of my house that I could see from there, the front step, the windows of the bathroom, kitchen, and Robin's room. "No!"

"You don't see it?" Bonnie's voice was disbelieving.

"See what?"

Kaboom! An ear-splitting blast rattled the neighborhood, every window in my house shattered, and a horrific fire exploded through them. I jumped back, gasping for breath, and stared in disbelief at the huge flames and black smoke pouring out.

Sue rushed outside. "Oh no!" She threw her hands to her face. I was standing in her driveway trembling. "Pam, stay right there. I'll call the fire department." Three minutes later, she came over to me and put an arm around my heaving shoulders.

I felt as though my head had separated from the rest of me. My legs were weak and wobbly as I watched red and orange flames consume the place I once loved. Fire erupted from the front and back of the house, its destructive arms tearing at the roof, ripping at the exterior walls, clawing our backyard fence, and suffocating the life out of the scraggly tree near Robin's bedroom window.

Sirens screamed their warning call. I hated and feared that high pitched sound of distress. Emergency workers traveled the well worn path to our house and began the well practiced routine. Men clad in black hats, yellow coats, and black boots disembarked from the shiny, red fire engines. They wasted no time pulling their heavy, yellow hoses from the back of their trucks and dragging them up to the front door.

"Let her go!" A fireman yelled to another and a powerful spray surged through the hose while another opened the door. A wall of fire pushed toward them. They hit it hard with the water before disappearing into the dense, black smoke.

Sue's front yard filled with worried neighbors. Mother arrived home and in a panic rushed over to Sue and me. "Pammie, where's your sister?" she said.

"Joy," Sue said. "Robin's still in school. Do you think someone should bring her home?"

A woman who lived several houses up from ours told Mother not to worry about Robin, and volunteered to go that minute and get her.

Smoke billowed up from behind our house. "The dogs," Mother said. "They're not still back there, are they?"

"They've been taken care of. They're in my backyard," Sue said. "One of the firemen brought them over." Sue rubbed her forehead. "I need to check on my little guy. I don't mind coming back if you need me to."

Mother didn't answer.

She put a hand on Mother's shoulder. "Joy, do you need me to stay?" Her syrupy voice sounded melodious and calming. "Hon, I can come back in a second. I just need to see how Mark's doing. He's just five and I shouldn't leave him." She leaned in closer to Mother, making eye contact with her. "He's watching T.V."

"We'll be okay."

Sue stared at the flames leaping through the windows and the smoke spilling out of every opening. She shook her head. "It's really awful. I'm so sorry for all of you. This is just—just too awful. But if you need me, I'll be right back."

Mother waved her away and huffed. "Sue, I'm fine. Pam's fine. We're fine."

People swarmed around us as neighbors and total strangers asked lots of unanswerable questions. Mother turned around and spoke with someone behind her. "I don't know. I have no idea." Her icy-cold voice was edged with stress. "I just got home." She tsked. "My husband will be here soon. You'll have to ask him."

The neighbor from down the street arrived with my sister. Robin ran to me, tears streaming down her colorless cheeks. "While I was still at school, I heard sirens and I knew they were coming here. Why does this keep happening?"

A short while later, a fire investigator approached with clipboard and pencil in hand. He looked down at me. "Were you in the house?"

I heard him, but I couldn't speak. I understood, but I couldn't answer. I smiled. *Why'd I smile? He'll think I'm weird. No one else is smiling.* Staring at my house practically engulfed in flames, I thought how stupid it is to smile.

Bonnie, on the other side of Robin and me, spoke up. "Pam didn't go in the house," she said to the investigator.

He stooped down and, looking in her eyes, spoke to her. "What makes you so sure?"

"I saw her."

"What did you see?"

"She walked up there." Bonnie pointed at the open door through which inky black smoke poured.

"Did she go inside?"

Bonnie shook her head. "No. She ran over here."

"And then what happened?"

Bonnie's voice trembled. "It exploded."

The fire investigator turned to me. "Do you know how the fire started?"

I didn't answer.

"How long were you home before the explosion?"

Mother was behind me, speaking to someone. She stopped in mid-sentence. "Excuse me," she said politely to a neighbor and swung around, her eyes glaring, and pointed a finger at the fire investigator's face, almost touching his nose. "Leave *my* daughter alone!"

Two hours later, the clear sky had become a soft grey in the fading sunlight. I stood near Robin and Mother on Sue's lawn. Smoke no longer poured through every crevice, and most of the firemen had returned with the large engines to the station, leaving a smaller truck and crew at the scene.

Max approached a fireman, watching for flare-ups near the house's front entrance. "All right if I go in?" he said.

The fireman nodded. "Better be careful in there. Wait a minute and I'll go with you."

Several minutes later, Max came over to us, shaking his head and wiping black soot from his hands. His wide eyes were dilated. "Well," he said without meeting Mother's steely stare, "maybe Dad will loan me the money to fix it." He clutched his head and gazed at the ground. "Oh, I almost forgot to tell you. Pierre and Suzette are back in our yard. I guess Sue will feed them again." He stared at our fire damaged home. "What's going on here?" He cleared his throat and mumbled, "The whole thing's about gutted." He dropped his hands to his sides and glanced at Mother, a look of defeat on his face. "I'll be at my parents," he said, walking away.

Suddenly, I wanted to hug him. "Daddy Max," I called.

Max faced me. "Kid?"

I stepped toward him, but Mother grabbed my hand and held me there.

"See you later, Kid," he said, getting into his Corvette.

Mother's hand around mine trembled. I felt the tremble. Why? I wondered. She was bigger than me and incapable of weakness. Did she feel as I felt—small and vulnerable? Is she as afraid as I am? Then who could I turn to for help? I needed Mother to be strong. I needed her strength.

CHAPTER EIGHTEEN

Robin and I returned to Aunt Marylou's and Mother stayed across town with her friends from The Vagabond, Ed and Patti. Two weeks after the fire, in early March when the wind howled incessantly and whipped the branches of the bushes against the living room windows, Mother came by to see us. "Marylou, I can't visit today. Max is out in the car waiting for us. We're taking the girls with us to see the house." She had a white knuckled grip on the strap of the black leather purse on her shoulder and a frown on her glossy red lips.

A wave of dizziness hit me just then, brought on by the suggestion of entering our burned out house, and I wanted to protest, but knew it wouldn't help.

My aunt who sat crocheting in a living room chair looked up from her work. "Joy, really? I don't think that's a very good idea."

"Girls, come on," Mother said, ignoring her. "We don't want to keep Max waiting."

She flicked her long finger at me and, even though I was terrified of going with her to see our burned out house, her non-audible command brought me from the floor to my feet and outside to the waiting Impala.

A half hour later, Max pulled onto Wyant Way and parked along the curb of our house. I peered at the light blue exterior walls, swagged with ashy grey, and the charcoal edged window openings, covered with boards. Alarm signals hammered my body, making it shake. "M-m-m Mommy. D-d-d don't..." I tried telling her I didn't want to go inside but speaking had become difficult.

"Can Pam and me stay in the car?" Robin said.

Max turned off the ignition. "Kid, you better come and see if there's something you want."

I had missed our dogs and wanted to go to the backyard and see them. "Can I g-go see Pierre and Suzette?"

"Come on, kid," Max said, ignoring my question.

We stepped cautiously into our home's entryway of black walls, bubbled and cracked paint, scorched wood, and into the awful stench of acrid smoke. I covered my nose with my hand and scrutinized the disaster around me. Robin and I inched our way toward Max and Mother, near the kitchen.

Max gasped at the destruction. "We won't find anything in there." His joyless voice, without a trace of hope, increased my feelings of anxiety. Mother shook her head and averted her eyes to another part of the house.

The house felt unsafe, like it would erupt into another blaze any second. Robin and I clung to one another as we tiptoed around blackened debris scattered over the carpet and went from one room to another and stared with round, frightened eyes at all we had lost.

An inferno had burned the front part of our home. It scorched a trail up the entry hall, walls of the kitchen, and living room. I glanced at the ceiling. The blaze swiped a wide swath of black and grey across large portions of it. And I looked across the room to where Pierre and Suzette should've been waiting for us. They always sat just opposite the glass door, wagging their stumpy tails at us, but not this time. They weren't there.

My teeth were chattering. "M-m-m Mommy," I said.

"Shush," she said.

"M-m-m Mommy."

"Pammie, not now."

Max headed down the hall. He stopped and turned back toward us. "Joy, you better see about the photo albums and kids, if you're going to take anything with you, you better go and get it."

From across the room, I stared at the empty back step. "Robin, wh-wh where's Pierre and Suzette?" I said.

"I don't know," she said.

"At Sue's?"

"I don't know where they are."

We stepped carefully over the smoke saturated carpet, littered with rubble, our hands over our noses, and peered out the glass door. Black charcoaled pieces of once useful things lay on the lawn and patio.

Robin shook her head and whispered. "Pam, I can't believe this happened. How did this happen?"

I stared at our burned sofa on the patio, my mind spinning around and coming up with possible causes. *Maybe the stove was left on. Maybe the heater did this.* Then it dawned on me. *Maybe my prayers caused this. Maybe asking Jesus to protect us from fire made all this happen. This is my fault. Is it possible? Did my prayers make this happen?*

A couple of minutes later, we stopped outside the shut door of my bedroom. I was afraid of what we'd find, and I didn't want to go in. Robin turned the knob and opened the door. For a couple of seconds neither of us moved. We took inventory of my room's contents. *Nothing's burned. Not my bed. Not my dresser. Not my curtains. Could my prayers have caused the fires? Nah, that can't be. My room's safe and we weren't hurt.*

Robin brought me back from my thoughts. "Everything's ruined," she said. "Look at it. The ugly smoke stains are everywhere." That same hideous smoke, throughout the rest of the house, had entombed my bed and toys in an odorous, dark grey shroud. She scrunched her nose. "There's not something you want is there?"

We looked through the closet. The dresses made by Nana, and everything else, were ruined. "They won't wash," Robin said. She knew this from first hand experience. Her entire wardrobe was thrown out after the fire in her room. "Might as well leave them."

I took my doll that had comforted me during our season of crisis, and Robin's former blanket from my bed, the one Mother had swaddled around her in her infancy, and we left my room.

Robin and I rode in the back seat on our way back to Aunt Marylou's. We passed Alicia and Bonnie's house with its finely manicured lawn and Henry's, too. His bicycle lay on the driveway beside a pair of his blue and white sneakers, and I wondered if I'd ever see him again. We rounded the corner and went by the Lutheran church.

Finally, I could ask Mother the question about our dogs. "Mommy, where's Pierre and Suzette?"

"Max?" she said, looking across the front seat at him.

He ran his hand through his hair and rubbed the back of his neck. "Well, Kid, they've run off."

The shaking of my legs and stomach had calmed, and only a slight vibration remained. "They wouldn't do that! They'd never leave us!" I scooted to the edge of the bench seat and touched Mother's arm. "Mommy, did they get hurt?"

Mother glanced over her shoulder at Robin and me "Pammie, sit back! What if we had to stop suddenly, you'd crack your head open on the windshield."

I scooched back and sat up straight.

"That's more like it," she said, a slight smile on her lips. "Girls, you get to stay a little longer with Marylou and Uncle Bud. You and your cousins will have loads of fun."

Robin nodded once.

"Bingo with Uncle Bud on Saturday night." The pitch of Mother's voice rose. "Remember how much fun that was?"

I pressed my nose against the side window and searched the scenery for two poodles, our white curly furred Suzette, and black curly furred Pierre.

"Pierre wouldn't leave," I said again. "He'd never leave us."

"Pammie. They're okay," Mother said. "I'm sure both dogs are safe and sound with another family. By now, someone must have found them."

The cars and trucks ahead of us screeched to a stop. Over on the left side of the street, the garage door went up on a firehouse. We passed this same station dozens of times on our way to The Green Parrot and Aunt Marylou's. A shiny, red truck pulled out onto the road. A loud siren blasted. Mother winced. Robin trembled. I sucked in my breath and buried my face in my hands.

We continued on our way, and after the sound of the ear splitting wail faded, I watched for our dogs again, but when I didn't see them, my eyes filled with tears. *They might be lost. Maybe they won't find us.* For the first time since the beginning of the whole awful ordeal of blazes and fleeing for our lives, I cried.

CHAPTER NINETEEN

J swung alone on the jungle gym in Aunt Marylou's back-yard. The sun was warm on my face and I shut my eyes and pointed my chin up at it. A white dove perched on an overhead telephone wire and cooed.

Only the week before, I had gone with my family to view our home's remains and Mother had said we'd never again live there. Her words lifted the weight of a hundred fears from my shoulders.

Here, with my aunt and uncle and cousins, I experienced a different world where children were the priority. That's how it's supposed to be, I decided. *When I grow up, I'll have a little boy and a little girl, and I'll be just like Aunt Marylou.* I leaned back on my swing, soaring as high as the two chains holding up both sides of the seat allowed, and reviewed recent events.

I counted the fires. *The curtain was one. Robin's closet, two, the garage, three, and the whole house, four. Geez. Four fires?* I pumped my legs, lifting myself into the air, and considered a possible cause. One of my older cousins had suggested an electrical wire failure. *Maybe the wires inside the walls got too hot.* My stomach muscles tightened and began quivering. *No, that's not it. There aren't wires in Robin's closet.* I didn't like the anxiety beginning inside me. *We don't ever have to go back there, and I'm never sleeping in that house again.*

Max and Mother had separated. He lived with his parents and Mother was still staying in the home of her Vagabond friends, Ed and Patti. Soon after we reviewed our burned out house, Robin and I went with Dad to a Chinese restaurant. He also took us roller-skating before returning us to Aunt Marylou's. While I swung, I thought about Dad and wondered what he was doing? *Probably working.* And I remembered he said he works for the State of California in the payroll division.

Then I thought about Max and a pang of longing shot through me. *I miss him.* Mother saw us every couple of days when she dropped by for a visit with Aunt Marylou over cups of coffee, but Max never came by.

Days later, my mother and aunt visited at the dining table. It was morning and Cindy and I were in our pajamas, curled up in blankets on the living room floor, watching Saturday morning cartoons.

"Joy, how did the meeting go?" I overheard Aunt Marylou say.

"With the school?"

"Oh," she said, sounding surprised. "I didn't know about the school. Was there another meeting? Last time I tried talking to you about your appointment with the investigator, we were cut off or something. I don't want you leaving until I've heard everything they told you." Aunt Marylou chuckled. "Before your Uncle Bud left for work this morning, he made sure I'd remember to ask you."

"Marylou, didn't I tell you what the investigators said? I'm sorry. We learned nothing...absolutely zilch, and the meeting about Pammie was to talk about her educational plan."

"There's nothing wrong with her, Joy, she's a bright child. She just needs to be taken care of."

"I know." Mother sounded annoyed. She coughed and cleared her throat. "Pammie's teacher is concerned that she's still writing words backwards. But I'm really not too worried about it. She'll catch up. Dyslexia, whatever her teacher wants to call it, it's just a word they use when their cookie cutter teaching doesn't work."

"Give her some books, Joy. She looks at Cindy's all the time—some children's books with big print should help. Okay, so back to the investigation. I know your Uncle Bud will want to know more about it."

"Really, there's not that much to report." Mother sighed, and then she brightened. "Tell my uncle to put his badge on and run it." She snickered. "We could use his FBI know-how."

"Right, Joy." Aunt Marylou laughed. "I'll tell him you said so." For a few seconds they were quiet. Then Aunt Marylou told Mother how strange it seems that the police are scratching their heads and no one seems to know the reason for the fires. "Bud and I are worried," she said.

"Marylou, thank you for your concern. Really, I promise, the girls and I will be fine...we are fine."

"I'm not as worried about Robin and Pammie as I am about you. They're resilient little girls. They'll bounce back, but Joy, I need to tell you something; before your mother died I made her a promise to look after her girls." Aunt Marylou lowered her voice, but I still understood every word. "You're not doing right by your children. When Pammie got home from school, you weren't there. She was alone with that last fire. Think Joy. Can you imagine what would've happened if she had gone inside your burning house?" she said, her words edged with alarm. "She might not be here with us now."

"Don't be so superior," Mother snapped.

"You should've been home, but you weren't. You were drinking at the bar. Your drinking's out of control. Joy, don't you think you should be home with your children?"

The silence that followed meant Mother hadn't wanted to hear the truth. She didn't want to admit she'd done something wrong and she disdained being told what to do. Then there was the sound of keys jingling and a dining chair rubbing against the carpeted floor. "I'll be by in a few days to see the children," Mother said, coolly. On her way out, she looked down at me and a forced grin appeared on her face. "Pammie, I have some errands to run. I'll see you soon," she said and left.

That night while Cindy slept beside me and Robin slept with Kat in the bed across from us, I rolled over on my side and considered what Aunt Marylou had told Mother. For the first time, I felt ashamed of being the daughter of a woman who went to bars and got drunk, and I remembered Aunt Marylou saying that if I had entered our burning home, I might not be here.

It struck me then that something amazing had happened to me during the fourth house fire. "Jesus," I whispered, "You told me to run away from the house before it exploded." A sense of awe came over me. "You saved my life." Then several seconds later, I asked, "Why?"

Near the first of April, Mother called on the phone. "Darling," she said to me, "I'll be by in about an hour to get you and your sister." A nasty edge crept into her voice. "Your aunt's such a busy body. You and your sister will stay with me at Ed and Patti's until we get a place of our own."

Ninety minutes later, we stood with Mother across from our middle-aged host and hostess in the dining room of the richest place I'd ever seen. It had two floors, a tile entryway, and oak kitchen cabinets. The living room had a huge brown shag carpet, mahogany and leather furniture, and a tall ceiling to floor bookcase loaded with hardbound books.

Ed and Patti greeted us with unwelcoming words and pretend smiles. I studied their faces. Patti's eyes, blue like Mother's, lacked warmth and laughter. Right then, I distrusted her and moved my eyes quickly from her to Ed and found him looking at me with a slight smile. Somehow that smile didn't put me at ease. I moved my eyes away from them and stared at a spot on the carpeted floor, just in front of my sneakered feet.

After introductions, Patti told us we'd sleep upstairs and I liked the sound of that. Then she began listing off the household rules. "We have our own way of doing things here. While you're under our roof, you'll pitch in and help. There's always something needs done. Understand?"

"Okay," Robin and I answered.

"Don't leave any of your things in the entry hall," she said. "Every Saturday, you stay in your room until it's clean. Quiet voices downstairs and never any yelling. You'll eat all your food on your plates, all your food, even your vegetables. Understand?"

I glanced up at Mother. She never forced Robin or me to finish the food on our plates. Mother didn't seem too happy with Patti. She had one of those expressions I knew well, the one I especially dreaded. It said she'd let you have it if you didn't straighten up immediately. Her large eyes narrowed and her jaw line tightened. Hers was the look of true annoyance and, second by second, a shortening wick. If Patti kept it up, Mother would silence her flapper. She knew how to punch the air right out of over-inflated windbags. I dropped my eyes back to the spot on the floor.

"There'll be no waste," Patti said. "You'll go to school at the new elementary down the street. Your mom's enrolling you Monday morning. No dirty shoes in the house. Please take them off at the door."

Patti dished out orders like a drill sergeant, in long breathless sentences. "The girls help with the kitchen and living room. Dishes are washed by hand, dried, put away, the floor's swept, the table and counters are wiped off. A clean room has no dust. The carpet's vacuumed. Everything's in its place. I'll only ask you to do something one time."

I had already forgotten the first item on Patti's list. I studied the spot on the floor and worried about what would happen if I forgot a rule.

Next Ed took a shot at it. "Look at your elders when spoken to."

I lifted my eyes from the floor and blinked a couple times at his face. He still had that grin, and it still made me uneasy.

"That's the way." He sounded practically happy. "It's not your fault, you've never been taught any different." Ed, self important, and three sheets to the wind, picked up his drink from the kitchen table and sipped it. The ice clinked against the glass. "Looking at the floor when an adult is speaking shows disrespect, remember that."

I glanced over at Mother, the muscles of her face twitched, and I thought she'd let him have it any second.

Ed sipped his drink again before setting his glass on the kitchen counter. "Our boy, Ralph, mows the lawn," he said. "Our daughters Denise and Sherry do dishes and a few other things. You'll help Patti with the household chores, and if there's any trouble from either of you, we'll deal with you like we do our own children." Ed looked sternly from Robin to me. "If you mouth back or do something sneaky, I'll send you outside to get a switch from the tree and you'll get a whipping."

Mother stepped toward our host and hostess. "Ed!"

Robin met my eyes and smirked. I raised an eyebrow and nodded slightly. *Here she goes. This'll shut their traps.*

Mother didn't need to yell to make a point. She did just fine using her authoritative demeanor, body language, and words. She placed both hands on her hips and narrowed her eyes even more, while gritting her teeth. "I don't believe in spankings. *My* daughters have never needed to be spanked. You will never switch them. You won't lay a hand on them!" She pointed a finger at Patti. "And *my* daughters are never forced to eat. When they're through, they're through!"

Ed chuckled nervously and raised both hands in front of his face. "Joy," he said, "wait. Hold your fire. I'm just kidding."

She maintained her position with that same furious look in her face.

"Can't you take a joke?" he said.

This was not the best day of my life but it wasn't the worst, either. It was somewhere in between. We had just moved from a happy home where adults actually liked kids to a glorified work camp.

CHAPTER TWENTY

*I*n the middle of April, on my ninth birthday, Mother took Robin and me to the apartment where Max lived. We knocked at his door and he opened it. "Hi," he said. Before I realized what I had done, I threw my arms around him. "I miss you," I told him.

He patted my back. "Me too, Kid," he said.

Mother's eyes darted nervously around the room. She cleared her voice. "This is nice."

"It's not much. Well, you didn't come by to see my place. Presents are this way," he said on his way to the kitchen. We had chocolate cake before I opened three gifts, Tinker Toys, a plastic ladybug house, and a butterfly net. They were the first toys in my possession since the fires, and I was elated to have them. "Thank you Daddy Max and Mommy," I said, hugging them both.

Mother smiled at my manners. "You're welcome. You girls go outside and play for a few minutes." Mother opened the door and shooed us outdoors. This meant she and Max needed adult conversation without our listening ears, and I hoped they'd make up and get back together.

I went to the edge of the second floor balcony overlooking a courtyard of lush, green grass, and ducked under the wrought iron security railing. "Robin, watch this," I said, leaping off the edge. A split second later, I stood on the soft ground, beaming a broad smile at Robin, staring down at me.

"Come on!" I yelled. "Your turn!"

"Pam, are you sure?"

"Yeah! Come on!" Once when Max and I watched television on his day off from work, I saw skydivers jump from a plane, way above the earth, hurl toward the ground, and bend their legs upon landing. "Bend your legs a little when you land, like parachuters do!"

She stood on the ledge of the second floor, looking at her landing pad, the grassy yard, and I could tell she was weighing the possibility of injury. "Promise you won't get hurt," I said.

Robin leapt from the edge and landed on her feet and said how much she enjoyed flying to the earth like that.

We ran up the flight of stairs, jumped, ran up the stairs, jumped again, then Mother came outside and ended our fun. "Girls, that's how you'll break a leg," she said, "or your neck."

Two weeks later, on April 28th, 1973, Patti's children, Robin, and I had just completed our Saturday morning room cleaning assignments. We sat on the floor and took turns moving tiny, plastic, figures around a game board. Suddenly, we heard a thundering, distant boom.

"Uh-oh," I said quietly to Robin who sat at my left.

"What was that?" Denise said.

"Beats me," Sherry said. "Maybe dynamite."

"I don't think so," her younger brother Ralph said. He got up and dashed to the window. "That was too big for dynamite."

Another great blast occurred and we hurried down the flight of stairs. Two more explosions followed. We went outside just as a fifth massive boom sounded. Far off to the north, thick columns of smoke streamed upwards, filling the sky.

"It's the end of the world," Ralph said, running to the tree that grew in the middle of their yard. He wrapped his arms around a low hanging limb, pulled himself up to a sturdy branch, and spoke excitedly. "Come on! We'd better get up here so we can watch for enemy jets."

Another bomb exploded.

Ralph pointed up at the blackening sky. "Whoa! Look at that!" He climbed to a higher branch and called down to us. "Hurry up you guys!"

The tree had dense foliage and large, spreading branches. A slight breeze rippled the leaves. Ralph's two sisters pulled themselves onto branches, then Robin and I did the same. Perched there like so many birds, we stared with wide-eyed expressions at the rising smoke plumes.

It was the Vietnam War era and Ralph's imagination ran wild. "It's probably the Viet Cong. It's a Communist takeover," he said, shaking a large overhanging branch.

"Hey! Knock it off!" Sherry said, annoyed. "Ralph, would you stop it?" Her voice softened. "Viet Cong. Communists. Then what? What'll we do?"

"If they come this way, from here, we'll see them, and hide in the house, and barricade ourselves in my room," he answered.

"We can't hide in your bedroom. They'll find us there for sure."

Another bomb exploded.

"Man! Did you see that? That was huge," Ralph said.

"Seven," Robin said.

Kaboom!

"Eight!" she said.

A fraction of a second later, another bomb blasted.

"Nine!" We all yelled.

Sherry and Denise sat on branches below Ralph. He dropped leaves onto their heads. "Those could be Vietnamese bombers dropping missiles on our base." He pressed his bottom lip over his top as he always did when mulling something around in his head. "Maybe they're bombing downtown."

Two more explosions rumbled the sky.

"Ten! Eleven!" We shouted.

The way ten-year-old Ralph and his twelve-year-old sister Sherry handled the whole situation reassured me. At least they seemed to know what to do in an emergency like this.

"Any fraidie cats here?" Ralph said and we all said we weren't scared, though my heart beat fast with excitement and my stomach muscles quivered.

Next, a succession of booms and blasts rattled what seemed like the whole world.

"Twelve! Thirteen! Fourteen! Fifteen! Sixteen!" We yelled in unison.

"Maybe it's not Vietnam. It might be the moon and sickle."

I didn't know what the moon and sickle meant, but I agreed with Ralph and the rest of the kids that this could be the moon and sickle.

Another sequence of explosions thundered and gigantic mushroom clouds hung in the breezeless sky. Sherry and Ralph spoke some more about their survival plans. We'd hide in the food pantry, live on canned food, and emerge from our hiding place when the American and communist armies pronounce a cease-fire.

We had been in the tree for several minutes when Robin said there's supposed to be a huge war that ends the world. "Our Aunt Marylou told us about it. Then Jesus comes and takes us to Heaven. It's in the Bible."

"She told us that angels are going to fill the sky," I said.

Ralph's excitement grew. "Oh, man! It really could be the end of the world. Maybe that's what this is."

"It could be," Robin said.

There weren't any more explosions, but columns of thick, black smoke continued rising on the dark, northern horizon.

Patti called us inside for lunch. We kids left our perches, went inside, and sat around the dining table with bowls of soup and grilled cheese sandwiches. Patti had the radio tuned to a news station and we discovered then that all our talk about war didn't apply to the present crisis.

The voice of the newscaster filled the dining room. "Boxcars carrying six thousand, MK 81's blew up at the Roseville, California Southern Pacific rail yard. The trainload of artillery for our troops was on its way to the Naval Weapons Station in Concord, California, and from there to Southeast Asia. Remarkably, there haven't been any reports of fatalities."

"You mean to tell me a train blew up?" Ralph thumped his hand against his forehead. "We've been in the tree making plans to hide from exploding trains?"

CHAPTER TWENTY-ONE

*T*he corners of Mother's mouth quivered as she resisted the tears filling her eyes. It was Friday and she had come upstairs to speak with Robin and me in Sherry and Denise's room. She sat on the bed beside us, crossed her legs, and I smelled the lemony fragrance of her perfume. "I have some news I want to share with you." She rushed into the reason for her visit. "Mommy needs a rest and, with summer coming, I'm going away for a while to a resort. You girls are staying here with Ed and Patti until I get back."

"Going away?" In a flash, the impact of her words struck me, and I threw a hand to my forehead. "Oh no! Mommy, please don't leave us here."

Since our arrival, Mr. and Mrs. Dictator had often badgered Robin and me. Once when Mother wasn't home and Robin, sick with the flu and delirious with fever, lay on the sofa, Patti told her to go upstairs and clean the girl's room. "I can't," Robin said, moaning. Her head pounded.

"Yes, you can, and you will," Patti said. "Robin, you're just trying to get off working. Get up and get going." Robin had climbed up the flight of stairs, leading to the bedrooms, on her hands and knees, and she blacked out on the way. Patti yelled from below her. "You're not sick! And you better do a good job!"

Robin stared unblinking at Mother. "You can't leave us with Ed and Patti."

Mother sighed and nodded sympathetically. "It won't be for long, promise."

I'd heard that resorts are vacation spots for the wealthy. I wasn't sure what we'd do at a resort, but I sure as anything didn't want to stay here. "Mommy, may we go with you?" I said, hopefully.

"This resort is not for children."

It dawned on me then, without Mother's presence, Ed and Patti could do whatever they wished. Ed might even switch me. "Mommy, please?" I tried one more time, but arguing was pointless. Robin and I both knew that once Mother clamped down on a decision, she was like a dog with a bone. She wouldn't give it up. She never budged from her decision once it was made.

"In the middle of May, just after breakfast, Mother, Robin, and I stood in Ed and Patti's driveway. A stranger wearing dark sunglasses pulled up in a shiny, grey, four-door sedan.

Mother's swollen eyes brimmed with tears. Her sadness wasn't what I had expected from someone leaving on vacation. "Oh look, it's my driver," she said. It seemed to me she was trying to sound happy. She even tried smiling, but the corners of her lips trembled. "Girls, I better be on my way." She bent down, and kissed my sister standing beside her, and rubbed the lipstick from her cheek. "I love you."

"Love you, Mommy," Robin said.

She turned to me—her mouth quivered as if any second she'd fall to pieces—and she stooped down and brushed my face with a kiss. "I love you. Pammie, be good for Ed and Patti."

Her mixed signals confused me. Mother, leaving for vacation, should be joyful, but her eyes, moist with tears, conveyed sorrow.

"When will you be back?" I said.

"After a while."

Her answer didn't satisfy me. "When's that?" I said, walking with her to the waiting sedan.

She ducked inside the car, sat in the passenger seat, "Pammie, soon," she said through the open window. "Go back to your sister."

The sedan eased down the driveway, and we walked beside it to the sidewalk, and watched it leave with our mother. She waved and we waved back until the car was out of sight.

Dad had begun dating Big Pam the year before the first fire—the curtain fire. A year or so later, she moved in with Dad and his dog, Trixie, a mixed Chihuahua. They lived in an apartment in Fair Oaks, a Sacramento suburb.

Big Pam wasn't very tall, but she made up for her squat stature in every other way. She had sparkly blue eyes, short red hair, a bulbous stomach, short puffy arms and legs, and a round face with skin as white and smooth as the petals from the roses that grew along my former home on Wyant Way. Whenever we saw her, every two or three weeks, Big Pam gave Robin and me lots of affection. Hugging her was like being squeezed by a soft marshmallow and I liked her hugs very much.

Fourteen days after Mother departed on her "vacation," Dad picked us up at Patti and Ed's and brought us to his place. "You'll be staying with me until Joy's back," he said.

"Dad, great," I said. "Way to go. Ed and Patti will have to find someone else to be their slaves."

One evening, after we climbed into the bunk beds that Dad set up for Robin and me in a spare bedroom, I pulled my white blanket, stained with smoke, up to my chin, snuggled Baby Tenderlove against my side, closed my eyes, and whispered. "Now I lay me down to sleep." I stopped and considered adding a second request. "Please protect Mommy," I continued. "And Dad, Big Pam, Robin and me. Please protect all of us and every room from fire. Amen."

For a long time, I thought about Mother and then added to my prayers the words, "Jesus, I want her to come home."

The next morning, I met Dad in the kitchen. "When's Mommy coming for us?"

"Your mother will return when she's ready," Dad said.

I frowned at Dad and crossed my arms.

"Little One, don't worry about it. Worrying about what you can't change won't do you a bit of good."

Staying at Dad's wasn't the same as staying at Uncle Bud's. Here Robin and I didn't have other kids to play with. The hours dragged on and I ached for Mother's nearness. At the end of June, Mother still hadn't come home and none of us had heard from her. Then one afternoon, Big Pam gave Robin a letter. "This was in the mail for you and Pammie," she said, handing Robin a letter. "It's from your Mother."

Robin read out loud from the letter on cream colored stationery. I leaned over her shoulder and recognized Mother's stylish cursive.

Darlings,

How have you been? I miss you both so much. Have you done anything fun this summer? I've enjoyed swimming and laying out in the sun by the pool. I've met some other ladies here and have enjoyed playing cards and checkers with them. Please tell your daddy and Big Pam I said 'hi.'

X O X O X O

Love and miss you,
Mommy.

P.S. You can write me at the address on the enve-
lope.

Robin and I didn't waste any time writing back.

"Dear Mommy," I wrote on white, lined paper, misspelling nearly all the words. "How are you? I'm fine. I miss you. Me and Robin swim in the pool, but not a lot. Daddy works. Big Pam watches T.V. I hope you come home soon. I love you. I miss you.
X O X O X O
Pam."

Sunday evening, right after watching Mutual Of Omaha's "Wild Kingdom," Dad called from the kitchen, "Pammie, come in here a second."

"Yeah," I said.

He pointed to the four burner stove. "This darned pilot light keeps going out and your hands are the perfect size to reach it." Dad offered me a pack of stick matches.

I put my hands behind my back and shook my head. "I don't want it."

"It won't hurt you. Why are you afraid of a little match?"

A knot formed in my throat and I backed away from Dad. "I don't like them."

"When you fall off a horse, you gotta get back on."

This wasn't a horse. I had never told Dad "no," and weighed my options. I could disobey and maybe he'd send me to my room or I could get it over with, light the match, and stick it under the burner. My insides quivered. "No. I won't do it."

"Here," he took a stick match from the tiny box. "Trust me with this. I wouldn't ask you to do something that would hurt you," he said. He struck the red and white tipped end against the striker on the side. A tiny flame appeared and I inched toward the living room. "Little One, come back here. I understand why you're scared, but don't you know you can't run from your fears?"

Dad lit another match, and coaxed me into coming near him and holding it. When the flame traveled up the stick, I felt a growing warmth against my fingers, and blew it out. Dad gave me the box, a stick match, and told me to light it. I struck it against the box and actually felt a sense of accomplishment when a tiny, orange flame leapt out on the end.

Dad held my wrist and directed my hand, putting the lit match near the sound of a hissing sound coming from near the stove's front burner. Puff! A blue flame flashed. "See," he said. "Now was that so bad?"

"Yes. It was super, super scary."

"Super scary?" He chuckled. "Sure you were afraid, but it's much better for you to face your fears than run from them. You looked it right in the eye, didn't you?"

"I guess so."

"Wasn't that better than avoiding what makes you scared?" He ruffled my hair. "I'm proud of you," he said.

The Huffy bikes, having been in the backyard, weren't destroyed in the fires, and Max brought them to Dad's place. Max didn't stick around long enough for a visit because he had to get to work, but I liked seeing him. I hugged him before he left. "I love you," I said. He patted my back. "Me too, kid."

A short while later, I rode my blue Huffy around the block of apartments, and pedaled past several neighborhood kids kicking a ball out in the street. I turned the corner and coasted downhill where I spotted three girls walking ahead of me. I hoped they'd want to play. "Hi," I said, coasting to a stop. "I'm having a club. Do you wanna help? You can bring other kids." The little girls, ages eight to ten, had glum, wide-eyed, expressions.

"We'll have fun. Come to my apartment at two o' clock. They'll be games, and—" I tapped my finger on my lips, trying to think of fun activities. "—and stories, stickers, and treats."

The biggest girl scrunched up her freckled face. "What'd you say?" she said.

Speech therapy had helped to improve my speech, but I still had difficulty with words containing the letter "R". For their benefit, I repeated myself. "We'll have stowies, stickahs, and tweats."

The big girl's face was still scrunched up. "Today?" she said.

"At my apatment ovah theh." I pointed to the first building closest to the swimming pool. "On the gound."

The big girl looked sideways at me. "Huh?"

"I mean down stahs."

At two o'clock, the three girls showed up for the first club meeting. We played Old Maid. Big Pam read to us from a book of children's fables and we ate Vanilla Wafers. My three club members received gifts for attendance, stickers, and rub on tattoos that I had saved from boxes of Cracker Jacks. As long as I had cool giveaways, they returned, but when I ran out, about two weeks later, they quit and the club ended.

The T.V. stayed on all day and night at Dad and Big Pam's apartment. Until now, television wasn't something for which I had much time. Besides, Mother enjoyed music more than the boob tube. When she did let me see a program, she switched on cartoons or *Sesame Street* and *Mr. Rogers Neighborhood*, although I did get to watch sports shows with Max. Dad liked sports, too, and war movies. For the first time in my life, while watching a movie with Dad, I saw men blown to smithereens. Dad said the soldiers hadn't really died, that they were actors pretending to have died.

That night in bed, I remembered Nana's death and, after seeing the movie, understood more fully why she never came home. Tears dripped down my face. *She's dead like those soldiers. Nana can't come back because she's dead.* I wept for a long time. Then, I wondered why leaving for vacation made Mother sad. *Maybe she's not at a resort. She could be in the hospital. She could be dying.* It crossed my mind that she and Dad would hide this from Robin and me.

Six weeks after Mother left for the resort, in the middle of July, Dad loaded up the Oldsmobile with fishing tackle, a green metal ice-chest, folding chairs, Trixie, Big Pam, Robin, and me. "We're getting out of Dodge," he said with a grin. That's what he called Sacramento—Dodge. "And we'll catch us some fish."

We drove over an hour to a mountain lake. Dad gave Robin and me fishing poles, and helped us cast our lines. He stood on the bank between us with Trixie sniffing the ground nearby, and explained the river's rapid downstream flow. He said the water originated from the ocean, streams, and snow-melts in higher elevations, and was returning to the ocean. He pointed at a grebe, floating near the shore. "Watch him and he'll disappear." Soon, the little bird dove underwater. "Where'd it go?"

Robin and I had all sorts of ideas.

Dad shook his head and chuckled. "Can you find him? He'll pop up downstream a ways." Dad was right. The grebe showed himself downstream for a second before disappearing again.

"It swims underwater?" I said.

"More like flying with his mouth open. The grebe's hungry and he's catching tiny fish." Dad knew about all kinds of interesting things and I loved hearing him explain how they worked.

He looked at my fishing pole's bobber, about a third of the way across the river, moving up and down with the current. "If you leave your line in the water long enough, a big fat fish will smell dinner on your hook, and then swim over to your wiggly worm, then bite it." He pointed to the red and white plastic ball shaped thing attached to the string's end, floating on the water's surface. "Little One, keep your eye on the bobber. When you catch our dinner, it'll go under the water for a second and come back up. So, watch it."

Robin fished twelve feet from me and another fifteen feet or so down from her, Dad cast out his line. Big Pam fished several feet further down the river from him. Dad balanced his pole on the prongs of a stick, took a beer from the cooler, sat down on a mesh chair, and patted Trixie lying in his lap.

The lake was pretty and several hundred feet to the right of us, logs drifted along a cove that jutted into the shore. The forest of white fir, Rocky Mountain douglas fir, and pine trees grew everywhere except where we were. On our side, there were no trees, just a long stretch of grey, pebbly, moist ground. A breeze rippled the water and wispy white clouds moved across the blue sky.

Five minutes after Dad sat in his chair with his beer, dog, and pole, the anticipation of catching a fish got the best of me and I began turning the reel handle. The translucent string entwined itself around the spindle and gears, and I kept cranking.

"Daddy! Daddy!" I hollered.

He put down his can of beer and ran over with Trixie at his heels, and panting for breath, he stared at my pole. "How'd you manage to do this?" he said, shaking his head. Dad untangled the knotted line and cast it back into the water. "Pammie, leave it right there. Don't touch it until you got a bite," he said.

The breeze picked up speed and waves lapped against the shore, thrusting the red and white plastic ball at the end of my line. I clutched the pole between my hands and waited for a bite. Ten minutes later, I could no longer stand the wait, and cranked my reel as I hollered for Dad. When he came to see what I needed, he found the same scenario: tangles, knots, and no fish. After the two reprimands, I still hadn't learned patience and transgressed a third time, the line of my pole spilling onto the ground.

"You're done fishing," Dad's voice was calm and firm. "I'm not spending all my time fixing your messes. I'll work on your pole at home. Go wait inside the car."

I pouted in the car. *I shouldn't have done that. Why can't I be more like Robin? She's never in trouble.* The clouds had changed from thin wisps into heavy, white, puffy shapes resembling animal ghosts. I gazed at them through the windshield. There was an elephant in the sky with a long nose and round belly, and a long winged bird, and another cloud formation that looked like a steep mountain, and then I spotted a vapory woman flying through Heaven.

My thoughts turned to Mother. *Maybe she's not coming home.* The ghost woman's brilliant white form, long flowing dress, arms, hands, and round face reminded me of her. Tears ran down my face. *What if she's dead?*

CHAPTER TWENTY-TWO

*J*t had been a long, sultry summer. By early August, the delta breezes that had consistently cooled the valley at night, quit blowing, and now both days and nights were hot. One evening, ten weeks after Mother went away, Big Pam answered a knock at the door, letting in a blast of heat. "Brenda," she said, surprised, "long time no see."

Brenda entered with a little, blond headed boy, another long legged boy in high water pants, and a chubby girl. Brenda smiled at me, sitting on the floor with a coloring book and crayons. Her blue-green eyes sparkled and faint lines turned up at her jaw and temples. "Is this Pammie?"

"Yup," Big Pam said.

Brenda poked Big Pam's squishy shoulder and smiled at me. "I'm her sister and these are my brats, Markie." The blond headed boy wrapped his arms around her leg and avoided my gaze. "Roger," she said, flipping her fingers toward the boy in high water jeans. "And this here's Marcella."

"Hi," I said.

Markie grinned shyly, Roger lifted his hand and met my eyes, and Marcella wrinkled up her nose.

"We've come by to meet Keith's daughters," Brenda said.

Big Pam pointed to her niece. "Pammie, Marcella's your age." She headed for the kitchen and called over her shoulder.

"Brenda, want a Coke? Let's go in the kitchen. What about the kids?" she said, opening the refrigerator.

"Mine don't need more sugar. They're hyper enough."

"You young'uns want some water?" Big Pam asked us.

Of course no one wanted water, not when the adults were drinking soda. We all shook our heads and stared longingly at the two cans on the dining table.

Brenda sat across from Big Pam while her children and I hovered nearby. "So, where's Keith?"

"He's at his brother's, working on his car," Big Pam said, crossing one extra wide and stubby leg over the other. She pulled the can's tab and it released a whoosh of air.

"Robin's with him?"

"She's in her room."

"Uh-oh. Sounds like trouble." Brenda took a cigarette from a pale blue case and lit it with a Bic lighter. "Marcella's going straight to her room when we get home for mouthing off again." She rolled her eyes toward her daughter, standing beside her, and blew a trail of white smoke in that direction.

I wondered what Brenda meant by "mouthing off" and felt sorry for Marcella, and figured her mother shouldn't blab this kind of personal information with me and Big Pam right there.

"Robin hasn't been bad," Big Pam said. "She got a nose-bleed from the heat, that's all. I don't know what's taking her so long to come out of her room. Maybe she's napping." She tightened her lips and waved us kids away like we were annoy-ing pests. "Okay, all you young'uns get out from under foot. It's nice outside. Go play."

It wasn't nice outside. It was hot. And I didn't want to play with her niece and nephews. "Do I have to?" I pleaded.

Big Pam frowned. "Pammie, go play."

"Robin gets to stay inside."

"Are you Robin?" She pointed toward the other room.

"Now, do as you're told."

Brenda's two oldest children, Roger and Marcella, were quarreling in our yard. I couldn't stand their loud, angry voices, and took off on my Huffy, and rode several laps around the complex. I pedaled slowly and thought about Robin. *Her nosebleed stopped a long time ago. It's not fair that she gets to stay in the house. Maybe I can sneak into our bedroom and hide there until Brenda and her kids leave.* I devised a plan, decided I'd enter the apartment quietly, tip toe across the living room, and sneak into my room.

I neared a block of a hundred, brass numbered tenant mailboxes housed in a black frame beside the swimming pool and across from Dad's apartment. Near them, Marcella and the two girls from my "club," Helen and Jill, were talking in a huddle.

Marcella's head jerked up, and seeing me, she stiffened. A look of contempt spread across her face. Helen saw me, too, and her bottom jaw fell open. Jill looked over at me as I approached them and her eyes grew large. I pedaled slowly past them on my way to Dad's apartment.

From fifteen feet away, Helen stepped forward from the group and called to me. "Hey, is it true?" Her eyebrows were raised in disbelief. "Did your mother really set your house on fire?"

I turned my handlebars and headed in their direction. "What did you say?"

"Marcella told us..."

I felt my face turning hot. "She lied." My eyes darted from one girl to the next. The two girls looked like they had swallowed a nasty tasting secret. "Marcella, you're making it up."

Marcella blew out a noisy breath of annoyance. She put a hand on one hip and cocked her head. "Well, just ask my mom. Your mother's in jail."

This was the cruelest thing anyone had ever said to me. I hated Marcella at that moment for slandering Mother's name and glared. "Well, you're a liar."

She mocked me, making fun of my impediment. "Well, yow a liah."

My eyes burned with bitter tears. I charged home on my bike, dropped it on the dirt just outside the door and burst inside the apartment. Big Pam and Brenda had tall glasses of iced Coke on the kitchen table beside two cigarettes, smoldering in an ashtray. A swirling cloud of smoke hung near the ceiling.

Brenda sized me up and down, her eyes roaming from my tearful eyes to the clenched fists at my sides. "Pammie, what's wrong? Is Marcella being mean?"

"She made up stuff about Mommy," I said in a small voice.

"Marcella has a problem with that." Brenda turned to Big Pam. "She's had almost as much soap in her mouth as she's had anywhere else. I'm sorry she upset Pammie."

Big Pam raised a palm into the air and shrugged. "I'm not the one she lied about. Don't tell me." She picked up her cigarette and held it. "Maybe Marcella needs to be in here apologizing."

"Pammie. Baby," Brenda said. "I'm sorry, honey. I'll have Marcella come inside and say she's sorry."

"No, that's okay." I unclenched my fists and wiped my eyes with the back of my hands. I never wanted to see Marcella again, or hear her pretend apology. I felt certain she wouldn't mean it.

Brenda held an arm out to me. "Honey, come over here." She put it around my waist. "What'd she say?"

"It doesn't matter."

I watched the smoke trails from their cigarettes, and suddenly I flashed back to the blaze in Robin's bedroom closet and the shocking truth behind what caused the fires began to surface. By this time, Robin was watching television in the living room. As soon as the memory surfaced, I made my escape and headed for my room. A pressure built in my chest and I thought I might cry loud and hard. "The fires weren't accidents," I whispered, my words coming out halted and trembling. I curled into a ball and sobbed.

Dad called me out of my room later that evening after Brenda took her children home. He sat in his living room chair and reached out to me. "Little One," he said, beckoning me with his hands. "Come on."

I walked into his thick, hairy, arms and while he held me close, I buried my face in the warmth of his chest, and wept.

"It'll be all right."

While my face was still against his shoulder, I told him what happened. "Marcella said Mommy lit our house on fire." I gasped for air. "She told my friends." Tears and snot ran onto his shoulder. "They won't want to be my friends anymore." I cried and my shoulders shook. When I had gained control of my emotions and was able to speak, I told Dad that I hadn't known how the house fires happened. "Now I know. I forgot how, but now I remember."

My dad held me close and ran his hand rhythmically across my back.

I flashed back two summers earlier and I remembered the afternoon of the second house fire. The thing that captured my curiosity, pulling me away from my sister's side at the bathtub was Mother. She carried one of the kitchen chairs to Robin's bedroom and I had wondered why. I watched her put it in front of the closet, and stand on it. I saw her open the upper cabinet and then she got down. Mother left with the chair and I returned to Robin, soaking in the warm water. Five or ten minutes later, something pulled on my heart and I looked down the hall at Robin's room. That's when I saw the smoke.

I cried a long time on Dad's shoulder. Soon, I was able to catch my breath and while my head lay against his warm neck, wet with my tears, he questioned me.

"Which fire did you see her light?" He rubbed my back. "It's good for you to talk about it. I don't want you holding anything in."

I sat up in his lap and looked in his sad, tender eyes as he listened to me describe the details of that Saturday afternoon. After I told him everything, I asked the most pressing question. "Why? Why'd she do it?"

"Your mother's not well. She *really* didn't know what she was doing." He paused for several minutes. During the quiet that followed, I remembered the fights between Mother and Max and her moodiness, how one day she'd seemed happy and the next, irritable and angry. "She saw a psychiatrist a week or so ago," Dad continued. "And he said part of her problem had to do with the bitterness she's held onto toward her own mother, your Nana. It's never good to hold grudges. Do you understand what a grudge is?"

I shook my head.

"It's when you're angry at someone. Forgiveness will bring healing, but sometimes people don't want to forgive. She's been angry at your grandmother for a long time. She never talked about what was going on up here." He pointed to his head. "She's always been so stubborn and prideful. I don't ever want you to be like that. I don't want you to keep pain bottled up because it'll make you sick. You can talk to me about anything. All right?"

"Okay," I said.

"Talk about things when they bother you and forgive."

I thought about Marcella and Dad's words. If I wanted to stay healthy, I should forgive her and, although I had no anger toward Mother, I should forgive her, too.

"Mommy's not at a resort?"

"No, honey. Your mother's in prison." Dad had a far-off look in his eyes. "If those cops had done their job right the first time, she would've been there a lot sooner and there wouldn't have been a fourth fire." Dad scoffed. "They couldn't see the noses on their faces. The evidence was right there all along."

Robin came out from our bedroom. She went in there when Dad had called for me. He held her in his arms and told her the truth about Mother. Robin cried like I had, long and hard, and her pain brought my own sorrow to life all over again. We both sobbed on our father's shoulders.

Big Pam brought us Kleenex, and we blew our noses. She pulled her short, chubby legs under her, and sat on the sofa like the Buddha statue near the hall, and explained how Marcella learned the truth. "I was telling Brenda about Joy. That was after you kids went outside, and she said that Marcella put her ear to the door and listened. Robin and Pammie, I'm sorry. Your dad and I, and your mother, wanted to protect you from this."

After my memory had returned of Mother starting the fire in Robin's cabinet, and then learning that she wasn't on vacation at a resort, but that she was in prison, I walked around for days with an indescribable ache far more severe than any pain I'd ever known.

Not many days later, Dad came home from shopping with
a bulging round thing in the pocket of his lightweight jacket.
It moved and I squealed. "There's something alive in there."
"Where?" he teased.
I pointed at his pocket. "In there. Dad, it's alive."
"What's alive?"
"What you have in your pocket," I said.
Dad reached inside his pocket and brought out an orange
hamster. "It's a baby and she needs someone to take care of
her." He held the ball of orange fur at eye level and stared
into its beady eyes. "Don't be afraid. I won't hurt you," he said
softly, sweetly. Dad's smile met mine. "Want to hold her?"
I clasped my hands around the hamster's soft, warm body
and pressed her against my chest.
Dad put an arm over my shoulder and watched me stroke
the hamster's smooth fur. "I'm too busy with work, and, well,
she wouldn't get the care she needs. I wonder who might want
a baby hamster."
"I do," I said. "Can I name her?"
"She's yours. Name her whatever you want."
"Sunshine," I said, "for her orange fur."
I looked up into Dad's sparkling eyes, and the grin on his
face, and I knew he loved me.

CHAPTER TWENTY-THREE

*M*other was charged with arson and incarcerated at The California Institute for Women. She was released ninety days after she left for "vacation." At the end of August, reunion day had finally arrived and she returned to Ed and Patti's.

All the way there, I chewed my nails until they bled. Mother spent the summer locked behind bars with criminals, I surmised. While there, she wore black and white striped clothes, like prisoners do on television, I imagined. *She had to be in handcuffs, and policemen with guns ordered her around.*

Robin and I entered Ed and Patti's home and followed the voices coming from the kitchen. I couldn't wait to be with Mother, and I hurried toward the kitchen. Patti was rattling on non-stop and Mother, seated at the table, was listening. "Sounds like I didn't miss much," Mother finally said, her voice low and weak.

Mother pressed a hand against her forehead. Her undone hair, a short boyish style, dark circles under her eyes, and the morose expression on her makeup-free face depicted the story of months of anxiety and crisis.

My knees went weak. Her appearance frightened me. She didn't look like my mother. That feeling that I had carried in my heart all summer, the unbearable longing for her, now became a sense of panic. *Something's really wrong with Mommy.*

What happened to her? She's different, angry, sick. The food in my stomach pushed up my throat. *She's looking at me. Her eyes are on mine. What do I say?*

"Girls, it's good to see you," Mother said in a tired voice.

Her physical appearance had so altered and her voice was so flat that I felt I didn't know her. Where were her Marilyn Monroe mole, smile, red nail polish, high heels, and the fun energy she typically carried?

My body fired distress signals at me, heart pounding in my chest, blood draining from my face. Pretending I didn't know where she spent the summer wasn't something I wanted. I couldn't live in deception. Lies create barriers and I longed for a close relationship with her. "Mommy, I know the truth. You weren't at a resort. You were in prison for setting our house on fire."

My words were ice cold water to her face. She tensed and her head jerked. Since I hadn't planned on saying these things, I was as shocked as she that I had said them.

"Okay, Pammie," she said in that same hollow voice. "Why don't you and your sister go play with the other kids."

I dropped my head, stared at the floor, and felt my shoulders slump. After an agonizing wait, the reunion with Mother had arrived and had ended. *Mommy didn't miss me and maybe she doesn't even want me.*

After staying with Ed and Patty for a few weeks, we moved into The Barkley Square Apartments in Carmichael. I awoke Saturday morning and heard Mother singing, her strong soprano voice filling our new apartment with beautiful sounds. For several minutes, I lay there listening to her and thinking about my last conversation with Robin.

The night before, after we nestled under the blankets, Robin said she hoped there wouldn't ever be another fire. "Pam, I won't fall asleep while Mommy's up, so close your eyes, and don't worry, okay?" Knowing she would watch out for us had comforted me and I had slept peacefully.

Our apartment, one of sixty or so units, faced a courtyard. It had two bedrooms, a bath, a narrow kitchen, and a living room big enough for our few pieces of used furniture. The swimming pool and parking lot were just outside our kitchen window. Robin and I shared a room that faced the patio and grass covered yard in the center of the complex.

The sizzling aroma of bacon from the kitchen made my stomach grumble. Warm sunshine streamed through the window beside where I lay on a double bed beside Robin. She sat up and mumbled something about the good food smells coming from the kitchen.

"Isn't it great?" I said.

Robin stretched and yawned. "What? Breakfast?"

"That, and it's just you and me, and Mommy."

The last house fire had destroyed practically everything in our home, including our clothes. Someone gave Mother some nice used clothing, but I only had a couple pair of pants, shorts, two tops, some underwear, socks, and a pair of shoes. Robin's wardrobe wasn't much better. During our summer stay with Dad, he bought us some new outfits and then told us to leave them at his place and said we could wear them when we came back over. After I got up, I pulled on a pair of loose fitting jeans and a top.

Mother yelled cheerfully. "Pammie, Robin, breakfast's ready." We went to the dining table in a tiny area off the living room. From the kitchen, around the corner, I heard Mother softly humming. A cabinet door clinked. "The food will be there in a jiff," she called to us. "How about we go sometime today and see if we can find Poppy?"

Robin and I stared into one another's eyes and nodded knowingly. "That's *just* what I want to do," she whispered and rolled her eyes, letting me know that's not really what she wants.

A metal spatula scraped the bottom of an aluminum pan. Plates rattled. "Hope you girls are hungry," Mother said cheerfully. She entered the room with the platter of steaming food and put it on the table. "I feel like celebrating. Isn't it nice to be in our own place? Okay, girls help yourselves," she said.

We were loading our plates with eggs and bacon and before we had time to reply, Mother went on about the apartment. She commented on its small size, that it needed a plant, and joked about getting a Wandering Jew because, after all, "We're part Jewish," she said, giggling. "This is a far cry from my Auntie Mame house, but it's just the beginning of better days."

"Auntie Mame," Mother said, "is a really old movie starring a sophisticated woman, like myself." She giggled again and leaned toward Robin and me, and folded her arms on the table. "Mame wore expensive clothes and gorgeous jewelry. She had a huge house decorated with beautiful, lavish furnishings and, all the time, she entertained lots and lots of company. Dahlings," Mother said, stifling a laugh.

Robin and I giggled.

Mother smirked. "Dahlings, this is how Auntie Mame spoke. She said 'Dahling.' One day, we'll have an Auntie Mame house with a extravagant veranda and we'll sit there, sipping tea, and admiring the setting sun."

I believed in Mother and in her Auntie Mame house. "I can't wait!" I said, chewing on a mouthful of bacon and eggs.

"We'll live in a big house with lots of pretty things. Can we have a horse?"

She frowned at me, "Pammie, where are your manners. Be ladylike. Don't talk with your mouth full. We'll see," she said. "If there's room, then you girls can each have your own horse."

After breakfast, Mother went to the kitchen and got a can of beer from the refrigerator. "I have good news," she said on her way over to us. "Why don't we sit on the sofa and I'll tell you all about it." We sat beside her as a delicate smile appeared on her lips. "Next Tuesday, I'm interviewing for a job." She rapped her knuckles on the coffee table. "Knock on wood." That's what Mother did whenever she didn't want her plans backfiring. Knocking on wood would bring us luck, she had said.

Living in an apartment was temporary, Mother explained. It was a little piece of the bigger picture. "I need to do two things to move on up in the world. I'll get a job and I'll find you girls a daddy. Then comes my Auntie Mame house." She giggled.

I admired the way she balanced a cigarette between her two fingers. Once again her nails were long, red, and shiny. She had crossed her legs and by putting her elbow into her thigh, she kept the cigarette pointing in the air. Mother stared at the glowing end. "I have more good news," she said. "I've been trying to think of a way to tell you, but I think the best plan is to just come out with it."

I couldn't imagine what could be better than being here with Robin and Mother. I shot my sister a split second glance. I don't know what she thought, but I didn't want a new daddy. The one we had suited me fine, and I hoped Mother's news had nothing to do with marriage proposals or weddings.

166 Mother had only taken a couple drags of her white and tan cigarette when she smashed it against an ashtray, straightened it, and saved the rest for later. "Do you want a sister or brother?"

I laughed. "Our new daddy has kids?"

"Geez, Pammie," Mother said. "You're hilarious. No."

Robin's eyebrows scrunched together. "You're having a baby?" she said.

"You got it," Mother said.

I had no idea where this baby came from, didn't even wonder, and shrieked with joy. "A baby! We're getting a new baby."

"Mommy, really?" Robin said. "Does this mean you and Max are getting back together?"

For the next five minutes, Mother explained that the problems between she and Max were beyond repair and she told us about her pregnancies with Robin and me. The same doctor who delivered us would deliver this baby, too. She said the baby would be small and arrive earlier than the doctor's due date of February because all her children were little and early. Somehow this made us special, but I didn't know why.

"Robin, you were a preemie and weren't even five pounds when you decided it was time to be born," she said. Then Mother looked at me. "Pammie, you were a little bigger."

Mother patted her stomach. That's when I noticed the round bulge under her shirt and asked permission to touch her belly. She placed my hand on the warm bump and it seemed a miracle to me that a human being was actually underneath her skin.

Two months later, we celebrated Christmas Eve with Dad and all his kissing relatives at his brother's home where Santa Clause made a live appearance, passing out presents to Dad's nephews, Robin and me. And we spent Christmas day with Mother in our little apartment.

Mother clutched her protruding belly with one hand and finished putting a few items in her travel bag. It was the end of December and her labor pains had begun. "Mother Gwen's on her way over," she told Robin and me. Since Gwen and Nana would be the same age, Gwen got the parent title attached to her name. "She's driving me to the hospital. When you get home from school, wait here for Gwen. You'll stay with her and Ted while I'm in the hospital."

After school, Robin and I hurried home. We crossed the street, leading to our apartment complex. "What do you think it is?" Robin said, excitedly. "A boy or a girl?"

"A girl, or, maybe a boy. I don't know." I ran across the parking lot behind our unit. "Come on, let's hurry and find out."

We threw open the apartment door and stopped in our tracks. Mother lay, resting on the sofa, her huge, round belly looked extra watermelon like. "False labor. I had them with both you girls." She looked emotional, mascara ran under her eyes, and she sounded exhausted. "The doctor ordered me off my feet."

Within the week, Mother had more contractions and Gwen hurried over again, loaded Mother into her car, and took her to the hospital. Within two hours, my still pregnant mother was back home.

Robin and I attended a school across the street from our apartment, Mission Avenue Elementary. Early in January, sheets of water descended upon the campus, turning the playground into a huge pond. A few minutes before the lunch bell rang, Miss Pratt, the school secretary, spoke on the intercom system. "This message is for Pam and Robin Williams." At the mention of my name, I gasped. Everyone in my class quit working and stared at the speaker jutting from the wall, near the chalkboard. Even the kids who always fidgeted stopped moving. "Pam and Robin, your mother's gone to the hospital to have her baby. Go straight home after school."

When school finally ended for the day, I walked in a drizzle to where the school's entrance and parking lot met, and tried to ignore what I saw. Kids in nice clothes, rushing to their waiting parents, parked in cars at the curb. I dropped my eyes to my stained jeans with the hole in the knee and then to the grey pavement, hiding my envy, my pain. *We're getting a new baby. None of those kids have new babies.* That evening, Gwen brought home my still pregnant mother.

Near the third week of January, Robin and I arrived home from school and found a note on the table in Mother's handwriting, explaining the reason for her absence.

Dear children, Gwen's rushing me to the hospital.
She'll be by for you later this evening. Please wait in
the apartment for her. I love you, Mommy.

CHAPTER TWENTY-FOUR

*S*oon, Gwen came over. Her goofy grin showed the silly gap between her two front teeth. "Guess what?"

Robin grinned. "Well, you're here and that can only mean one thing."

I jumped up and down, "Mommy had the baby!"

"What'd she have?" Robin said.

"You have a new brother."

"Oh yeah!" Robin and I said, smiling, then laughing. "When can we see the baby?" Robin said.

"Your mother and baby brother should be home in a couple days. She's pretty tired and the doctor wants her to stay an extra day or two and get some rest."

Seeing our concerned faces, she told us that Mother's labor had been long, that she was dehydrated, and that she and the baby are fine. "She better get the rest while she can. Newborns are a lot of work," she concluded.

Gwen and Ted were the oldest people I knew. Gwen had pewter grey hair, a smidgeon longer than Ted's white buzz job. They both had sagging cheeks and Gwen had wrinkles the size of the Grand Canyon. When they laughed, which wasn't often, the loose folds of wiggling face skin creeped me out. I was apprehensive and quiet around them.

Mother had said she'd only have "natural childbirth." She told Robin and me there'd be no cesarean section, no strong painkillers, just a lot of panting and blowing, and her doctor's gentle guidance, but nothing unnatural. "I've had all my babies the natural way," she told us with that special nose of hers in the air and a smug grin on her face.

Robin and I caught the bus near Gwen and Ted's and rode it to school. We stayed in their home for three days. The afternoon after my baby brother's birth, I shivered with cold under the eaves of my classroom during recess. I leaned against the wall, waiting for the lunch bell to ring, calling us back into class. A north wind blew. The dark, overcast sky threatened rain. Large goose bumps covered my bare arms.

The longer I stood against the wall, the cruddier I felt. I pretended not to stare enviously at the kids climbing on the jungle gym, or the girls giggling and chattering in groups, or the boys kicking a soccer ball to each other across the field, shouting and running for the goal.

My third grade teacher, Mrs. Dowdy approached. "Pam, where's your coat?"

"I don't know," I lied. The house fires destroyed the one I had owned, but I didn't want her knowing this. She might ask questions and then I'd have to figure out something to tell her. Mother's sins made me feel dirty and ugly, and I didn't want anyone to know that she lit our home on fire or that she spent time in prison. I didn't want anyone judging me for her behavior.

Mrs. Dowdy had thick, black hair and wore large hoop earrings. She had on an ankle length corduroy skirt, a brown coat, fur-trimmed hat, and tall black boots. She put a hand on my shoulder and pointed me toward the swings and jungle gym. "Go play. It'll do you good to get your circulation moving."

My eyes dropped to the ground. I thought the other kids saw flaws in me and I figured no one wanted to play with a flawed girl, and so I hadn't even tried to get a friend. "Please, don't make me."

"Don't make you? Of course, I won't make you." She rubbed her hands together to warm them. "Can't you participate with the other children?"

I kept my eyes on the ground.

She knelt beside me. "Don't you feel well?"

"Uh-huh."

"Don't you want to play?"

My eyes met her intense stare and I shrugged.

"Why don't you?"

"I don't know."

"Well, there must be a reason. Is it something one of the children said?"

I nodded and bit my bottom lip to keep from crying. A boy in my class often pinched his nose and made animal sounds as I entered the classroom. That morning, he had told one of our classmates that I stunk.

"Who was it?"

"I can't tell. If I do, that'll make me a rat fink, and besides, he'll clobber me."

Mrs. Dowdy said I could tell her anything and she'd never let anyone know how she obtained the information. Her empathetic voice and warm eyes alleviated my anxiety, but I kept my secrets to myself. "Well, okay, if you don't want to tell. But remember to bring your coat to school. It's supposed to rain all next week and for goodness sakes, bring an umbrella." She smiled and her stern eyes softened.

Mother came home from the hospital with our baby brother wrapped in a blanket like a sausage. She reclined in an easy chair, cradled him in her arms, and gazed at him with warmth in her eyes. "He's named after my cousin Steve," she said, softly. Robin and I stood on either side of her, staring at the tiniest person we'd ever seen.

I studied the baby's contented face, porcelain like, with rosy cheeks and the smoothest skin I'd ever seen. Steven's eyes were shut and he had long lashes. One little hand stuck out of the blanket, his fingers so tiny and curled tightly around one another. I rubbed the back of his hand. "He's perfect," I said.

"Isn't he?" Mother said. She looked more peaceful than at any other time, holding him, a gentle smile on her lips.

"Look at all that pretty hair," Robin said, stroking the back of his golden brown hair. "It's so soft."

Not many days later, Mother hurried Robin, me, and ten-day-old Steven out of the rain and into The Green Parrot. "It's a family place," she had said and sure enough, she was right. People we knew surrounded both sides of the L-shaped counter. Uncle Ernie, Brother Bob, Mother Gwen, and Poppy were among them. Having come here myself since infancy, this was the life I knew, and the people with whom I felt most comfortable.

We entered the barroom through the saloon like doors that separated the pizza order area from the drinking area.

"Joy!" the gang said.

"There he is," Uncle Ernie said, snickering Paul Lynde style. "The new baby," he whined. "Joy, he's a cutie."

"Here's to Joy and Steven," Brother Bob said, lifting his half full mug of beer in the air. Others around the bar lifted their drinks and cheered, "To Joy and the baby!" Then those that had been Mother's friends over the years rose from their warmed seats and surrounded us. I could smell their after-shave, cologne, the heavy scent of beer, and cigarettes.

Everyone oohed and ahhed over Steven as Robin and I stood within the gathering and agreed with the endearing accolades. Yes, he looks like a darling little cherub. Yes, his eyes are especially blue and we also hoped they'd stay that way. I nodded in agreement, but in truth I secretly hoped his eyes would someday be the same as mine, dark as coffee. Yes, his hair feels soft as goose down, and no, there certainly couldn't be a cuter baby anywhere, and yes, Robin and I were proud to be his big sisters.

"Edie," Poppy called heartily, his cheeks red from having consumed too much alcohol over the years, "give me daughter a beer and me granddaughters sodas." Poppy chuckled and lifted his stein toward Steven asleep in Mother's arms. "Young man, you're too little for a drinkie. He's a good-looking lad, that he is." Poppy drank a fourth of his beverage in a single gulp and sputtered. Saliva appeared on his lips. "Fellas, have you seen me handsome grandson? Takes after his ol' grand-dad, that he does," Poppy said, laughing.

Brother Bob slapped his shoulder. "You son of a gun," he said. "Congratulations!"

All that month and the next, having a new baby in the family brought about a second blessing. In place of the all day beer marathons at the bars, which Mother had reduced greatly during pregnancy, she took Robin, me, and our infant brother with her to The Green Parrot where she sprinted through two or three beers, as many as she could consume, while Steven slept. When he awoke, his cries were an alarm calling us into action. Mother grabbed her purse, and Robin carried Steven as we hurried from the bar, climbed into the Impala, and went home where Mother fed him and changed his diaper. Then, we stayed home for the rest of the day.

And this—Mother's attentiveness to Steven, her presence in our home, and the times Robin and I had with her—all of this changed. It happened so gradually I didn't see it coming.

"Girls, I'm going out this morning for a while," Mother said. She held a grocery list in one hand, her purse and car keys in the other. "Robin, Steven's just had a bottle and he'll sleep a few hours. I need to run some errands. I'll be back within the hour. Cross my heart." Steven was three and a half weeks old the first time Mother left him with us.

Then one Saturday morning, Mother came to Robin and me with her purse slung over her shoulder. "I'm going out for a little bit. Watch your brother."

I walked with her to the front door.

"My hairdresser's squeezing me in today at three," she said. "Then I'll be at The Parrot for an hour or two. Okay?"

It wasn't really a question. It was more of an understanding of the way it would be. We would stay home and babysit Steven.

My sister lay on the sofa with her head in a book. She glanced over at Mother, standing at the door with her hand on the knob. "Really?" she said, "you're leaving the baby with us for that long? But what if he wakes up before you're home?"

"Robin, you are eleven and a half, that's old enough to babysit an infant for two or three hours. Check his diaper and if it's wet, change it. Give him a bottle and burp him. You girls have helped me with him enough to know what to do. You'll be just fine. Lock the door and don't open it for anyone."

As she left, I watched her through the living room window. She walked down the sidewalk leading to the parking area behind our unit, her heels clicking on the pavement. Two hours later, she returned. Fortunately, Steven had slept the entire time of her absence.

Almost instantly, Mother began increasing the frequency and duration of her trips away from our apartment. "You and Pammie are staying home from school today to help with your brother," she announced one morning in early spring. I liked the idea of no school and grinned up at her. She stood in front of the bathroom mirror and applied mascara, lipstick, a little blush, a pretend mole. "Girls, you'd never believe what I heard on the news the other day. A family of children was taken from their parents and put into foster homes."

Robin stood beside me in the bathroom doorway. Her eyes grew wide and I felt mine do the same. "Really?" she said. "That's such a mean thing to do."

Mother teased her short hair and combed it into a pumped up style. "That's what the state social service department does. They tear children from their parents and make them live with strangers." She sprayed her hair with Aqua Net and smirked at Robin and me, still staring with our eyes wide and worried. "So, anyways I'm going out for the day. I'm meeting your granddad and Luke at The Vagabond."

We accompanied her to the kitchen. "If you need something call. Here's the number." She handed me a slip of paper with a phone number. "Darlings, keep the door locked and whatever you do," she said, her voice raising, "don't let anyone in, and don't tell anyone that you're home alone."

By the time Mother returned to us, an entire day had passed, and the sun had sunk down low. She entered the living room, singing and smiling. "Girls, guess what? Things are really starting to look up. Luke asked me out on a date. We're going out to brunch this Saturday." She giggled. "Maybe he's your new daddy."

Not many days later, while I played on the living room floor—My plastic cowboys were fleeing from my plastic Indians—Mother said she was going out for the morning and, since it was the weekend, Robin and I wouldn't need to miss any school. "After I run a couple errands, Luke's taking me on that brunch date I told you about," she said.

Mother had on a knee length dress with a belt around her slender waist. A sweater lay across her arm and her purse and car keys were in one hand. I thought how I hated it when she left us, and, without realizing I'd done it, shook my head.

"Pammie, you and Robin will do fine," Mother smiled down at me. "You've become such capable young ladies."

Robin's back was toward Mother. She showed me her rolling eyes and silently mouthed, "Oh, brother."

I folded my arms and frowned. "But you're never home anymore and I wanted us to be with you."

"Pamela Jean Marie, pouting is unbecoming on young ladies. I'll be home in a little while."

Minutes after Mother left, Steven awoke from his nap. Robin changed his diaper and gave him a bottle of warm formula. We took turns holding him, patting his back and, when he fell asleep, we lay him on his side in the bassinet, at the foot of Mother's bed. By bedtime, Mother still wasn't home. Robin gave Steven another bottle and then she and I went to bed.

Long after dark, the sound of jingling keys woke me from my sleep. Rain splattered against the window and Robin slept soundly beside me. I heard Mother enter the apartment. She bumped into something and giggled. She went to her room and shut the door.

Mother served Robin and me eggs and bacon for breakfast a day or two later. "Girls, you aren't going to class this morning. I want you to stay home and help me with Steven. Luke has the day off and he's taking me out on the town." She wiped a bit of milk from Steven's mouth with a cloth. She tapped the tip of her shiny, red fingernail against a slip of paper on the dining room table. "Here's the number where I can be reached," she said. "You can call *only* if you need something."

Staying home with Steven so that Mother could maintain her social life became the new normal. Just before the beginning of spring break, she kept Robin and me out of school two days in a row. "Girls," she said, "I'll be at Luke's until Monday." This was the first time she left Robin and me alone overnight with our baby brother. "Steven has plenty of formula," she said and handed Robin the baby, dressed in clean pajamas. Answering machines and cell phones didn't exist yet and we had no way of reaching her quickly if necessary. "I'll call tomorrow. Call me at that number I gave you, but only if it's urgent."

She returned Monday morning as promised, but a couple of days later she departed for another overnighter with Luke. There were few groceries in the house. For dinner that night, Robin and I ate bologna with mustard spread on it and some iceberg lettuce. There wasn't any bread. The next morning, Mother still hadn't returned and she had been with Luke so much that I wondered if she loved him more than us. "Why doesn't she come home?" I asked Robin.

"Beats me," she answered. "She'll probably be home later today."

I shared the last of the Frosted Flakes with Robin, filling two bowls halfway with it. "The milk's almost gone," I said.

"Let me see," Robin said, peering through the opening of the cardboard milk carton. "Do you mind if I add water to it?"

"Robin, you're brilliant!" It was decided. We'd have Frosted Flakes with a little milk and a lot of water.

Later in the day, Mother called. "Pammie, how are you and your siblings?"

"Steven's okay, but me and Robin are hungry."

"There's been a change in plans, darling. Luke and I are having a great time. I'm sure you and your sister can take care of Steven for one more night." She hurried on with scarcely a break between words. "Pammie, give your brother and sister hugs from me. Uhm-mah," she said, making hugging sounds.

"But, Mommy," I said into the receiver, "there's nothing to eat." I fought against a sudden urge to cry. "We're hungry," I said again.

"Check the cupboard and produce drawers. I know there's not much there, but I'll get more groceries before I come home. Cross my heart."

The bologna was gone, but we had a small head of lettuce, and spread mustard on the leaves, and ate them for dinner. I thought mustard and lettuce tasted good, but my stomach ached with hunger and I was sad.

Two days later, Mother called again. Robin pressed the phone against her ear, "Steven's last diaper's on him and we're out of food."

There was a pause and Robin's face went blank. "Didn't you hear me?"

Robin hung up and flung herself onto the sofa. "Pam, I don't know what to do. Why isn't she coming home? She's with that Luke guy. That's why. Well, what about us? This is sure a rotten thing to do to your own kids." A bitter tear rolled down her cheek.

Our baby brother ran out of disposable diapers before the day ended. We did the best we could and improvised with a small stack of kitchen towels and when we were out of these, we used regular towels folded into makeshift diapers. The bulging apparatus went from his tiny thighs to his collarbone.

Steven seldom complained. Whenever he whimpered, we gave him a bottle or changed his diaper. We held him until he fell asleep, then we put him in his bed. Early the next morning, five days after Mother left on her supposed overnight date, Steven's whimpers turned into ear-splitting cries. Robin brought him to our bedroom and laid him beside me on the bed.

"What's wrong with him?" I said with a voice louder than his screams.

Robin's face was worried. She unpinned his urine soaked towel, stared at him, and gasped. "Oh, no!"

"What is it?" I said as I saw for myself.

"I'm not sure, but we better call Mommy." She pinned the last available clean towel around Steven and handed him to me.

We went to the living room where Robin dialed the number that was just for emergencies. "Mommy," she practically yelled into the receiver. "Steven's crying," she said as if Mother couldn't hear him. "There are sores on his bottom. When are you coming home?" She slammed the phone down in frustration. "In a little while. That's what she always says."

It seemed to me that our situation would never change and I wondered if Mother had moved out of the apartment and whether she would ever come home. Steven refused his bottle and cried all day. Long after dark, he fell into a fitful sleep, waking every couple of hours to tell us the only way he could that his bottom hurt.

In the morning, Robin dialed the phone number Mother had left with us, but no one answered. After noon, while the baby slept, she called The Vagabond. "Is my mother there?" She paused for a second and then spoke into the receiver again. "Mommy, we need you home. Steven's sores are worse. It's really bad. White stuff's coming out of them." Her brows drew together and she rubbed her forehead. "No. Wait. Did you hear me? Steven didn't sleep good last night because his bottom hurts him." Her voice trembled like she might cry.

"Pam and me had lettuce for dinner a few nights ago." Her voice was thick with sarcasm. "What did you have? Mommy, please come home."

She banged the receiver down and huffed. "Pam, I'm so mad at her! She told me the same thing she's been saying. I can't believe she's doing this."

The next day, Mother still hadn't returned to the apartment. We washed Steven's bottom in cool water, and wrapped him in a smelly receiving blanket. All of his clothes and blankets stunk of urine and sour milk. My insides ached with hunger and I was lightheaded. I wanted to go to bed because of the hopeless feeling in my heart, but I wouldn't leave Robin alone to care for Steven.

Robin and I discussed calling Aunt Marylou or Dad, but we had strict orders from Mother not to tell anyone we were home alone. The baby's shrill cries put me on edge and I walked around the house with my hands over my ears, feeling useless and frustrated. Eventually, Steven's cries quieted, then he opened his mouth and his face was scrunched up and bright red, but there weren't any sounds.

Spring break was over and school resumed, but Mother still hadn't returned to us, so we stayed home to care for our brother and make due with what we had. The sores on baby Steven's bottom were worse than ever, but he didn't cry as much and he drank a little milk, enough to convince us that he wouldn't starve to death.

More than a week after Mother left for her date with Luke, a knock came at the door. I peeked out a crack in the curtain. "Oh man," I whispered loudly. "Robin, it's the school nurse."

"If we don't answer it, she'll just come back later." She paused for a moment with her hand on the doorknob. "We might as well open it."

"Good morning," the nurse said, smiling. "You've missed a lot of school and I'm here to see if there's anything wrong. Are you ill?"

"Yes. We've had the flu," Robin said, sounding like a grown up.

The nurse eyed us suspiciously. "May I speak with Mrs. Williams?"

"You mean our mother?"

"Yes. Is she home?"

"She's sleeping. Come back later."

After thanking the nurse for her concern, Robin shut the door and walked over to the phone. "That does it. I'm calling Aunt Marylou."

CHAPTER TWENTY-FIVE

J wrapped my arms around Aunt Marylou's hips. A flood of relief washed over me. Someone who could help had finally arrived.

Aunt Marylou chuckled and reached toward three-month-old Steven, crying in Robin's arms. "Here let me see him."

He stopped crying, took a breath, and relaxed his head against the nook of her elbow.

She smiled down at him. "Aw, isn't he a cutie?"

We stood in the living room of our apartment, making excuses for Mother's absence, trying to give Aunt Marylou a logical reason why Mother had left us alone. Steven squeezed his eyes tight, coughed a couple times, and yowled.

Aunt Marylou raised her voice over Steven's earsplitting cries. "You girls get your things together." She held our baby brother against her shoulder and rubbed his back. "Robin does your brother have some dry pajamas? What about a bottle and formula?"

"Everything's dirty and he has a little formula."

"Bring your laundry and we'll do a load."

Soon, Robin was back with a bag of things. "Mommy won't know where we've gone."

"Your Uncle Bud's contacting her. Taking care of the baby and you girls is Joy's responsibility. If she's abandoned you, that's not your fault." Steven was still crying and Aunt

Marylou was still speaking loudly. "And if she returns and you're not here, maybe she'll learn her lesson."

We went with Aunt Marylou to her home. She and Uncle Bud hovered around Steven like he was of especially great value. She opened his makeshift diaper, a folded towel, and shook her head. "This is terrible. I've never seen a diaper rash so bad." They worked on him together, bathing him in water, patting him dry, and covering his entire diaper area with cornstarch.

In my heart, I accused someone severely for the rash—not Robin, not Mother, but I blamed me. *Steven wouldn't have this rash if I took better care of him. I'm the reason he's sick. Maybe I could've done something to keep Steven well. I should've, but I didn't.*

Aunt Marylou turned toward Robin and me with tender eyes. "You girls wait and see. Very soon Steven's diaper rash will be gone." She continued with the baby, putting a diaper on him and lifting him to her shoulder. The bath, cornstarch, and new diaper made him more comfortable and he relaxed in her arms. "You both look like you're about to cry. Steve will be okay. You did the best you could. This isn't your fault. It's Joy's." The love in her eyes and the warmth in her words relieved some of my emotional pain.

Robin and I took baths. We dressed in freshly washed clothes and filled our stomachs with Aunt Marylou's home cooked meals. Two or three days later, a car stopped outside the house. Then came the click-click-click of heels. Mother tapped once on the door and entered.

"Joy, there you are," Aunt Marylou said. Her eyes met Mother's shifting gaze. "I wondered when you'd be by. Steven was out of diapers and Robin and Pammie didn't have anything to eat for days. Your Uncle Bud and I are unhappy with you. You left a tiny baby with two little girls." A look of confusion filled her face. "Joy, I'm surprised you would do that. Steven isn't their responsibility and your children need you."

Mother clenched her jaw tight and, without any explanation, she retrieved Steven and flicked a long finger at Robin and me, directing us out the door.

The new normal continued. At the end of the month, Mother and Luke went out for dinner and ballroom dancing. That night, I couldn't sleep. *What if she loves Luke more than us?* Rolling onto my side, I peered out the window at the courtyard lit up by the full moon. *What if she doesn't come back?* Far off in the distance, a siren wailed and I winced. Several neighborhood dogs howled mournfully. *Mommy said everything happens for a reason. What's the reason for being abandoned?*

The early morning sunlight, filtering through my sheer curtains, brightened the room with a pale yellow glow. I stretched, rose from bed, and headed for the bathroom. Just then, Mother's bedroom door swung open and a shirtless man, a total stranger, froze in place and stared at me, blinking with unfocused, puffy eyes. He rubbed his unshaven jaw and hurried past me on his way out the door.

My heart beat fast. "Mommy!"

She came out of her room in her bathrobe.

"A man was in your room," I spoke excitedly. "He scared me. What was he doing here?"

"Pammie, it's all right. My car broke down in the middle of the night and he gave me a ride home." Mother yawned, covered her mouth, and studied my face. "It was late and he stayed. Don't look so worried. He won't be coming back."

Summer arrived and Mother spent more time at the bars and with Luke than she did with Robin, Steven, and me.

During her frequent all-day-and-night absences, my insides pained with loneliness as I longed for her return.

From the middle of June until the beginning of the school year in September, Robin and I fell into a monotonous routine of caring for the baby and trying to survive without enough food. At various times, when there wasn't so much as a piece of bread in our apartment, my sister and I became seasonal fruit pickers, picking ripe peaches, nectarines, plums, and apricots from trees in the neighborhood and bringing our harvest home where we devoured the delicious fruit and satisfied our gnawing hunger.

Staying inside the apartment with the sunny, warm weather calling us outside tortured us. We grew bored and broke up our monotony by playing tickle torture, contests of dominance in which we fought to overpower each other. We'd wrestle to the carpeted floor, sit on each other's stomachs, and while pinning legs and arms to the carpet, we'd tickle bellies, sides, and knees, and laugh hysterically until one cried out, "Uncle!" Sometimes, we had indoor water fights, or turned on the radio to the "oldies" music station and sang with all our hearts as we danced through the apartment.

A few days after the new school year began, Mother, Robin, and I had just finished eating dinner when we heard neighborhood children playing on the courtyard. I peeked at them through the open window.

"Red light. Green light. Red light. Red light," a girl yelled,

"Mommy," I said. "Can we go outside?"

"It's may we," she said.

"Okay. May we go outside?"

"If you'll be back by dark."

I recognized the kids gathered in the courtyard. Several lived in the apartment complex. A couple lived in a house nearby. The oldest in the group, Judith, a girl Robin's age with shoulder length hair the color of butterscotch, spotted Robin and me walking toward the group. She stopped the game.

"Oh good," she said and trotted over to us. "Y'all wanna play?"

Robin nodded. "But not for too long. Our Mother says we have to be home by dark."

"Why don't we play Hide-and-Seek across the street," Judith said to the group of seven or eight girls.

We crossed the street and huddled on the massive green lawn of Mission Avenue Elementary School and the neighboring Lutheran church.

"Hide anywhere this side of the church or school," Judith said. "Y'all can't cross the street or leave the school grounds."

The sun dropped down toward the western horizon. "Gosh," I mumbled to Robin, "this'll take all night." I figured Robin and I wouldn't get to play if Judith kept on yammering. "It's getting dark."

"Pam, shh," Robin said.

"Who wants to be *it* first?" Judith's eyes darted from one girl to the next. "No volunteers? Oh come on, y'all. It aint always gotta be me."

I fidgeted with the drawstring of the only shorts I owned. Just then, from my place in the huddle beside Robin, I heard a deep male voice shouting from far away and turned away from Judith, and scrutinized someone walking briskly toward us.

A white haired girl with blunt bangs that hung just above her brow line stood across from me in the circle. "I guess I can be it," she said.

"Give us enough time to hide," Judith said.

Another girl pointed at the mysterious person approaching us. "Hold on a minute. Listen. Who's that?"

The sun sat at the horizon and the landscape was covered in the greying light of the closing day. Some of the girls in our huddle with their backs toward the approaching stranger turned around and peered into the half-lit distance. Some shook their heads and others shrugged their shoulders.

He shouted again.

"Y'all understand him?" Judith said.

And again, the stranger yelled.

The white haired girl scrunched up her nose. "Sounds like, I'm highanivanife."

I glanced from one girl to the next. Everyone peered at him, some with squinted eyes and brows drawn together. The smaller girls regarded the older, bigger girls, and, I supposed they, like me, waited for answers.

The stranger came closer and shouted again, "I'm highanivanife!"

He drew near and, from a few hundred feet away, I finally saw him more clearly. He looked to be one of the high school boys in faded jeans and t-shirt. He held something small and slender in his right hand over his head.

He came to a patch of lawn and a narrowing shaft of golden sunlight and the object in his hand glinted like metal. My eyes darted from him to the motionless girls, then to my sister. "Robin," I whispered. "Whatta we do?" She stared curiously at him, her eyebrows scrunched together, her head tilted to the side. I could see she was straining for understanding, trying to figure out what he was doing, and why he kept shouting at us.

"I'm highanivanife," he said.

I tried deciphering his words. *What does he mean? I'm highanivanife?*

He stopped a few hundred feet in front of us and swung the metallic thing, back and forth, in the air.

"Y'all, know what he's doin'?" Judith said.

He yelled. "I'm high!" And he laughed. "Man, I'm high and I have a knife."

This time, I got it and apparently the other girls did too. Mouths dropped open and all our eyes fixated solely on the teen and the knife held above his head. The questions ceased and we didn't move or make a sound.

Why's he telling us about his knife? What does he want? My mouth went dry as a cracker and my legs trembled. I had a sudden urge to flee, but, since Robin hadn't moved, I figured we were safe. The stranger advanced and I stepped a little behind my sister. He marched closer to our group of girls, his knife swinging wildly above his head.

From fifty feet away, he shouted. "I'm high. I have a knife and I'm going to kill you."

Is this a joke? I gazed at Robin and searched her unflinching eyes for answers. She and the rest of the girls stood stock still, shocked into a frozen, immobile state.

He came closer and my heart beat so hard my neck throbbed. My legs were so heavy I couldn't move them and my mouth so dry I couldn't swallow.

The boy kept swinging his weapon, slicing the air. "I'm high. I'm high. I'm so high." He laughed a wicked, cruel laugh. "I'm gonna kill you."

None of us girls moved.

"Did you hear me? I'm high and have a knife." He gripped the black handle and stabbed the stainless steel blade at us from a distance. "I'm gonna kill you." He drew back his arm, and hurled the knife into the air. End over end, it flew toward us and landed flat on the grass in front of our feet.

We girls had been so entranced by this boy's insane behavior that we hadn't moved, but when that knife struck the ground, we woke up, we shrieked, and Judith gave the order. "Hurry! Get the knife!"

The girl with pigtails threw her hands over her mouth and recoiled. The oldest among us—Robin, Judith, and another girl, Lizzy—sprinted for the weapon, lying fewer than ten feet away.

"No you don't!" the boy said, charging them.

Lizzy reached the weapon a mere second before the boy. She picked it up, screeched, and, as if it were on fire, tossed it away from her toward some of the other girls. Judith picked up the knife awkwardly, and threw it toward the school building.

Just like that, we came alive and, in a fevered sprint, the girls took off in a dead run for home. But I ran in the opposite direction, toward the church, and Robin, not wanting to leave me alone, followed.

We ran as fast as our legs would carry us and ducked down along the church building behind a row of evergreen shrubs. For several seconds, we kept as still and quiet as possible. I could only hear one thing in the perfectly calm, night air—the beating of my heart pounding in my eardrums.

The sun had set and in a couple minutes the afterglow of day would be gone. We peered through prickly branches and searched the distance for the whereabouts of the drug-crazed assailant. A crescent moon hung in the sky above our complex across the street, and dozens of little windows reflected the soft yellow glow shining through them. I wondered what Mother and baby Steve were doing at home.

Robin tapped my shoulder. "When I tell you to run," she whispered, her eyes large and frightened, "run home."

I became aware of the sound of my own breathing and was certain I'd give away our hiding place. I tried taking shallow, unperceivable breaths, and searched the darkness. A car drove slowly down the road with its stereo booming. Nearby someone whistled a melodious tune I didn't recognize. The whistling came nearer and I peered into the darkness that had fallen all around us. My eyes caught the movement of a dark silhouette less than fifty feet away.

"Run!" Robin shouted.

My sister and I sprang to our feet from behind the bushes and made a mad dash for home. On our way there, Robin tripped on a sprinkler head, fell, and shot up into a sprint. She raced ahead of me, leading the way toward all those lights shining from the windows of our two-story complex.

We neared the street and didn't even stop to check for traffic. We didn't slow at the curb, but kept up the pace, and ran as fast as possible. It took every ounce of my strength to keep up with her. My tired lungs ached. We reached the black asphalt parking lot directly behind our apartment and ran by the vehicles there, including Mother's red Impala. A white glow illuminated our kitchen window not more than two hundred feet in front of me.

Robin arrived at the courtyard entrance and glanced back at me for a split second before zipping around the corner. In ten seconds, I could do the same. I panted hard and slowed my pace, glanced around for her and, when I could no longer see her, I became suddenly overwhelmed with a terrifying sense of being lost and alone.

A dim light at the top of a pole barely lit the small parking area. Robin was no longer with me, leading me to safety, and I panicked. A dumpster to my left had one end against a high chain link fence. I dashed over to it and crouched in the small space. *He won't find me. He can't find me here.* It wasn't cold, but the muscles in my legs quivered. I covered my nose to muffle the sound of my rapid breathing as I tried to catch my breath.

Voices came from one of the apartments. Dogs barked in the distance. *Maybe I can go home.* I stood, listened for footfalls, and trembled with fear. *Maybe I should stay here. Robin might come back for me.* Another minute passed.

The ominous sound of whistling began again. It came closer and closer. My mind blanked out and my head went light and fuzzy. The whistling came even closer and then it stopped. A silence fell and I shrank back and held my breath. Suddenly, the boy jumped out at me, his knife held high over his head. "There you are, and this time there's no escape."

CHAPTER TWENTY-SIX

*M*y attacker held his drawn knife over his head. He stepped toward me and sneered. I inched back, trying to put some space between us and backed into the chain link fence, the metal hard and cold against my bare calves.

He raised his knife high and glared down at my trembling body. "I'm going to kill you."

I had a spinning sensation, my legs shook violently, and I felt the color drain from my face, and then I began screaming.

"You little—" he began to say.

I screamed again and he dropped his arm, turned on his heels, and left me there. Seconds later, the terror I felt hadn't lifted and I screamed once more. Then from far away, I heard click-click-click. Mother was running toward me and her heels clicked wildly across the pavement. From somewhere nearby, I heard her panicked voice. "Max, that's Pammie. Pammie," she yelled, her voice high and shrill.

The street lamp cast a soft, light on the pavement. I stepped into its soft golden glow, and Mother engulfed me in her arms and I cried into her shoulder. Then Max appeared beside us. The last time I saw him was a year ago when I had just turned nine. He put his warm hand on my back. "Kid, you all right?"

"I was almost killed."

Mother stood me up in front of her, stooped down, and gazed into my eyes. "What do you mean?"

"A creep tried to kill me," I said with chattering teeth.

"Who tried to kill you, kid?" Max said. He looked tenderly down at me, his eyes wet with tears, and he placed his hands on my shoulders. "Who was it?"

"I don't know."

"Kid, what happened?"

I told Max and Mother everything, describing the boy's features, and explaining how he chased my friends, Robin and me. "He wanted to stab me with a knife," I said.

Max called the police station and before long, a sheriff arrived at our apartment and interviewed Robin and me. Later, after he left, Mother carried Steven in her arms and went with Max outside, and stood under the porch lamp. I watched them through the open window, Mother rocking Steven the way parents do to sooth their restless infants, and Max standing beside her, with his hands in his pockets and a boyish grin.

Robin called from the kitchen, "Pam, you want a glass of water?"

"No!" I fell into the sofa, laying my head against the back cushion, and squeezing my eyes shut.

Mother and Max visited outside the open window. "Well, the divorce should be final in a couple weeks," Mother said. "Are you going to marry her?"

Robin came over to the sofa and sat near me. "All that running made me thirsty. You sure you don't want some water?"

"No. Thanks," I said and pointed to our parents standing outside the window. "Mommy and Max are divorcing. I don't want them divorcing."

She raised her chin. "I didn't think they'd get back together."

We listened to their conversation. Max's voice didn't contain a trace of malice. Mother's did. His voice, soft, and gentle was hard to hear, but hers carried just fine into our apartment.

Robin leaned toward me. "I want to know something. You were right behind me all the way, then I got home and you weren't behind me." She swept a long strand of her dark blond hair from her face and tucked it behind her ear. "What happened?"

"I got scared."

"But you were right behind me."

"I couldn't see you any more."

My sister searched my eyes questioningly.

"It was dark," I said.

"You were with me all the way. I made sure of that by looking back several times. You were behind me when I turned the corner."

"I didn't know what to do."

"Come home!" Robin sounded exasperated, "that's what. Pam, you should've come straight home."

"It's not my fault."

"I'm not blaming you. It's just that you scared me so bad I nearly threw up."

"I couldn't see you," I insisted.

"Okay, I got it. You couldn't see me. That's because I came home. When I got here, I left the door open and waited for you. Mommy asked me where you were and I said I didn't know. Then we heard your awful screaming." Her eyes filled with tears and she moved across the sofa to me. "Geez, Pam, don't ever do that to us again, okay?"

"Don't worry, I won't."

"I mean it. Next time, come straight home. Okay?"

I nodded. I didn't plan on there ever being a next time.

Robin threw an arm over my shoulder, and I rested my head against her and tried not to cry.

"I love you, and if anything ever happened to you," she said, "I don't know what I'd do. Well, we're both safe now."

She brightened a little. "Never again. I'll never leave you like that again."

Hearing her say this made me feel safe. I kept my head on her shoulder. "I love you, too," I said. "And, Robin—"

"What?" She said softly.

"I'm sorry."

"For what?"

Tears rolled down my face. "I went the wrong way, didn't I?"

"Why didn't you run straight home to begin with?"

"I don't know."

We sat there with my head on her shoulder, and neither of us said anything. Crickets chirped outside somewhere in the darkness and our parents spoke in low tones. Mother told Max he could come by anytime to see Steve. I heard his brief reply, and then I realized why I ran the wrong direction.

"Robin," I said several minutes later, "I was just thinking about something."

"What?"

"Something."

The neighbors, a couple of weed smoking hippies, stomped on the floor over our heads. Mother said goodnight to Max. A breeze played with the edge of the living room drapes.

"Home isn't safe," I whispered to her.

"And church is?"

Whenever I had attended church services, the peaceful atmosphere had relieved me of worry, fear, feelings of worthlessness, and shame. "It was supposed to be."

CHAPTER TWENTY-SEVEN

"*Y*ou don't have to tell me anything," Dad said to Robin and me, one Sunday evening, shortly before Mother picked us up from his apartment. We had been watching television in the living room and Dad went over to the T.V. and turned it off. "But if you do," he said on his way back to his chair, "I won't tell your mother how I found out." He took a deep breath before continuing. "Is it true that you go to school without breakfast? Your school principal called last week and said he's worried about you. He said your mother's not feeding you enough."

Robin and I attended school without breakfast often enough that being hungry had become a typical condition. On a couple of mornings, the principal got me out of class, welcomed me into his office, and served me a full meal. If I had known he'd tell Dad, I would've refused his offer.

I cradled my hamster Sunshine in my hands against my chest and scrutinized Dad's unrelenting gaze. Telling on Mother sounded like a bad idea and I shook my head. "Dad, I can't. I don't want Mommy getting in trouble."

Dad put one arm around Robin and another around me. He drew us close and sat us on his lap. "Your mother's not in trouble, but she needs help. Neither of you has to tell me anything, but I can't help unless you do."

There were Robin's feelings to consider. She and I made eye contact. In our private moments together, she had echoed my own loyalty. Neither of us wanted Mother's neglectful treatment of us exposed. We communicated without words. There was the slight nod of our heads and a certain look of uncertainty in her eyes. We wouldn't rat on Mother.

"Sometimes you have to do what's right even when you're afraid," Dad continued. "Even if the consequences are painful."

"But we can't tell on Mommy. You'll be mad at her, and she'll get mad at us," I said.

"Your mother's not in trouble, and I didn't say telling me would be easy, but if she's not feeding you, then you're the ones being harmed and that's not right. Little One, going along with a bad situation because you're afraid of the reaction you might get is cowardly. Didn't I promise you that I wouldn't tell her how I found out?"

I didn't want to be a coward and made up my mind, I'd tell Dad one thing, and if he still wanted more information, he'd have to get it someplace else. I could feel the warmth of tears beginning to build up inside my eyes. "Sometimes," I said in a voice above a whisper.

"Sometimes what?" he said.

"What you was talking about."

"Sometimes you don't have breakfast?"

"Uh-huh." All of a sudden, a lump formed in my throat. I closed my eyes for a second, pressed Sunshine against my chest until I could feel the comforting warmth of her tiny body, and fought against an urge to weep.

Dad hugged us gently to himself and a thin smile appeared on his face, revealing his pleasure in my answer. "Is food in the cupboard?" he said with his eyes moving from Robin to me. "Well?"

Robin looked up at his face. "No, Dad."

He winced. "How about in the refrigerator?"

"Not really," she said.

"Is there beer?"

"Uh-huh," I said. Instantly, I questioned myself. What's wrong with me? I wondered. Why did I tell him that?

"Has Steven ever gone without milk?"

Robin and I communicated with each other through our eyes again. We wouldn't disclose this information. Aunt Marylou and Uncle Bud knew Mother had left us alone for over a week, but I didn't want them or Dad discovering the bigger secret of Mother's consistent and frequent absences. I could tell the conversation was headed in that dangerous direction.

"Pammie and Robin." He spoke softly, gently. "I want you to trust me. I know this is hard, but if you can help me with this, maybe I can do something to help Joy," he said, calling Mother by her name.

We sat quietly for a few minutes as Dad waited for a response. I wanted to say lots of things about what the last four years had been like, but I didn't want to betray Mother. Even after the fires and all that had happened, I didn't blame or hate her. I had a love for Mother that went beyond reason, and I felt that telling Dad much more would be a betrayal of that love.

"If Steven's going without food this is very serious," Dad said, breaking the silence. "Has he ever been without milk?"

I was thinking hard, trying to come up with an answer that would appease Dad and end his questioning. Reluctantly, I finally spoke up. "Robin walked all the way to The Green Parrot and got money from Mommy for formula. We've carried Steven on that walk before—to The Parrot." I dropped my eyes from Dad's tender gaze. "To see Mommy. It took us a long time and our feet hurt."

"Twenty minutes?" he said.

"Or a half hour," Robin answered.

"She let him run out?" he said.

A tear trickled down Robin's cheek.

Dad hugged us. "I'm proud of you both."

I stared at my feet in the new tennis shoes I had to leave here when Dad took us home and hoped this conversation had ended. But it hadn't.

"You needed food. Steven needed formula. What else do you need?"

Robin and I sat there on his lap and neither of us spoke.

"It's okay. You don't have to say another word," he said, "if you don't want to."

I knew what we needed and the thought of it made me feel like I would lose all control and begin wailing in agony. "We need Mommy," I whispered.

Dad's eyes filled with tears. He nodded and let out a long sigh. "I know," he said. His words, filled with anguish, seemed to come from a place of intimate, personal knowledge.

A short while later, we heard the familiar honk of Mother's car. Robin and I hugged and kissed Big Pam and Dad. We went to our Mother, waiting for us alongside the apartment building, and climbed into the Impala.

On the way home, Mother swerved through the traffic. I sat up stiffly and gripped the door rest with one hand. Robin gave my other hand a little squeeze and I looked over at her. "We'll be okay," she mouthed without making a sound, alleviating a bit of my fear.

Mother's drunk driving always threw me into a state of quiet dread. Who could say that we wouldn't crash into on-coming traffic or sail off the road and land upside down in a ditch? My heart was in my throat. The Impala weaved slowly into the lane of oncoming traffic, horns blared. Mother corrected her position, moving back into her lane.

When we were almost home, I thought about Dad's conversation with us. *I was only going to tell him one thing and I told him more. Why'd I do that?* I scolded myself and gnawed on the nail of my index finger until it stung and bled. *I shouldn't have told, but I did.*

The question must've lingered in me because the next morning, when the light moved slowly across the courtyard, I sat bolt upright in bed. "That's it," I mumbled.

"What's it?" Robin, lying beside me, said.

"I know why I did it. Why I ratted on Mommy. Dad said he'd help her and wouldn't it be great if she stayed home with us?"

Robin put the pillow over her head and covered her ears. "Why don't we have this conversation in a half hour? Go back to sleep."

"I thought of something else."

"Pam!"

"Dad's eyes get shiny when he's happy with us and his eyes got shiny when we answered his questions, and I want him to be happy with us and proud of me. I like how it feels when he's proud of us. Don't you?"

"Sure. Now, go back to sleep."

The next day when we came home from school, Mother's glaring eyes looked like two balls of blue steel. "So! You told your dad I'm never home." An open beer can was on the coffee table and beside it, a lit cigarette smoldered in a clean ashtray. "Never home!" She threw her hands in the air and walked away from us.

Mother stopped near the dining room table, reeled around, and sneered. "Well, where am I now? I can't believe you told him that!" She slapped one hand on her hip and came at us with her finger held high in the air like any minute she'd use it to send us through the wall. "Told him there's no food." She kept walking toward us, scolding us with her shaking finger, and gritting her teeth. "No food! You said there's nothing to eat. The cupboards are bare. The refrigerator's bare."

My sister and I were just inside the front door. I was mute as I considered how to answer in our defense. Past experience had taught me that anything could happen, and my answer would either improve or worsen the situation. "Mommy," I said, weakly.

Mother pressed her lips together and scowled. "Yes? I suppose this is a confession," she retorted sarcastically and got right in my face. "Go on. What other lies did you tell your dad about me?"

"We didn't," I managed to say.

"That's right," Robin said.

"Liars!"

I was afraid she'd strike me and stepped away from her reach. "We're not lying. We answered some of Dad's questions. That's all."

Mother kept waving her finger at us. "What did you tell him?" She pointed at herself. "That I'm a lousy mother?"

I hadn't seen her so angry since the fight with Max when she punched his nose and I was bewildered. Love doesn't hurt other people. She loved us—that's what I had always thought and I'd always believed that she would never deliberately hurt us. My mind raced. *The house fires were an accident, since she didn't even remember doing them. Or did she? Had she really blacked out?* Now, I questioned her love and I wondered about her capacity to harm us.

Mother stepped closer to me, gesturing wildly with her hands, her face reddening with anger. I felt threatened, unsafe, and at risk of suffering physical harm.

I wanted to defuse her hostility. "You're not a bad mother," I said. "Dad asked us if we have enough food."

"What else?" She went to the sofa and stood there, and I thought she might sit down, but then she came at us. "What else did you tell him?"

"He said he wanted to help." Robin's thin voice trembled.

Mother marched across the living room. The memory of Nana's rage and suicide played in the back of my mind. For a moment it seemed Mother might storm from the apartment and flee in her car. She lowered her voice and spoke flatly. "Your father told me everything."

I felt betrayed. *Dad said he wouldn't do that. He promised.*

"Maybe he'll call the state," she yelled. "They'll rip our family apart and put you in foster homes!" Her voice softened. "Bet you didn't think of that."

She stared at Robin and me standing near the door, her hands on both hips. "What is it you want?" she said. "I know what it is, you love Big Pam more than me."

"We don't love her more than you," I retorted, thinking how ridiculous it was for Mother to suspect such a thing.

Mother ignored me. "Do you want to live with them?" Her voice rose and her eyes narrowed suspiciously. Soon she was yelling again. "Go ahead! Leave! Go ahead! Go live with him and your *stepmom*! Is that what you want? Leave! Get your stuff together and leave!" She marched across the room and grabbed the phone hanging on the wall near the dining table. "I'll dial the number for you. I'll call your dad and tell him to come and get you."

"Mommy," Robin said tearfully. "We're not lying. Daddy asked us a few questions. We didn't say awful things about you. Really, we didn't." There was a plea for calm in my sister's voice. "It didn't happen like you think," she finally said.

It began in my belly, a tense, anxious vibration. It turned into a tremble and moved up my torso to my arms and down my legs. Soon my entire body shook. My mother was about to tell my dad to take us from her. Staying together as a family meant more to me than anything, even more than having three meals a day, or one meal a week. I stepped away from the front door and took a few steps toward her. "Mommy, no. Don't call Dad." My head felt faint. "Please, don't make us leave. Don't make us go. We love you and Steven."

Steven slept through the entire scene. Moments after Mother's final words, she stormed out of the house. I heard the heels of her pumps click on the walkway, and the rumbling of the Impala's engine, and then she drove away.

Tears splashed on my shirt. "Robin, what if Mommy does what Nana did?"

"She wouldn't do that. At least, I don't think she would."

"What if she does?"

"She won't."

"But she's drunk and really mad. Nana was like that."

"Mommy will probably just go to one of the bars."

CHAPTER TWENTY-EIGHT

*A*ll night I listened for Mother's steps on the walkway, her key in the door, her bedroom door shutting, and when those familiar sounds didn't come, I wept. The screaming scene from the previous afternoon reminded me of Nana's rage-filled departure. None of it made any sense and I wrestled with the questions. *Why'd Dad tell on us? Why'd Mommy behave like that? What did Robin and I do wrong? What if she doesn't come home? What if she comes home and does something horrible? Maybe she'll light another fire.* Then, sometime in the predawn darkness, she returned to our apartment.

Weeks later, near the end of March, there was a knock on the door. Mother wasn't home and Robin, who was sitting on the sofa holding fourteen-month-old Steven in her lap, said, "Pam see who it is."

I was playing with Ken and Barbie dolls, gifts from a neighbor girl who had outgrown them. I got up and peeked through an opening in the drapes. Immediately, I recognized our visitor. "Looks like Aunt Cindy," I said.

Robin stood with Steven on her hip. "Really?"

I nodded and kept looking through the crack in the drapes. "Tall, brown hair, tons of dark blue eye shadow. Gee, it has to be her."

We last saw Aunt Cindy when Robin was seven and I was five. She had changed a lot in four years. Her straight brown hair went below her shoulders. In addition to the heavy layer of eye shadow, she wore shiny lip gloss, bell-bottom jeans and a long sleeved, buttoned, polyester shirt. She had gained weight and her hips were extra wide.

Robin, Steven, and I greeted her in our gosh-awful clothes, uncombed hair, and bare feet.

"Hey, can I come in?" she said.

For several minutes, it was like show and tell. We all sat on the sofa. Robin held Steven in her lap and showed Aunt Cindy the cool stuff he could do. "He's started saying all kinds of words," she said. "And if he holds onto my fingers, he can take a few steps."

"Watch this," I said, tickling Steven under his arm. He turned away as if embarrassed and grinned. "He's supposed to laugh. He always does."

"Where's Joy?" Aunt Cindy said.

"Getting us a daddy," I replied matter-of-factly.

She sat up straight and blinked a few times. "Oh, I see." Her voice didn't carry a trace of condescension and there wasn't a hint of judgment in her tone. "That sounds *just* like Joy." She stroked Steven's blond curls while watching his contented expression. "So, how've you guys been?"

Funny, the depth of meaning in five little words. She might as well have said, "I've heard what Joy did and that she's drinking too much and she's practically abandoned you and I'm worried about you. Tell me why I shouldn't be concerned?"

Robin and I didn't hesitate. "We're fine," we responded, as though two children alone with a toddler was normal and expected. Truth is, Mother wasn't home much, ever. We lost her to booze and a boyfriend, but if we wanted to stay together as a family, we couldn't tell the truth to Aunt Cindy or anyone.

After Aunt Cindy left, she moved into an apartment across from ours. She and Mother rekindled their relationship and we saw her sporadically when we'd go to her apartment for a quick chat, or when she'd stop by just to say 'hi.' She worked and dated, and wasn't around enough to know about the severity of our situation. It seemed like no one really knew and we wanted to keep it that way.

On my way home from school in early spring when the weather had begun turning warm, one of the boys in the grade above mine, yelled at me. "Hey, you!"

I didn't respond.

"Freak!" he said, laughing. "Super sci-freak!" The boys around him shoved one another. They hooted, whispered into one another's ears, and then laughed, loud and hard.

All their loud-mouthed behavior was meant to upset me. I wouldn't give them the satisfaction of knowing that their bullying stung and I concealed my emotions. They wanted a rebuttal, a tear rolling down my cheek, an expression of shock, anger, or pain. Well, I didn't want them getting pleasure from my pain. My unexpressive features, eyes that looked down at the sidewalk, lips nearly straight, and cheeks relaxed, gave the impression that their words weren't received or understood.

"It's not fair," I told Robin when I got home. "Why was I born so awfully ugly?"

"Who told you that?"

"The kids at school tell me I am. They say it all the time. I hear them whispering and sometimes they call me names. Today a boy called me a freak."

Robin's words helped build a deflector around my heart that protected me from the full impact of mean words. "Pam, ignore them. You *are so* beautiful," she said. "Don't let their words hurt you. And if I ever catch those big meanies bothering you, they'll be sorry."

Spring break arrived again and, including weekends, Robin and I were off from school for nine whole days. The first Sunday of our freedom, we went with Dad to his brother and sister-in-law's for dinner. Aunt Carolyn, Aunt Gay, Aunt Kathleen, and Aunt Merle hid several dozen painted Easter eggs outside in the front and back yards.

Three of Dad's siblings had kids and there were seven of us cousins, including Robin and me. When we had collected the brightly colored eggs, we sat at an extra long table and feasted on ham, turkey, mashed potatoes and gravy, yams, green beans, strawberry Jell-O with miniature marshmallows, buttered rolls, and chocolate cake.

Later that night, the sun had completely set when Mother pulled into the parking lot of Dad's apartment and honked twice on her horn. Robin and I said goodbye to Big Pam and Dad, then headed outside to the Impala where Mother and Steven waited for us. A spring storm, moving into the area, covered the sky with charcoal grey clouds. It sprinkled lightly. Robin climbed in the front beside Mother, and I sat in the back beside Steven strapped in a car seat. When he saw me, he smiled.

"I'm happy, to see you, too," I said. "Isn't it great to be together again?"

Steven grinned and reached for me. "Out?"

"We have to wait until we're home."

Robin turned around and looked at me with large eyes. She raised her brows and roller her eyes toward our mother, warning me to be careful, and even if Mother asks me a question, to say very little.

"Girls," Mother slurred, "did you have a nice time?" We said it was good. Not great, lest she get her feelings hurt. Just good. We had learned to never speak about the fun we had with Big Pam and Dad. Doing so could result in a disapproving scowl from her or a self-pity tirade about how we loved Big Pam more.

Mother eased the Impala, at an incredibly slow speed, from the parking lot into four lanes of traffic. I watched horrified through the window as automobiles swerved around us. It seemed Mother's car was on a movable surface. Like a vehicle on ice, it slid slowly from the center of the lane onto the right side, crossed the bike lane, and practically fell into a ditch before moving to the left and barely missing a passing motorist. I gripped the edge of my seat. The roadway, wet from the light rain, glistened. Horns blared and the Impala floated in and out of the lane. Automobiles with windshield wipers keeping up with the light rain whizzed around us.

The Impala slowed even more. Then, it stopped. Mother parked in the bike lane and turned off the ignition. A steady stream of traffic approached, their lights reflecting off the wet, black pavement. The traffic curved around our vehicle. I sat on my knees and gazed over the headrest out the front window. Porch lights from residences along the four lanes cast a pale glow on the street. There was the sound of the rain splatting against the pavement, the swoosh of tires on the wet roadway, but complete silence in our car.

I had no idea why we had stopped and wondered if the car had just quit. Within seconds, lights flashed all around us, inside the Impala and outside on the roadway, in front of our car, and alongside of us. A highway patrol officer stepped to the driver's side. He looked through the window at Mother with the beam of a flashlight. She stiffened and opened her door.

"Stay in the vehicle," the officer ordered. "Roll down your window."

After Mother rolled down the window, the officer beamed his flashlight in the front and back seats. "Ma'am, are you aware that you were drifting and going fifteen miles under the forty mile speed limit?"

She gripped the steering wheel with both hands. "No," she said. "I'm a little tired, officer." She had trouble speaking and sounded like she had just returned from the dentist with her lips full of numbing medicine.

"Have you been drinking, ma'am?"

"I had two beers."

I felt like I did when Mr. Reese, the congenial owner of the local drugstore, caught me eating candy I hadn't paid for. He called it stealing. Humiliated, I cast my eyes to the floor, confessed the offense, and left his store. From then on, every time I saw Mr. Reese my face felt flush.

Had she been drinking? Yes. I answered in my mind. And I realized our dire situation. *We're in trouble. Then what? What'll happen to her? And to Robin? And to Steve and me?*

A second policeman came over to the driver's side of the Impala and waited.

"Ma'am, I need to see your driver's license and registration," the first officer said.

Mother fumbled around awkwardly in her purse and tried giving him her entire wallet.

"Take your license out, please."

She gave it to him.

"And I still need your registration."

There weren't many papers in the glove compartment, but Mother appeared to have trouble finding the requested document.

"Can I help you?" the first officer asked. He came around to the passenger side, opened the door, and pulled out the document at the top of the small stack. "Here's what we need," he said, passing it and her driver's license to the second officer, standing behind him.

I turned around and watched the second officer through the back window streaked with rain. He took Mother's documents to a squad car with bright, rotating lights.

Meanwhile, the first policeman returned to Mother's open window. "Ma'am, I need you to get out of the vehicle."

Mother opened the door. She stepped out of the car and onto the road in her pumps.

We had already been in a few minor car accidents when Mother, intoxicated from having drunk too much beer, had slowly banged into stopped cars on the road ahead of us. The highway patrol officers who had responded to the scene had only ticketed her. This was different. *They know she's drunk.* "Robin," I whispered, "what's going to happen?"

"Pam, I don't know," she whispered back to me. "This is just awful. I'm really scared."

Steven didn't make a sound. He didn't even move. As I waited nervously to learn what would happen next, through the opened window, I heard the first officer giving Mother directions.

He spoke to her gently, as if speaking to a child. "I want you to walk on this line. Here let me show you, like this...good. I want you to close your eyes and touch your nose like this. Good. Good."

I thought the tone of his voice and word choices, telling her that she had done something "good" meant that she could get back into the car and drive us home. But that wasn't the case.

"Step over to the car and Officer Higgins will read you your rights."

The first officer opened the Impala's door and slid in behind the steering wheel. He looked at Robin sitting on the front seat and greeted her. Then he looked back at Steven and me. "I'm taking you home," he said. "Your mother needs to spend a night at the station. Where do you kids live?"

A rush of relief hit me. We were really going home.

"On Mission," Robin answered.

In a tool belt around his waist, there was a long flashlight, a gun, and a radio. Voices and static came over the radio. He turned down the volume and pulled away from the curb. "Here we go. I'll have you there in a jiffy." At The Barkley Square, he parked under the soft glow of the street lamp. Another squad car pulled up across from us at the curb. I stared at it, trying to make out Mother through the window, but it was too dark, and the back passenger window was splattered with rain, so I couldn't see her.

"Will you guys be all right by yourselves?" he said.

"Sure we will," Robin said.

He escorted us to our apartment door and looked down at us, Steven in Robin's arms and me standing beside her. He grinned. "Do you need anything? You sure you can manage on your own?"

"We got it covered. Thank you," Robin said. She opened the door, turned on the porch light, and the three of us entered our apartment. We knew exactly what to do. Lock the door. Warm Steven's jar of baby food. Change his diaper, and in another hour, put him to bed. This was our life—it was all a very familiar routine.

CHAPTER TWENTY-NINE

*T*wenty-four hours later, Mother returned to the apartment. The first order of business was to schedule an appointment with her hairdresser. The next day, she went out for a couple of hours and came home with her hair frosted and styled.

When Poppy stopped by our apartment, Mother boasted about her drunk driving incident. "I couldn't out run him this time, Daddy." This was back in the 70's, before strict driving laws were passed, when motorists could collect traffic tickets like trophies without losing their licenses. "That makes nine," she giggled, "or maybe, there are ten. Geez, I've forgotten how many tickets I have." She smirked and tilted her nose toward the ceiling. "Your daughter's just like her ol' dad."

"It's the lead foot. You got me lead foot," Poppy said in his Irish brogue. He raised his beer glass to her. "I outran a copper, I did." He chuckled and took a sip. "The other day I out smarted him, that I did. The ol' boy didn't know where yer ol' dad went. I did the one, two disappear trick."

Dad and Mother had agreed to let me bring Sunshine home and I was playing with her on the floor while listening to the grownup conversation. I hurried Sunshine to her plastic rodent house and shoved her inside. Then I ran over to my grandfather. "Oh boy! That's neat," I said exuberantly and plopped down on the floor nearby him. "Poppy, you can drive faster than the cops?"

He chuckled in a deep gravelly voice. "Yep. Yep. That I did."

"You really outran a cop?"

He smiled proudly and patted his chest.

"How'd you do it?"

"Disappeared, I did."

It dawned on me: my granddad had achieved greatness. I stared at him in amazement. Then, thinking he could've gotten in a lot of trouble for speeding away from the cops, my jaw dropped. "Gosh, Poppy."

He rubbed his thumb stump against his greying head. "Now, now." His pink cheeks reddened. "Weren't the first time. Won't be the last. No copper can catch me, by golly."

Mother knocked lightly on the coffee table. "Daddy, knock on wood," she said.

Not many days later, Mother came to Mission school and excused Robin and me from class early. The dental appointment hoax had always worked, and it achieved the desired results this time, too. I climbed into the Impala beside Robin, smiled at Steven strapped in his car seat and hooted. "Score! Mommy, where're we going?"

"Gwen invited me out for pizza and a beer. We'll drop by her place for a visit and then we'll all head over to The Parrot."

At Gwen's house, she and Mother visited at a round kitchen table. Robin, Steven, and I, fifteen feet away in the family room, sat on the floor, stacking checkers into towers for Steven to push over. He giggled when they swayed and laughed when they toppled.

"Every job application I've submitted has been rejected." Mother was frustrated. "My darned criminal record clouds their eyes. If they would only let me try. It's not like I'll ever again do what I did." She pressed her hand against her forehead. "Gwen, I still don't remember any of it. Honest to goodness, I don't."

Gwen reached across the table and patted Mother's hand. "Honey, I know."

"It's hard for me to believe I did what they said. When I was in prison—" She stopped in mid-sentence. A second later, she began again. "I hope to never go back there." She shuddered. "At first they put me in a jail cell with women who used words a lady should never say. They were mostly in for prostitution. A couple days later, two very nice policemen transported me to a women's institution. The accommodations were sure a heck of a lot better." She chuckled and took a swig of beer. "For the first time in a week, I slept between crisp sheets."

"Joy, I didn't know you were in the city jail for two days."

"A week."

"A week? Ted and I could've made a visit."

Mother leaned toward Gwen and lowered her voice. "I met with a psychiatrist at the prison who diagnosed my problem. He told me I had a complete nervous breakdown, said I had bottled up deep grief. It was a mental illness. I needed psychiatric help, not imprisonment. During our sessions, I got everything out in the open with him and, knock on wood, I'm fine now."

Since Mother never spoke of her past, an involuntary gasp came out of my mouth. She wasn't a criminal. Not that I had ever thought of her as one, but it was good hearing her say she didn't start the fires on purpose. Dad gave a similar explanation, but hearing it from Mother drove the point home.

"Honey," Gwen said, "did it have to do with your mom?"

"You got that right." Mother frowned. "Did I already tell you about my childhood rheumatic fever?"

Gwen nodded and sipped from her can of beer.

"When I was bedridden, she mistreated me." she waved her hand as if it had been so long ago as to be insignificant. "That was ages ago, but I was angry at her for it, even after her death. When she died, I didn't grieve because I wouldn't let myself."

Gwen, her mouth turned down, her eyes full of tears, shook her head gently. "I'm so sorry, honey."

"That's not all. My first marriage failed, then I married someone who battered me, but I never spoke of it. Abused wives do that. They keep it to themselves, you know. It's typical."

Robin looked up from Steven and the checkers. She rolled her eyes in disbelief at Mother's last remarks about being an abused wife. Without making a sound, she cocked an eyebrow at me and mouthed the words, "Yeah, right."

When Gwen and Mother finished their one can of beer, we went to The Green Parrot for lunch and more beer. I stood in the small space between Mother and Gwen and picked at a piece of dehydrated gum, stuck to the underside of the bar. I pried it off with my nail and popped it in my mouth.

Music came from the jukebox at the back of the room. Mother smiled down at me. "Pammie, where'd you get the gum?"

I pointed at the bar. "I do it all the time."

She laughed. "Geez, Pammie, your stomach's tougher than mine. Don't chew gum from under there."

"Why not?"

"It's not ladylike and besides, darling, it's very unsanitary." She giggled and shook her head. "I swear you must have an immune system made of steel."

Mother was giving me something that I yearned for and I wanted to talk with her some more. Interacting with her was the one activity I craved more than any other and I hoped she'd let me remain beside her. She looked at my beaming face. "Someday, when you're old enough, you can sit up here and have a beer. I promise. Cross my heart. Go over to the picnic table with Robin and Steven. Our pizza will be ready in a second."

I had no intention of spending any more time than necessary at The Parrot and I hated the smell of beer. A whiff of it reminded me of everything I had lost. Nana had been drunk when she locked me in the closet and also when she killed herself. Mother had been drunk more times than I could count. Beer odors repulsed me and, if I could, I'd dump all the cans of beer Mother kept at home down the drain.

"Mommy just told me I get to sit at the bar and drink beer someday," I told Robin with exaggerated sarcasm to lift the disappointment from my heart. "Drinking beer," I said, licking my lips and rubbing my belly, "yummy. That's what I dream of."

"*You* dream of it?" Robin's eyes glittered with amusement. "Me, too. I can't wait. Can you?"

"No," I said. "Just think, instead of getting jobs, like regular people do, we can sit in here all the time and drink until we walk funny and talk weird. Like them."

We both checked out the adults seated around the bar. "They need to grow up," Robin said, laughing. "No wait, then they wouldn't be having so much fun." She laughed even harder and Steven, seated between us, giggled. "We're all having such a blast." She laughed still harder.

Our words were the opposite of how we really felt. Robin held her belly, laughing hard, tears forming in her eyes. "Robin, really," I said giggling, "just think—someday when we grow up, we *get* to spend all our time here." I laughed out the words.

"We've hardly ever been here and it's so wonderful." I practically fell over laughing.

The electric company shut off the power. The telephone went next, then the gas. Mother received two checks every month, one for public assistance and a second from Dad. She didn't manage this money very well, and typically ran out of cash a week before the next check arrived. Then one morning, the apartment manager served her with an eviction notice.

Mother had a history of writing bad checks and then scrounging up the money from relatives to pay them just before she was charged with fraud. While she had many strikes against her, somehow she acquired the references needed to qualify for an apartment at The Continental Gardens, just ten minutes away from The Barkley Square.

And then, a few days before we moved, one morning I got up and looked inside Sunshine's cage. Her stiff body lay beneath her exercise wheel. I wept as I carried her from our apartment to a nearby patch of earth, my tears splashing on the dirt as I buried her.

The day after we unpacked, Mother came into the bedroom Robin and I shared. "Rise and shine, sleepyheads," she said. I heard her, but I wanted a few more minutes of sleep and lay motionless. She came over and shook my arm. "Wake up. It's almost time for school."

I moaned. "Do we have to?"

"You don't want to miss your first day at the new school."

"Yes, I do."

Robin dropped her feet over the side of the bed and headed for the bathroom.

I sat up and stretched. "I hate being the new girl."

"You'll do fine." Mother went to the window across from our bed and opened the drapes. "Look. It's sunny. At recess, you can play out in the sun. You always enjoy playing outside."

"Not by myself."

She stood at the end of my bed with both hands on her hips. "Pammie, making friends isn't that hard. Win them over with your smile and don't be afraid to introduce yourself."

"Please don't make me go."

"Come on, lazy bones. Get up." She looked back at me from the hall outside my door. "Get dressed and come out for breakfast."

After breakfast, Mother marched confidently into the front office at the school with Steven balanced on her hip, and Robin and me in tow. A lady behind the front desk was busy at the typewriter and didn't notice us. Mother cleared her voice. "Excuse me, I need to enroll Robin in sixth grade and Pammie in the fourth."

The woman came over, leaned against the long counter, and sized us up. "Do you have their records?"

"No, but they can be placed without them. The school they were last enrolled at was the best one in Carmichael. My girls passed with bells and whistles." She smiled.

The principal, in an inner-office with the door open, overheard Mother. He sauntered over to where we stood and ogled us. His eyes moved from my sister, who had washed and brushed her hair, to me. Mine was unwashed and tangled into dense knots. The last bath I had was at Dad's, over a week ago. I thought the dirt on my forearms looked like I had been tanning and hoped the kids would think I had been to Hawaii. Robin and I wore ill-fitting, threadbare hand-me-downs. As the principal looked us over, I wondered what went on between his squinting eyes.

Next, he scrutinized Mother, holding Steven in her arms. Mother's makeup and nails were done just right. Her hair, professionally styled, shone under the glaring office lights. She wore a knee length skirt, matching blouse, and two-inch pumps.

The principal called for an office girl. "We can get their records later. Show our new students to their classes."

Entering a new class more than halfway into the academic year felt a little like squishing into a closet with a crowd of strangers. Several months before moving from The Barkley Square Apartments, Robin and I squeezed into a telephone booth with eleven other people. A college student had asked us to help him get his name entered in The Guinness Book of World Records. Telephone booths weren't intended for more than one person at a time. There was pain and tremendous social discomfort as Robin and I squeezed into the group of world record makers.

Going into a room full of kids I didn't know felt a little like that. My new teacher, poised at the opened door of his classroom, extended his hand to me. "I'm Mr. Donnelly Onnelly."

I gave his hand a little shake and studied him thoughtfully. I'd never known someone with a rhyming name. My new teacher was the tallest one I'd ever had, and I'd already had six. He was the seventh.

Mr. Donnelly Onnelly had on tan corduroy jeans and a matching vest over a long sleeved, shimmery shirt with multi geometric shapes in browns, yellows, and oranges. I checked out his brown suede shoes before meeting his smile with my grin.

"Come on in and let me show you where you'll sit," he said, directing me to a class, unlike any I'd seen, and I'd seen plenty. It had tables arranged in two semi-circles around the teacher's long desk, and two overfilled, furry, beanbag chairs at the back of the room.

I walked with Mr. Donnelly Onnelly to a vacant spot at a table, but the kids didn't look at me. They were rowdy, everyone speaking at once. Their lack of attention relieved me of some of my new student anxiety. I sat at a table with a girl, and looked at the walls with posters of running cheetahs, blue striped zebras, Einstein with his Law of Relativity dancing above his head, and colorful hot air balloons.

In Mr. Donnelly Onnelly's class, we competed in spelling bees, played games, solved math problems with dried beans, painted on huge sheets of paper, and made mosaics from recycled items. Once a week, Mr. Donnelly taught us Vietnam protest songs. He strummed the tunes on his guitar and we all sang the sad lyrics of soldiers dying and their girlfriends crying. And every day, we worked on different forms of writing.

A few weeks after I'd started at the new school, Mr. Donnelly leaned over my shoulder and observed me writing a poem. "Can I see that?"

I handed it to him and he silently read my poem, all the while nodding and rereading it, and nodding again. "This is cool." He looked at me with raised eyebrows. "Did you write this yourself?"

How could he ask me that? I wondered. He just saw me writing it. I nodded.

He cleared his voice and read softly. "On a spring day, I lay in the hay and pray away. Awake I take my soul to Thee."

Heat rose up my neck and spread to my face. I didn't know why, but his reaction and the reading of my poem had embarrassed me.

"This is an excellent example of what I've been talking about this morning. Write a poem about something you've experienced." He returned the poem to me. "Great job, Pam," he said. "I really like this. Keep writing."

Robin and I visited Dad and Big Pam for our scheduled weekend together, Dad told us he had something important to say. He and Big Pam were holding hands. "We're getting married," he announced with a broad smile across his face. His eyes sparkled like they did whenever he was especially happy. Robin and I began cheering and hugging them.

"Stop for a minute." Dad chuckled. "That's not all. There's something else. This June, we're going to have a baby."

I was very excited about having a new baby brother or sister. After Dad gave us the good news, it seemed to me that the weeks began passing slower than ever. Time was playing a cruel trick, making the wait almost painful.

On the final day of the academic year, during the second week of June, Big Pam was still pregnant, and I left the school campus with my excitement about the baby's soon arrival eclipsed by sadness.

Mr. Donnelly Onnelly was my favorite teacher. He cared about me, not just how I performed academically, but he was concerned about me as a person, as a child. His caring is what caused me to become attached to him, and saying goodbye hurt. I thought Mother would move us again or something dire would happen, and I'd never see him again.

CHAPTER THIRTY

$\mathcal{A}$t the beginning of the third week of June, Big Pam had a baby boy who they named Keith, after Dad. When the baby came home from the hospital, Robin and I stayed with them for two weeks. Baby Keith was beautiful, I thought, and reminded me of Steven—an adorable infant with downy soft hair who looked like an angel when he slept.

The three oldest aunts came to Dad's apartment to meet the new baby. They took turns holding him, babbled about his cuteness, and stared at him with stupid smiles on their faces.

Robin and I were invisible, standing near the television. The aunts and Big Pam acted like the baby was the most outstanding thing that had ever happened to our family. Sure, it was wonderful to have a new brother, but none of the aunts admired my eyes, the softness of my hair, or my attention span. I could focus on them for long periods of time without crying, too.

Then there was Dad. He was nuts about the baby and walked around with a dazed look on his grinning face. Forget that he hadn't slept in weeks. Dad told the aunts that he'd always wanted a son. Dad never said anything like that about Robin and me, and I thought he loved the baby most.

"Dad," I said, after the aunts left. "There's pheasants in the field back there." I pointed toward the back of the complex. "I saw them. They were real pretty." I recalled hearing

someone say dads and their sons hunt together. "Why don't
we go catch one and have it for dinner?"

"You can't catch one of those birds," he said.

"Can so."

"What makes you think one of those birds will let you
catch it?"

"What if I do?"

"Then, we'll have pheasant dinner."

He'll see what I can do and then he'll want me as much as
he wants the baby, I thought, grabbing a large shopping bag,
and running from the apartment.

The grassy field behind Dad's complex had anthills, wild
radishes, and small game animals. I ran there with my bag,
spotted a ring necked pheasant, crept up to it, swooped down
on it, and stuffed it in my sack.

The bird in the bag was heavy and I walked home with it
pressed against my chest. "Where's Dad?" I asked Big Pam
when I entered the apartment with my catch.

"At work. He left twenty minutes ago. Where you been?"

"Getting something for Dad."

She stood in front of me and eyed the bulging moving bag
in my arms suspiciously. Her eyes grew large. "Young'un, what
is that? Whatcha got in that bag?"

"A pheasant. Here, you can peek at it, but that's all. This
is for Dad. He said if I caught a pheasant, we'd have it for dinner."

I opened a corner and she peered inside it. "Well, this beats
all. Sure is a pretty thing. Your dad won't believe it when I tell
him." She grabbed the phone and dialed his work number.
"Keith, what am I supposed to do with a pheasant?" She paused
for a second. "What am I talking about? Your youngest daughter
brought a live one home for you." She put a hand on the side of

her face and a minute later, laughed. "You should know better than tell this young'un she can't do something. Okay, I'll tell her."

"Your dad said he didn't think you'd really catch one," Big Pam hung up the phone and she hugged me warmly. "I don't want your feelings hurt, but he wants you to take it back and let it go."

The idea of ending the life of any creature disturbed me. I'd have done it to win a place alongside Keith as a child Dad had always wanted, but I was relieved he didn't want my pheasant killed, plucked, and cooked. "I guess I'll be all right," I said, pretending to be sad. "Yeah, sure. I'll let it go, if that's what he wants. Sure was hard to catch."

Big Pam hugged me again. "I'm sorry. I wish he could've seen it." She opened the door for me. "Hurry along and don't dawdle. It'll be dark soon."

For the rest of my stay with them, every time someone came by the house to see the new baby, Dad and Big Pam told my hunting story, and I beamed.

On the final morning of our two-week stay, Dad came into the kitchen where Robin and I were washing and drying breakfast dishes. "Has Child Protective Services been by to see you?" he said.

"No," Robin said. "At least I don't think so." She wiped a plate with a cloth towel before putting it on a stack of dishes in an upper cabinet.

"Who's that?" I said.

"Those people from the state Mommy told us about," Robin replied and dropped the towel on the drain board. Her dramatic eyes grew wide. "Pam, you know, she said they put kids in foster homes."

I stopped washing the dishes and faced Dad. "Are they coming to take us from Mommy?"

"Come in the living room for a minute and we'll talk about it," he said.

Everyone knew not to sit in Dad's chair, across from the console television. From there, he had a direct, unobstructed, view of the T.V. screen, and a nearly effortless reach to the can of salted, mixed nuts on an end table beside it. Robin and I took our seats on the sofa with Big Pam. Dad sat in his chair.

"You haven't had a visit from anyone you don't know?" he said.

"I don't think so," Robin said. "But someone could have come by while we weren't home."

As I thought about Child Protective Services taking us from Mother, tears wet the corners of my eyes. "I don't want them taking us from Mommy."

"It's going to be okay," he said. "They might pay your mother a visit. If they do, I want you to call me."

Robin and I blinked back tears and breathed in shallow swallows, as though someone were sitting on our chests. Dad stroked his mustache thoughtfully. He turned to Big Pam. "I don't understand what keeps happening. Joy must have friends at CPS."

Big Pam pointed with a smoldering cigarette between her fingers at Robin and me. "Maybe they know."

He expected us to answer. "Well?"

"CPS?" Robin asked.

"Child Protective Services, the state social services department."

She shrugged her shoulders. Her lips trembled and tears ran down her cheeks. "Who knows? Mommy has lots of friends."

"Come here," Dad said, inviting us to sit on his lap. Robin and I were small and fit on either side of him. He wrapped his arms around us and I buried my face in his shoulder. "Everything will be all right. Don't worry." When we had composed ourselves, he stood us in front of him, a hand on each of our arms. "Can you help me with this? I want you to call when they come by or if your mother leaves you again. Okay?"

I nodded, not in full agreement but to show that I would obey, and then I looked at Robin for reassurance.

Dad gave my arm a gentle squeeze. "Now, don't worry. Worrying won't do you a bit of good."

When Mother came to pick us up from Dad's, I wanted her warned about CPS, but I'd have to divulge my information source, and then she'd get angry with Dad, and when he learned I'd told her, he'd be mad at me. I hoped we wouldn't have a visitor from the state and waited all week for the knock at the door. After there wasn't one, I obeyed Dad's instructions and tried putting it out of my mind.

Our summer vacation was like a super long weekend for Mother. Robin and I were out of school for three months and she could come and go as she pleased. Sometimes, when Mother returned home, after an extended absence, Robin and I'd leave and practically go anywhere we wanted. As long as we stayed together, Mother didn't worry about us. We'd wander the complex seeking out kids our ages, swim in the pool, or ask Mother for bus fare and ride it all over the city, stopping at the shopping mall on Sunrise Boulevard, the movie theater, the skating rink, and taking it downtown where we explored Sacramento's old buildings and quaint shops along K Street.

Sometimes, Robin and I walked to a nearby church and attended the Sunday morning service. Once the pastor gave me a white paperback Bible. I ran home with it and stuck my finger between the opaque pages. My eyes fell to a passage in Matthew.

> *He said to them, "Because of your little faith. For truly, I say to you, if you have faith like a grain of mustard seed, you will say to this mountain, Move from here to there, and it will move; and nothing will be impossible to you."*

I read this scripture several times and thought about it. *What's the mountain? It can't be a real mountain. No one can move something big like that.* I read the scripture one more time and noticed the word "impossible." *Mountains are impossible to move. I wonder if I can get the right kind of faith, the kind that makes mountains move.*

In August, one day when Mother wasn't home, just after one o'clock, I put Steven in his crib for a nap. Robin turned on the radio and as we danced in each other's arms the apartment began swaying. We stopped dancing and stared wild-eyed at each other for a split second before making a quick survey of the room. "The curtains!" I gasped and pointed at the waving drapes. "Gosh, the floor's moving." A thud came from the kitchen.

"Pam, come on!" Robin said, grabbing my hand. She threw open the door and pulled me out of our moving apartment and down the rolling flight of stairs. At the bottom, we planted our bare feet on the heaving earth and then it stopped, suddenly and completely. That's when it dawned on us we had left Steven alone in Mother's bedroom.

We ran up the flight of stairs, into our apartment, and peered through the crib rail at our brother still sleeping, peacefully. "We'll never leave you like that again," Robin whispered. "Sorry."

The phone rang just then. I grabbed it. "Hello."

"Pammie, did you feel the earthquake?" Mother said. In the background, I heard the distant rumble of a small crowd talking and music blaring from a jukebox.

"Yeah. Wasn't that neat?" I said.

She laughed. "Neat isn't something I thought of, but did you think so?"

"The floor kind of did this shake or roll thing. It's hard to say. But it was weird, really weird."

I heard someone in the barroom shout. Then that same male voice enthusiastic and jovial said, "Joy, we need your brilliant intelligence over here. Come help us with this puzzle."

"Are Steve and Robin all right?" Mother said.

"Sure they are. Steven's sleeping and Robin's right here. Wanna talk to her?"

"Not now, darling. Someone needs to use the phone. I better go. Love you."

"Mommy, wait. Can you come home? Please. There's no milk and I don't know what we'll have for dinner."

"Pammie, another customer needs the phone. I'll call later."

"You are coming home?"

Dial tone.

CHAPTER THIRTY-ONE

*T*wo days later, Robin called Mother at the number she left with us. "Mommy, Steven's almost out of diapers and there isn't anything for Pam and me to eat." Confusion appeared in her eyes and she shook her head. "But we're out of everything! There isn't any bread. No milk either. We're out of eggs. Cereal? We ran out of that three days ago."

I held Steven on my hip and waited eagerly for the ending of Mother and Robin's conversation. She put a hand over the mouthpiece and whispered to me, "She's really drunk." Her face reddened and she rolled her eyes. "I'm not exaggerating. There are two diapers in your room, that's all. And I am being honest. I wouldn't lie. There isn't anything to eat. Mommy, *please* come home."

Robin hung up the phone. "Pam, what are we going to do?"

We couldn't walk from the Continental Gardens to The Green Parrot to get money from Mother and buy diapers or food like we had done when we lived on Mission Avenue. It was too far.

My stomach ached with hunger. "I don't know."

"Should we call Dad?"

"I don't know," I said, impatiently. "I don't want the cops taking us away."

"CPS, Pam, and I don't either."

What Mother said about the state taking kids from their parents reminded me of what I'd heard about Hitler. As I'd later learn, Mother hadn't told the truth about the state agency that intervenes in child abuse and neglect cases. She never said that children living as we did are sometimes removed from their parents' custody until a safe living environment can be provided. In my mind, CPS and the Gestapo were the same.

My ideas about the Gestapo came from Mother. She told Robin and me about the Holocaust, said her grandmother was Jewish and what the Jews endured was horrific. We didn't know if our family wore yellow stars, or if the Nazis tore them from their homes, or stuffed them in cattle cars, or massacred them, but other Jewish families had experienced these horrors.

I hugged Steven and put him on the floor. If we didn't call Dad, I figured we'd go hungry, but it wouldn't kill us. The week prior, Robin and I had picked plums and apricots from neighborhood trees. We filled bags with them, and ate the fruit for breakfast, lunch, and dinner. Another time, I panhandled, stood outside the grocery store, asking for a dollar.

Robin picked up our eighteen-month-old brother from the floor. She bounced him on her knee. "This is the way the pony goes, trot, trot, trot."

Steven grinned.

"Gallop, trot, gallop, trot," she said, bouncing him.

He giggled some more, and Robin and I joined him, giggling and laughing.

I went to Mother's room, stood in the doorway, and stared at the phone beside her nightstand. *Dad told us to call when Mommy's gone. I said I would. A nod is the same as a yes. Robin didn't nod, but I did. I'm supposed to call. Maybe I will and if he asks about Mommy, then what?* My heart raced in my chest, and my mouth felt dry as paper.

I dialed Dad's number.

"This is Keith."

When I heard Dad's voice I almost hung up.

"Hello," he said.

My head began to spin. "Dad?"

"Hi, honey. Is your mother home?"

"No."

"All right, I'll make the call to child protective services. Little One, I'm really proud of you."

I wished I was proud of me too, but I wasn't.

"Love you," he said.

"I love you, Dad."

There were lots of things I should've said. I wanted him knowing we were home alone, but Steve and Robin were having fun, playing, and I'd go out and get us some food, and we'd be fine, and I wanted him helping us in some other way, but I didn't tell him any of these things.

I hung up, sat on the bed faced with my sin of betrayal, and wrapped my arms around my head. *Why did I do that? I can't believe I just finked on Mommy. Maybe I wanted to hear Dad tell me he's proud of me. Is that why I did it?* I closed my eyes, trying to clear my head. *Oh no! Dad didn't say to call when the state comes to our apartment. He didn't say he wouldn't let them take us.* My eyes stung with tears, and I gasped for air as I picked up the phone and dialed another number.

The phone rang once, twice, three times. "Hello, Green Parrot," the voice on the other end said.

My voice trembled. "Is my mother there?"

"Hold a minute."

A moment later, Mother came on the line. "This is Joy."

"Mommy, I just talked to Dad. He's calling CPS."

"What?"

"Those people who take children from their parents are on their way here," I said.

"Pammie. Close the drapes and lock the door. Don't answer it for anyone. I'll be right home."

Within the hour, Mother rushed in with two sacks of groceries and a jug of Gallo wine. I was happy to see her and followed her to the kitchen with my stomach growling and my face beaming a smile. "Yeah, you're home," I announced, feeling somewhat relieved. "Mommy they can't take us from you. You won't let them, will you?"

"No, Pammie," Mother said, unpacking those bags fast. She pulled out a small bale of diapers, a loaf of bread, cheddar cheese, a couple russet potatoes, two T-bone steaks, a head of iceberg lettuce, a few tomatoes, Frosted Flakes cereal, a half gallon of milk, and twenty four jars of baby food.

Usually Mother stuck to beer and wine, but she had recently begun drinking Smirnoff at night. Long after dinner, Mother put Steven in his crib, turned the lights down low, and filled a glass with vodka and tonic. She put a Barbra Streisand record album on the console stereo in the living room, and reclined on the sofa with her bare feet on the coffee table before her, crossed at the ankles.

"Memories
Like the corners of my mind
Misty water colored memories
Of the way we were," Mother sang, tears rolling down her face.

Robin and I crept away to our room. "What's that about?" I whispered, and clicked off the light. We climbed under our blankets and for several minutes, lay there listening in the pitch black of night. Mother's soprano voice rose and fell with emotion. I rolled over onto my side and faced my sister who was also lying on her side. "Gee, she sings pretty."

"Uh-huh, Pam. She really does."

"Robin, what if they come tomorrow?"

"Who are you talking about?"

"The cops."

"You mean social services?"

"Yeah."

"I hope not, but maybe it'll do Mommy some good. It'll probably scare her to death. Maybe even scare her into becoming a mother."

CHAPTER THIRTY-TWO

*O*ne dark, moonless night, I needed solitude and went out-side, walked away from our apartment, and stopped near a fence surrounding a field of orange pumpkins and gourds. I stared at the stars, twinkling and shimmering in space, and talked to Jesus.

"Mommy's never home anymore," I told him. "What if she doesn't come back?" Mother had left on a date three days earlier and hadn't returned. "Did I do something to make her hate us?" I wiped my nose with my sleeve and sat quietly for a while. A tear rolled down my cheek.

When I was six and a half, I had transitioned from reciting words to actual prayer, but I didn't know the reason for this. No one in my family was spiritual in any way, yet sometimes I told Jesus about my inner world, and when I couldn't relax, I'd pray and sing the songs I'd learned in church, and my anxiety would vanish. At those times, it seemed that love had touched me with a balm of peace, and I'd sleep.

I remembered the final fire, standing on the front step, and hearing someone urge me away from my burning house. "Jesus," I whispered. "I know it was you telling me to run. Why don't you talk to me right now? You know you can, if you want." A short while later, I returned home to Robin and Steven. I hadn't heard any answers, but the burden I had carried seemed a little lighter.

After another long absence, Mother came home with the usual two bags of groceries and a package of diapers. She handed me a jar of peanut butter and Robin a plastic bag of lettuce and tomatoes. "Put those in the fridge, please. Where's your brother?"

"Having a nap," Robin answered. "He didn't sleep good last night. I think he's teething again. Anything that'll fit in his mouth's game."

"And he's drooling. A lot," I said.

Mother poured herself a drink from the bottle of Smirnoff. "You can put a damp washcloth in the freezer. Give it to Steven when he wakes up. It'll feel good on his gums. I'm going out for a few drinks with my new friend. I'll be home later, after you children have gone to bed."

Robin stared disapprovingly at Mother.

"No, don't go. Please stay home," I said.

"Girls, I promise George will have me home before morning."

"George?" Robin asked. "Isn't he the guy who lives over at the other end of the apartments?"

A smug look came over Mother's face. "You got that right."

I thought she and Luke were dating. "You switched to George?" I asked for clarification.

"Luke broke it off." She sighed and crossed her arms. Dark circles were under her eyes and I thought she looked tired. "I didn't just meet George yesterday. He asked me out a couple weeks ago." She lit a cigarette and inhaled, blowing a trail of smoke away from us. "George and Joy, I think that sounds nice. What do you girls think?"

As the question hung in the air, Mother looked at Robin. She balanced her smoldering cigarette between her fingers and then she looked at me. I had only met George once, and only in passing, but when I heard his name with Mother's, I had the hair standing on end, goose bumps, makes my head swirl, creeps. What could I say? I was freaked out by the idea of my mother jumping from one man to another and something about George didn't feel right. After a long silence, I finally shrugged my shoulders. "I don't know," I said.

"I'm with Pam," Robin said.

"You'll like him." Mother lifted one eyebrow and grinned. "I do."

Not long after, Mother was home one whole evening and my heart nearly burst with the happiness inside it. We were together as a family over a dinner of Cornish game hens stuffed with seasoned rice, and steamed broccoli with melted cheddar cheese. I couldn't think of anywhere I'd rather be than right here with Mother, Robin, and Steven.

Mother leaned across the table and grinned. "Girls, I have some good news. I've finally found you a new daddy."

I swallowed hard and put my fork beside my plate.

Robin's eyes were wide like a deer's when a bright light shines in them. She was shocked, no doubt, like me.

"What's wrong, darlings? Don't you like George?"

Robin and I made eye contact before shrugging our shoulders. We had seen George with Mother a few times and something unidentifiable about his demeanor troubled me. "I don't think he likes kids," I said.

"Well, of course, he likes children. He has a son and daughter."

"Mommy, really?" Robin was incredulous. "You're going to marry George?"

Mother held out her hand and showed off her ½ ct. diamond engagement ring.

I disliked and distrusted George. Mother said he was a nice man. I doubted it. She said he was a good dad. I doubted it. She said we'd all be very happy together, but my gut told me otherwise. The whole idea of Daddy George sickened me. Right there at the table, I could've puked.

Sometime later in the summer, we were all at George's apartment. He and Mother were in the kitchen. Robin, Steven, and I were in the living room watching Saturday morning cartoons on his television.

George's voice rose. He verbally slammed Mother. Soon his voice was louder than Elmer Fudd saying to Bugs Bunny the game warden, *Oh, Mr. Game Warden. I hope you can help me. I've been told I could shoot wabbits and goats and pigeons and mongooses and dirty skunks and ducks. Could you tell me what season it weawwy is?*

Whatever was going on in the kitchen scared me. There was an escalation of emotions and George's volume kept going up. The cereal and milk I ate that morning, rose up in my throat. I tensed my muscles. "Robin," I whispered so as not to alert Steven. "I'm afraid."

Robin jumped to her feet. "He better not touch her." She motioned toward the kitchen. "Let's go in there."

We went to the kitchen and stood alongside Mother. "It's okay," she said to Robin and me. "Go back in the other room with your brother."

I felt a great stubbornness rising from my core and even though I always obeyed Mother, I shook my head and stayed with Robin where I joined her in glaring long and hard at George's reddening face. He kept railing at Mother and shouting accusations.

George, almost six feet tall, had broad shoulders and a barrel-sized chest. Mother, five feet five inches, one hundred fifteen pounds, looked small and vulnerable next to him.

He pounded his fist on the Formica counter. "You're seeing someone else! You can't admit it, can you?"

I couldn't believe my ears. I'd already heard this fight, years earlier when Max charged Mother with the same crime.

"I told you, he's a longtime friend." Mother motioned with her hands as she spoke. "George, you must believe me."

Perhaps Mother felt there was too much at stake to lose this relationship. George, a Vietnam vet, had a well paying job and had supplemented Mother with what she needed to keep up with the bills. "Bob and I've known each other for years. Years, George. We've been friends since I lived at home with my parents. He's a friend, like a brother. For goodness sakes, I even call him Brother Bob."

"There's more to it than you're admitting! Come clean with me, Joy."

She hesitated for a second before answering. "Honey, I'm not keeping anything from you," she said, in a soft voice.

"A friend, right! And I'm the president of *the United States*."

"Why would I be romantically involved with someone else?"

He accused her of sleeping with Bob and said he'd heard it somewhere.

"I swear to you," Mother said.

"You're having an affair," he said.

"I've never been unfaithful to you, George."

A vein on George's neck pulsed. Black hair framed a red-blotched face, his eyes bulged, and his jaw jutted out. He looked like he wanted to murder someone. "Sure. What else would you say?" George took a step toward her. "Why don't

you just tell the truth? It'll make your conscience feel better."
He shouted in her face. "Tell me the truth!"

Mother kept her eyes locked onto his. "Please calm down.
You're too angry to think clearly. We can talk about this later."

"Angry?" he said bitterly. "Well, lady you haven't seen angry."

Robin scowled at George's hate filled face. My heart
pounded in my chest and I clenched my hands into fists at my
sides. *I think he's going to beat her up. What do we do?*

Mother stepped back from him with a look of fear in her
eyes.

"Joy, this is not an unfounded accusation. This isn't about
something you haven't done," he said flatly.

"It's just like I've told you." She shrugged her shoulders
and shook her head. "I can't believe this is happening. You're
jealous of a friendship. Don't you think you're over-reacting?"

He shouted obscenities as he came toward her and drew
back his arm to strike her.

That very second, I rushed forward and got between
George and Mother. I stood on my tippy toes and pointed
my finger in his face, his warm pants of air striking my hand.
"You!" I hollered. "You will not hit my mother!"

George looked down at my petite body, my coffee colored eyes shooting daggers at him, my little finger pointing
up at his red face. He shook his head, dropped his arm, and
stormed from the room. The door slammed behind him.

Mother breathed in sharply. "That was too close for comfort." She looked up at the ceiling momentarily. "Thank Heavens that's over. Pammie, you shouldn't have done that. You
could've gotten hurt. But I'm glad you did."

At barely three and a half feet tall, I had moved my first
mountain.

Mother grasped the diamond engagement ring with a trembling hand. She removed it and placed it on George's kitchen counter. "He can keep it," she said. "Come on, girls. Let's get your brother and get out of here."

We walked up the sidewalk leading to our apartment at the other end of the long complex. "I'm glad that's over," Robin said. "We didn't like him anyways. He gave us both the creeps. Huh, Pam?"

My heart was still leaping about in my chest. "Yep," I said.

"Well, what's done is done, but I am a little worried about what George might do when he finds the engagement ring he gave me." Mother said, her voice sounding tired. We neared our apartment when she spoke up again. "If George gives me any trouble, I'll file a restraining order."

"A restraining order?" Robin said.

"Robin, it's a legal document forbidding him to come within five-hundred feet of me or something like that. I've forgotten the details, but I'm sure it would be just the thing to do the trick."

CHAPTER THIRTY-THREE

*A*t the end of summer vacation, a few days before school resumed, our landlady Mrs. Rothschild knocked on the door. It was very hot that day, close to a hundred degrees, and I stood inside the door's threshold beside Robin, who still wasn't very big, balancing our diapered, shirt-less, brother on her hip.

Mrs. Rothschild clutched a document in her hand that I presumed was for Mother. She craned her neck and peered around Robin and me, trying to see inside our apartment. "Is Joy here?" she said in a nasal sort of way.

"She's at the store," Robin said.

"I need to check on something in your apartment."

Robin cleared her voice. "Our mother said to never allow anyone inside while she's gone."

"The *owner* told me to stop by and personally take care of this," Mrs. Rothschild said, waving the folded document at us.

Robin faked a smile and juggled Steven, content in her arms, onto her other hip. "I'm sorry, but I can't disobey my mother. I'm positive she'll call the minute she's home." Robin began closing the door. "I need to take Steven inside now."

Mrs. Rothschild stepped forward, pressing a hand against the partially open door. "But this is the owner's request. I have to do this today."

Her overbearing demeanor and insistence frustrated me. I put on the sweetest smile possible. "Oh my gosh! Really? The owner? Gee, Mrs. Rothschild, that is the biggest, most important thing ever."

"If you can just let me in for an itsy bitsy sec," Mrs. Rothschild said. "I promise this won't take long."

The sun beat down on us and Robin's brow glistened with sweat. She backed away from the door. "Come on Pam," she said. And we both went into the living room followed by Mrs. Rothschild.

A short arrogant woman, she eyed our home disapprovingly, noting the clutter strung across our sofa—a dirty towel, Steven's bib, and his toys. Her pale blue eyes moved to the end table beside it, buried under cereal bowls, a plastic sippy cup, a magazine, and Mother's open novel lying face down. She glanced over the coffee table with its layer of whitish dust and the heart I had traced in it, and shook her head at the carpet, splattered with lint, dirt, and whatever else had traveled in on our shoes.

"This place is filthy," she said, walking to the kitchen, her short black hair with the ends curled under bouncing with each step. "It stinks like dirty diapers. When's the last time the apartment was cleaned?" she said with her back to us.

Call it looking through filtered lenses, but to my eleven-year-old eyes, our place was pretty spiffy. Granted, I realized it needed cleaning, but from my perspective, our apartment looked lived in, not filthy.

"We'll clean it up," Robin said, still holding Steven, who was watching with wide-eyed, speechless, curiosity.

I stood right beside Robin with Steven in the kitchen, and I wondered what Mrs. Rothschild wanted, and supposed it had something to do with that document she waved at us each time she spoke.

She opened our practically bare refrigerator and spotted a bowl of weeks old food with a layer of black, furry mold on top of it. "You can't keep spoiled food. Throw it out. And when's the last time the kitchen was cleaned?" She pointed at the sink piled high with dirty dishes.

"Mrs. Rothschild," Robin said. "Are you here to tell us how to clean the apartment?" She gave her no time to reply. "If so, you don't have to worry over it. We'll clean it up in a flash."

Mrs. Rothschild jerked her head around and faced Robin. "Actually, this apartment's in complete shambles and I'm thinking of calling social services. Children shouldn't be left alone and they shouldn't be alone with a baby. To think of it!"

Dad had already reported Mother's neglect to CPS and I knew if Mrs. Rothschild also called, they would certainly come to our apartment. *They'll take us from Mommy and maybe from each other.* "No, please don't," I said.

"We're fine, really. Our mother should be back any minute. Like I said, she's just gone to the store." Robin crossed the room with Steven on her hip and peeked out the kitchen window at the vacant parking space below us.

Mrs. Rothschild opened the cupboards and scrutinized our meager food supply. "I'm aware of what goes on around here."

"Please give us another chance," Robin said.

I chewed my fingernail and thought about our situation. *Daddy already called CPS. If she calls, they'll split us up. After all, lots of people would like to have our sweet brother. Even if they weren't sure they wanted a baby, Steven's wavy hair and pretty eyes would change their minds. He's no trouble at all, doesn't even fuss much like some babies do. They'd want Robin, too. She works hard and knows just what to do with a baby. Me? I don't think anyone would want a skinny, grimy girl like me.*

"Evicting you would be the owner's decision," Mrs. Rothschild said, interrupting my thoughts. "I'll have to let them know this place is just as I had suspected, a real train wreck."

She shook her head in disgust and headed for the door. "I haven't made a decision about calling social services."

Robin opened the door for her. "Mrs. Rothschild." She tried one last time. "Please don't."

As soon as the landlady left, I told Robin how I felt about her bursting in like she owned the place and telling us what to do.

"Pam, I know. Not now. Let's talk about it later, okay?" She went to the kitchen with Steven still on her hip, and sat him in his highchair near the dining table. "Want some milk?" He did and she placed a sippy cup on his tray before finding an oldies rock station on the stereo.

The rancid smell of fermenting food, old diapers, and soured milk came from a garbage can in the cabinet beneath the sink. On either side of it, there were cigarette butts, some rotting food from the previous week's dinner with Mother, and empty baby food jars.

I hauled the trash bag downstairs and dropped it in the dumpster while Robin got busy on the sticky kitchen floor, sweeping and mopping it. "The cabinet's yours," she said when I returned. "The smell's making me sick."

In the far recesses of the cabinet, where countless microbes lived, I wiped up garbage sludge, black mold, and other things that live on rotting stuff. It stunk, and I tried holding my breath while working. I spotted something grosser than the decomposing food and recoiled. "Yuck."

"I know, Pam. But I don't think I can do it," Robin said from the other end of the small room.

"Just plug your nose and come over here. The rice is wiggling." Tiny, rice like bugs wiggled on my cloth. "What is that?"

Robin scrunched up her nose. "Ew! Gross! Those are maggots."

"Maggots?"

"Fly larvae. Okay, don't panic."

I wasn't panicking.

This was war. We immersed hand towels in boiling water, and used them against the maggots, scalding them, and wiping them onto newspapers, and throwing them in the trash. After the bottom cabinet was clean, we scrubbed the mountain of dishes and every surface with soapy water.

When Steven wanted to get down from his highchair, we took turns dancing through the rooms with him on one hip and a moist cleaning cloth in the other. We sang full-throttle along with the tunes coming from the stereo, and tackled the dust, then put everything in its place, wiped down the television, and vacuumed the carpets in every room.

It seemed that Mrs. Rothschild's decision hinged on how clean we could get the apartment, and we worked hard, stopping for brief interludes. Steven needed his diaper changed and another snack. Then late in the afternoon, we put him down for a nap.

Three or four hours after Mrs. Rothschild's visit, a knock came on the door. "Well, Pam, this is it," Robin said, smiling meekly. "It shines. Don't you think so?"

"It's perfect," I said.

Our landlord entered, and walked through each room, clucking her tongue. "This'll never do," she said.

Hot tears filled my eyes. "But, it's so pretty," I said, wiping them with my grubby hands.

Mrs. Rothschild walked out the door and, stopping on the porch, she looked back at Robin and me. There was the absence of compassion on her face.

"Please, let us stay," Robin said.

"You can tell your mother that I'll return with an eviction notice. Don't know when, but I'll have it back sometime this week."

Just as Mrs. Rothschild began descending the stairs, I glanced over the living room. "Robin, I think we did really good." I plopped down on the sofa beside her and stared at nothing in particular. "Her mind was made up when she came here the first time," I went on. A sinking feeling came over me and I put my head in my hands. It all seemed so unfair.

"Pam, the eviction isn't our problem," Robin said, stroking my hair. "Mommy will just have to deal with it." She threw her head back against the sofa cushion and folded her arms. "She makes me so mad."

"I'm not mad at her," I said.

Robin's jaw dropped and her eyes grew large. "And why not?"

"I don't know. I guess I feel sorry for her."

"You feel sorry for her?" Robin's frustration grew. She nearly shouted. "Well, not me."

My stomach trembled from the day's events and now her outburst.

"Pam, Just look at us. Why would I feel sorry for her?" The pitch of her voice rose and she spoke rapidly. "She's the one having all the fun, wearing nice clothes, going to her weekly hair appointments, eating at restaurants. We're starving. And I have a constant stomachache from stress." Robin folded her arms, pressed her lips together, and down shifted. "I'm afraid of what might happen to us. Any minute, social services could come and take us away." She cocked her head and looked at me with a concerned expression. "Is Mommy worried about that?"

I drew in a breath and thought Mother might be more concerned than she'd made us aware of. "Maybe she is," I said. "Maybe she's real worried."

"If Mommy's worried about us, then where is she? She's not here where she belongs. Pam, do you know where she's at?"

"Not really. She might be at The Green Parrot."

"We can't say for sure. How do we reach her if there's an emergency? We can't. We can try, and do like we've done hundreds of times, call each of the bars and ask if she's there. It's embarrassing, and those friends of hers..." Robin's jaw tightened and she threw her hands up. "Ahhh! They act like they care about us. Well, where are they? We're hungry. I've lost weight. You've lost weight. Have you looked in the mirror lately? Your collarbone and ribs are sticking out."

I looked down at my ribcage and pressed my hand against my thin t-shirt and felt each of the protruding bones under my hand. "Isn't that the way they're supposed to be?"

"No! They're like that because you're not getting enough to eat. And Steven runs out of diapers all the time. My pants have holes in them just like yours and they're falling off my waist and so are yours. When was the last time we had new clothes?"

"A long time ago," I said.

"Where's the so called 'family' from The Parrot? They're getting drunk, just like Mommy." She blinked back tears. "Oh! Wait a minute! They're helping her do it." Robin's hands trembled and she wiped her eyes. She got up and clicked on the television. "We need our mother," she said. She slumped onto the sofa and stared at the screen.

There was something I hadn't told her. Not only did I yearn for Mother, but I missed hearing Uncle Ernie's whiny voice and the way Brother Bob banters with her. I missed Poppy, too. Even if none of these people spoke to me, I'd like to be near them. Maybe it was senseless to want to be near people who wished you weren't there.

Robin had made her point well and I knew she spoke the truth. I had questions of my own, though they were far less complex. Sniffing back tears, I looked deep into Robin's eyes. "Doesn't Mommy love us?" There, I'd said it. I had finally told Robin what had weighed on my mind for more than a year. "She doesn't. Does she?"

"Come here," Robin said, her anger subsiding. Extending an arm to me, she wrapped it around my bony frame. "Of course she loves us."

I leaned against her, laying my head on her shoulder, enjoying our closeness. "No, she doesn't. She'd be here if she did."

"She loves, you, me, and Steven," Robin said. She looked down at my eyes, filling with tears. "Pam, don't cry. Please. We'll be all right and someday, Mommy might come around to seeing things our way."

CHAPTER THIRTY-FOUR

"*M*rs. Rothschild came over yesterday while you were at school and evicted us." Mother dropped the news on Robin and me at breakfast before we left for school. Neither of us had told her about the landlord's visit and I had hoped she'd change her mind. We glanced up from our bowls of cereal and made eye contact before giving Mother our attention.

She ran her hands through her uncombed hair. "I don't know what we'll do. But remember this, everything happens for a reason." After a period of silence, she smiled. "Who knows," she said brightly, "maybe Poppy will loan me the money for deposits."

"Mommy! Roby!" Steven hollered from the other room. "Mommy! Roby!"

"Steven's awake," Mother said and looked at Robin. "Darling, I'll get him. Stay there and finish your breakfast." She was back in a few moments with Steven in her arms, smiling and talking to him in that special voice adults use with babies—soft, sweet, and cute-like.

A few short weeks later, we moved into a duplex within easy walking distance of The Green Parrot. Our new residence was on a four-lane street, lined by older homes, emerald green lawns, and trees. Summer was clearly behind us and autumn had arrived. It was my favorite season. Crisp, fresh smells filled the air and multi-colored leaves fell everywhere.

Robin didn't have to change schools. She attended the only junior high in the area, but I was switched to Whitney Avenue Elementary.

Within the first week at my new school, some of the sixth grade boys began to pick on me. They peppered me with their mean words like machine gun fire. As the school year progressed they took their name calling to new levels, singling me out in the lunchroom for more of their ridicule.

Mother's overnight absences increased and the neglect worsened. I had no idea who she dated, but whoever he was had her at his place several nights each week. It wasn't George. We hadn't heard from him since the day Mother left her engagement ring on his kitchen counter.

One morning when there was nothing more to eat than a few jars of baby food, I walked to school with my stomach grumbling. Robin and I had tasted Steven's pureed fruit and, once, after we had been hungry for several days, we shared a jar between ourselves, but we didn't go much further than this because we didn't want him running out of his supply of pureed fruits and vegetables.

I was a poor kid and everyday was a crisis. Food was such a big deal that I'd daydream in class about the hot school meals, but not anymore. That noon, when the lunch bell rang, I left my classroom and immediately went to the girls' bathroom where I hid from the bullies. When class resumed, I had missed lunch, but at least I hadn't been called names. The ridicule hurt far more than my pains of hunger.

On my way home from school in early spring, I spotted Dad's car parked at the side of the road ahead of me. He got out and waved. "Pammie."

I ran over to him. "Dad, what are you doing here?"

"I'll explain later. Can you go to the park with us?" He pointed at Big Pam seated in the car.

"Sure," I said, getting into his car. At the park, we strolled over the manicured lawn under dozens of ancient oak trees and headed for one of several redwood picnic tables. The smell of newly cut grass and dry leaves was in the air. A couple of bushy tailed grey squirrels crossed our path. One stopped to nibble on an acorn. Then the other chased it up the trunk of a tree. I tilted my head back and watched them scramble onto a densely leafed limb and disappear within a web of twisted branches.

"Come on slow poke," Dad said. "Don't dawdle. We haven't got all day."

"Honey," Big Pam said to Dad, "let's stop here." She sat at a table and waved for me to join them. "We brought you a strawberry milkshake," she said, handing me a white, Styrofoam cup and plastic straw.

I put my hand on her shoulder. "Thanks. Milkshakes are my favorite."

"That's what your dad said."

Dad stood beside Big Pam. He shoved his hands into the pockets of his navy blue slacks. His short sleeve, buttoned shirt was tucked into his pants. A thin, black belt held them on his slender waist.

"How'd you find me?" I said.

Dad chuckled. "That's what telephones are for. I called the school."

"Why'd you want to see me? I mean, you didn't come all this way to bring me a milkshake." I gazed at him, trying to discern his motives.

Dad gave a weak grin. "Has social services been out to see you?"

I kept my lips latched around my straw, guzzling strawberry deliciousness, filling my empty stomach, and shook my head.

"Then I'll have to approach this from a different angle. Since they never followed through, we'll go to Plan B. I had hoped they'd help me gain custody of you girls."

I let go of the straw and scrunched up my face. "Custody?"

"I need a court order signed by a judge saying you and Robin can live with us." He glanced up at Big Pam. "Your mother might put up a stink, though." He scratched his black goatee. "But if my idea pans out, that won't be a problem."

White clouds rippled across the powder blue sky, blocking most of the sun. It wasn't especially warm and goose bumps broke out on my arms. I shivered. Then I put my milkshake on the table and gazed in disbelief at Dad. Suddenly, I felt vaguely sick. He and Big Pam were watching me, studying my face and waiting for my reply.

"We want you and your sister to live with us," he continued.

My aspirations hadn't included moving in with them. I loved Dad very much and Big Pam was fun. She liked playing Scrabble and Monopoly, and sometimes she let me comb and style the wig she wore over her thick, super short hair. Going to their home twice every month had been adequate. Sure, I missed Dad between visits, but I didn't yearn to live with them as I yearned for Mother's presence.

I supposed Dad was waiting for me to say something, but I didn't know how to answer. "We drove by your duplex a little while ago," he finally said. "Your mother's there. At least, her car's in the driveway. We'll bring you home with us today, if that's all right with you." He smiled hopefully. "If I have your permission, I'll speak with her about it in a little bit."

My head began feeling as it had weeks earlier when I had the flu. I had a spinning sensation and a pressure began forming in my stomach. "Today?" I said, weakly.

He nodded. "When I take you back, I'll talk with her."

For the longest time, I had clung to a hope that Mother would come home for good and care for Steven, Robin, and me. If I went with Dad, I'd give up on any chance of this ever happening. "But, I can't leave with you now. What about Robin and Steven?"

The idea of leaving Robin, Steven, and Mother frightened me. It meant the end of being together as a family. Even when Mother wasn't with us, my siblings and I had each other. I dropped my eyes from his gaze to my drink, began bending the red and white striped straw, and stared at it.

Dad sounded far away. He was saying something about how Robin was more than capable of holding down the fort while I lived with them.

I blinked and looked up at Dad's face. He watched me while taking a cigarette from his pack of Pall Malls. He lit it and stuck it in his mouth. "Well?" he said through his lips clenched tightly around it. He inhaled on it before extinguishing it against the edge of the table. "What's your decision? Do you want to help with Plan B?"

I stared into Dad's eyes. They demanded an answer, urged me to agree to his plan, and beckoned me to trust him. My stomach began to quiver. "I'll live with you and Big Pam for good?"

"I'll arrange it with your mother and as soon as I can, I'll bring your sister to live with me too."

"I really love you, Dad. But I can't do it. I can't leave Robin and Steven."

"If you decide not to," Dad said. "CPS will eventually take you from Joy. It's really just a matter of time." He pushed his hands back in his pockets and said something about it being cold and that I should finish my milkshake because we'd need to go or Mother would worry.

"Dad," I said, "I *love* Mommy." I watched his eyes for understanding. "And I can't hurt her. I just can't."

"I knew I was asking you to do a hard thing." He put both hands on the end of the picnic table, leaned toward me, and looked me square in the eyes. "I had a phone call from your school this morning. The secretary told me to bring you some clean clothes and she asked me if I knew that you and your sister stay home alone with Steve. I'm not the only one who has called the state, and it's not the first time a school has filed a report with them about your mother. If I don't intervene and do something, sooner or later the state will. Do you understand how serious this is?"

I worried about Robin. How would she manage without me? Steven was sweet, and strong willed, and had become a defiant two-year-old, but with gentleness he complied. Would he feel rejected by my absence? I imagined the pain my leaving would cause Mother. "Daddy, please no," I said.

He stood and placed a hand on Big Pam's shoulder. She put her hand over his. "We want to give you and Robin a home," she said, smiling. "We'll take you shopping for new clothes, and you won't go to bed hungry, and we'll never leave you and your sister home alone at night." Her smile seemed hopeful. "Young'un, you and Robin need things we can provide for you. And think of Steven."

"I am thinking of Steven!" I snapped. I didn't mean to be so blunt, but I was afraid. "Mommy doesn't take care of Steven. Robin does and I help. That's because Mommy's drunk all the time. That's why we can't leave Steven with her." I turned to

Dad. "If we leave, Steven won't get fed." I felt panicked. "He'll run out of diapers. Dad, he could die. See why we can't leave."

"Can you just trust me?" Dad said. "Think about it. Would I leave Steven with Joy?" He stood up straight and shook his head. "Little One, you need to learn to trust me."

"But Steven," I said, my eyes filling with tears.

"Your Aunt Marylou said she talked with Max and he'll take Steven. If you'll give me permission, when I take you home, I'll talk with your mother and later this spring or summer, we'll go to court and let the judge decide where you and Robin should live."

"Please don't make me do it," I said. To my way of thinking, walking out on Mother would be the worst betrayal ever, and another great source of pain for her, my siblings, and me, too.

Dad put his arm around my shoulder. "Okay, come on, Little One." There wasn't a trace of disapproval on his face or in his voice. "We'll take you home."

A lump formed in my throat as we got back into the car. On the way home, I chewed my nails and worried. After I had found that scripture about mountain moving faith, I had often read and thought about it. On the drive home, a recurring thought came to mind. *Mountains are impossible. This is impossible. Mommy staying at her boyfriend's and her being drunk are impossible. Why is this happening? I want it to all go away.* Dad parked outside the duplex.

"I'll walk you to the door," he offered. We stood on the front porch for a few minutes where he watched me fidget with the edge of my top.

I had a sudden flight urge and wanted to run inside, flee up the stairs, and hide in my room.

"Little One, somehow everything will work out," Dad said, his voice filled with affection.

"But, you don't know," I mumbled and looked down at my chewed nails.

Dad touched my chin gently, lifting my face, and peering in my eyes. His gaze was soft and compassionate. "What do I need to know?"

My lip trembled. "About Mommy's Auntie Mame house. Robin and Steve and I are getting our own rooms, and then Mommy won't leave us anymore, and we'll have lots of clothes, and tons of good things to eat. Mommy said we might even have our own horses."

A familiar look came over his eyes. "Is that so?" he said. I'd seen that expression on his face before when he had told a joke and I didn't catch the punch line. That look in his eyes made me think that maybe Mother's talk of a better life and a beautiful home was as unreachable and fleeting as the wispy clouds slowly moving in the sky above us.

"She said she's getting us another daddy. That's why she's gone all the time."

Dad placed a hand on my back.

"It's not true, is it?" I said. I had never before doubted Mother's story. Then I was in his arms, sobbing on his shoulder. "Why does this have to happen?"

"Honey," Dad said gently. "I wish I knew. Sometimes life can be pretty hard on us. It's making you stronger."

"I feel like a weakling." I wiped my nose against his shoulder.

"Thanks," he said.

"Dad," my voice quivered, "okay."

"Joy," Dad called from the duplex's entryway. Just to our right, a staircase led to bedrooms and a bathroom on the second floor. I heard water running in the kitchen, directly ahead of us. Voices emanated from a television in the living room beside it.

Mother came from the kitchen. "Keith," she said, walking toward us. "What are you doing here?"

"Pammie has something she wants to tell you," he said.

My heart pounded in my ears and my head swirled. The sick feeling in my stomach worsened and I fought an urge to throw up. I turned to Dad. He had it wrong. I didn't want to ask her anything. He had said he would talk to her about me coming with him. "But—"

"You can do it," he said. "Go ahead, ask."

Mother pressed her lips together. Her eyes narrowed. Her jaw line hardened. I dropped my eyes from her steely gaze. She waited. Dad waited. Robin turned off the television and came over to us. She cocked her head, looking at me with her eyes full of concern.

Steven, in a crib in his room upstairs, banged his head against the headboard and rocked. It's what babies sometimes do when they're emotionally distressed. The crib had wheels. Every time he rocked forward, it screeched and moved along the floor, and every time he hit his head against the rail, the crib slammed into the wall. Bang. Screech. Bang. Screech. Bang. Screech. Bang.

I was so startled by Dad's words that I didn't know what to do. He put me in the position of having to stand up for myself, and it was too hard, too frightening, and such a great betrayal of my love for Mother, Robin, and Steven that I couldn't find any words. For several seconds, my eyes darted worriedly around the room, from Mother to Robin, to the ceiling, the floor, and back to Robin. *Maybe she'll hate me. I'm deserting her and Steven. Why wouldn't she? If she did this to me, I would be so mad. Mommy will think I love Dad more than her. She'll never speak to me again.*

"Go ahead," Dad said again.

"I want to live with Dad," I mumbled.

The shock on Robin's face was swiftly replaced by the pain in her eyes. Mother made a sound as if struck in the stomach by a great force. My eyes shot over to her face. Her eyes were on fire. She thrust a hand to her hip and glared. "Go get your things together."

On my way from the room, I glanced back at Robin. She looked from Mother, to Dad, to me. Her face had gone pale and her eyes filled with tears. I grabbed a brown paper bag and walked slowly up the flight of stairs. In my room, I shoved everything I owned into it before going over to Steven.

I put a hand on Steven's sweaty back and he stopped rocking.

"Down?" he said. His moist bangs clung to his forehead and a reddened face told the story of a long, hard cry. He stood in his crib and reached his arms up to me. "Down?"

"I'm sorry, but Mommy wants you to stay in bed." Tears trailed down the corners of my eyes. I tried hugging him over the bed rail, but he pushed me away, "Pammie, down."

"Steven, I can't. But I'm sure Robin or Mommy will come and get you soon." The tears kept coming and I kissed the top of his head. "I love you." When I got to his bedroom door, I looked back. He had resumed his earlier position, curled up into a ball against the crib's headboard. "I love you," I said again and then I left.

Leaving Mother, my sister, and Steven was the hardest thing ever asked of me. I waited at the top of the landing and fought for control over my plummeting emotions. I wiped my eyes, breathed in deeply, and went to Dad, waiting at the bottom of the landing.

That sound of my brother's distress began again. Screech. Bang. Screech. Bang. At the furthest end of the hall, Mother and Robin watched Dad and me. There were no hugs or loving farewells. When I finally spoke, my voice was above a whisper. "Bye, Mommy. Bye, Robin."

As I followed him out the door, Robin called weakly, "Bye, Pam."

CHAPTER THIRTY-FIVE

J woke up in the morning and stared out the window beside me. If I tilted my head back and to the left, I could see something other than the back of another apartment unit. There was the blue sky with streaks of white trailing across it and the scraggly branches of a bottle brush tree.

Baby Keith whimpered from his crib at the other end of the room, which wasn't anything new. I had a vague memory of him crying late in the night, and then of Dad soothing him with that particular vocal quality, once used just for Robin and me when we were hurting.

I lay flat on my back with my hands under my head. Was Mommy home? I wondered. What were Robin and Steven doing at this very moment? Whatever it was, it wouldn't be easy, I decided. My stomach growled. I was relieved to be where I no longer went days without food. The simple idea of three meals, every day, forever, seemed like a dream.

From the other room, Dad said something to Big Pam. Then she answered from somewhere else in the apartment. "I can't," she called. "I'm on my way to change Keith's diaper and get him up."

I was grateful someone else was taking care of the baby, holding him when he cried, changing his diapers, feeding him. It dawned on me then, and I smiled. *And they're taking care of me, too.*

Soon, Dad entered my room. "Come out for breakfast," he said. "We're taking you shopping in a while."

I lowered myself over the top bunk's edge, dropped to the floor, and ran after him. "Really? Dad? Shopping already?"

"Well," he chuckled, "we don't mess around."

In all my years, no one had ever taken me shopping for clothes or anything for myself, and I felt a sudden burst of excitement, and stared at Dad with my mouth half open.

"Don't just stand there gawking," he said, playfully. "Go eat your breakfast so we can go. Cheerios and milk are on the table."

Later in the morning, we dropped Keith off at the babysitter and went to K-Mart, Sears, and then Montgomery Ward. I was giddy with happiness. Dad and I took our orders from Big Pam. She had a knack for matching colors and fabrics. The variety of choices overawed me. I could have blue, green, tan, or brown slacks, t-shirts, blouses that buttoned, blouses with piping along the neckline, short sleeved tops or long sleeved sweaters. I ran my hands through the variety of slick, soft, and bumpy fabrics. All day, I tried on clothes while butterflies flitted around in my stomach. After a long day of shopping, Dad took us to dinner, and then we picked up Keith, and went home.

In bed that night, I thought of my pretty clothes hanging in the closet and tucked away in the four drawer dresser across from me, and I felt guilty for having new things when Robin still had the same old clothes she'd acquired just after the fires.

I rolled onto my side and curled in like a potato bug. The sounds were different here. There was the low rumble from the television and Big Pam and Dad talking. Far off in the distance, it thundered and then an emergency vehicle raced down the street with its siren blaring. I sucked in my breath, like it was the first air I'd had in a while, and tried to forget the reason for my sudden fear.

A couple days later, Dad attempted to enroll me in the school a few blocks from his apartment, but the secretary said there wasn't any room in the fifth grade. For a second, it looked like I might not have to go to school. "Sky Crest Elementary is a short drive," she said. "Just fifteen minutes. Look here." She showed Dad a map, pointed her wooden pencil at a certain spot, and glanced up at him over her wire framed glasses. "You'll find it's just off Madison Avenue and San Juan."

All that morning, I obsessed over the problem of being the new kid, figuring I'd be fresh meat for the bullies, but hoping I'd make a good first impression with my spiffy outfit. I certainly felt better about myself. I had on a dress and white bobby socks with light brown shoes that Big Pam had called Mary Janes.

Back in the car, I chewed nervously on the nail of my index finger.

"Stop worrying about school," Dad said as he pulled away from the campus. "And stop biting your nails."

My hand dropped on my lap and I covered it with my other hand.

"What's eating at you?"

I didn't answer.

Dad smiled in my direction. "Huh?" He poked my side playfully. "Cat got your tongue?"

"Eww!" I said, laughing. "That's gross."

"Well?"

"The meanies always find me and call me names."

"The meanies?" He asked. "What meanies?"

"There were these mean kids at school who called me names. They were at all the schools."

"Just ignore them. But if someone gives you guff"—"guff" was Dad's word for a bad time—"if he threatens to harm you, strikes you, or if you think he's about to strike you, make a fist and punch him."

"Punch him?" I couldn't believe Dad just told me to use violence and I felt my eyes go wide. "Really?"

"Would I joke about something like that?"

I shook my head. "Nope."

"Don't let anyone push you around."

"But, I'll get in trouble with the principal."

"Let me worry about that. My word's always over the principals and you have my permission to defend yourself. So defend yourself if you have to."

I looked down at my dress. It had a white bodice with tiny blue Forget Me Nots all over it and a navy blue skirt. I ran my fingers through my tangle free hair. There wasn't much of it left. Big Pam had cut it shorter than she or I had wanted. She said she had trouble getting the edges even, and she just kept clipping little bits off until the bottom edge of my hair was even with my earlobes.

"They won't tease me for my clothes, but they might for my wrecked hair," I said.

Dad chuckled. "If they call you names, ignore them. But, remember, if someone's about to hit you, double up your fist."

"Like this?" I showed him my closed fingers.

"Move your thumb around. Put it over your fingers."

"Oh, I got it. Like this." I held up my fist. "And then, I'll pop him." I swung at an imaginary bully. "Ka—Pow!" I said, laughing.

Dad became animated. His voice rose and he spoke excitedly. "Aim for the nose. Bop him right in the nose. Get the first swing in. Strike before he knows what's happening. If you get the first swing in, the kid won't bother you. Actually, none of the kids will bother you after that."

As we drove, I suddenly remembered my small size. "Dad?"

"Yeah?"

"Did you forget something? I'm kind of little."

"Trust me. It'll work. It doesn't matter if you're a runt. When I was ten, your Aunt Kathleen was eleven. That would've made Ross about fourteen and Merle was a year older than him. None of us kids were big." Dad smiled at me and his eyes sparkled. "We were kind of runty ourselves. Well, one time a great big kid was visiting his grandmother who lived down the street from us. He was eighteen or nineteen and he was on leave from the military." Dad paused.

"What happened?"

"We didn't have toys or many play things."

This was the first time I'd ever heard this. "You didn't?"

"Heck no!" he said. "My parents worked hard, but they never had money. But your Uncle Ross had some roller skates. I forget where he got them. He skated down the block and up that grandmother's driveway. Just then the big fellow stormed from her house and chased him all the way home. My sisters and I were playing in our front yard. Merle had the hose in her hand when the big guy chases Ross onto the lawn. He shouts at Ross and shoves him to the ground."

Dad turned a corner and entered the school parking lot.

"Then what?"

"Wait a minute. Let me park." He pulled into an empty space and turned off the ignition. "That kid towered over Ross. Merle had the hose in her hand, and guess what she did?"

I giggled. "Sprayed him."

"You got that right." Dad's eyes sparkled and he snickered. "She sprayed him. Kathleen and I jumped him, and while we were on his back, Ross decked him. He was so big that it took all of us working together to get our message across—Ross would not be bullied." Dad laughed until his eyes filled with tears. "That guy ran back to grandma's and we never saw him again."

I was proud of Dad, my uncle, and aunts, but I also realized Uncle Ross had three other kids defending him. I didn't have this advantage. "But it's just me."

"And?"

"Well, there were four of you."

"One normal-sized kid and you are not much different than that giant guy, verses four runty kids. Aren't you going to ask me what his name was?"

I hadn't thought it was important. "Okay, who was he?"

"Jethro from 'The Beverly Hillbillies.'"

I gasped and laughed all at once. "No way!"

"You know how big Jethro is?"

I had watched the Beverly Hillbillies on television lots of times and I nodded wildly.

Dad opened the car door. "Ready?"

"Sure I am."

Dyslexia made my schoolwork especially frustrating, and I felt like I was defective, inept—a moron. By fifth grade, I could read and understand a list of age appropriate vocabulary words as long as they weren't within a paragraph. When I read, my left eye would swing out and look at a word at the far left side of a page while my right eye was looking at words in the middle of the page. Both my eyes trying to read different words at the same time confused me. So, I closed my left eye and read with my right. Even with one eye, all the sentences on a page ran together, blurring into a tangled web of letters, not resembling anything.

I compensated for my reading difficulties by running my finger under the words on the page while I read them, but just because I could read didn't mean I comprehended the material. My social studies book might as well have been written in Arabic because my brain didn't understand the information coming to it through my eyes. The dyslexia also impaired my short-term memory, making it almost impossible to memorize spelling words and arithmetic tables. But there was some good news. I no longer had a speech impediment.

All the classroom doors at my new school faced a courtyard or the black top. After lunch, the bell rang, and my fellow classmates lined up outside our room, overlooking the courtyard. I believed what Dad told me about punching bullies in the nose. He had said I could only punch a meanie in self-defense and, once I did, no one would harass me. While we waited for our teacher, I had time to study the kids and think up a plan.

If I punch someone right now, then no one will call me names. I'll do it before the teacher comes. I chose a girl with hair the color of toffee standing in line near the door. I don't know why she had to be the one for my exercise. She was both taller and heftier than me.

I went over to the line of kids and made an ugly face at the girl. "This is my spot!" I said in my toughest sounding voice.

A bewildered expression came over her wide doe eyes.

"Didn't you hear me? This is my spot."

Instead of taking a swing at me, her bottom lip stuck out in a pout. "Is not," she said, whining.

I shoved her hard.

"Well, okay," she said on her way to the very end of the line.

Her yielding to my demands surprised me and I stood in her spot, wondering why she gave in so easily.

The girl standing behind me tapped my shoulder. I turned around to see what she wanted. "I'm Georgia," she said. Georgia had hair just like mine, boy short, except hers was orange, and freckles covered her white face. "Maybe, tomorrow you and I can hang out," she said.

I stared at her curiously. It looked like she didn't have eyelashes, then I realized she did, but they were white, and her eyes were pale blue. She was the first person I'd known with white lashes. From then on, Georgia and I hung out at lunchtime. Without meaning to, I had made my very first friend.

CHAPTER THIRTY-SIX

Robin was on her way to our apartment for her weekend visit at Dad's. "I hope Robin doesn't hate me," I told Big Pam. I last saw Robin when I told her and Mother good-bye. "I'd be mad at me if I were her."

"It won't be long before she's here," Big Pam said. "You guys can just talk it out."

Big Pam was watching "General Hospital," her favorite T.V. soap opera. Since moving in with her and Dad, I'd learned all about Luke and Laura, and had begun following their never ending drama. I thought it was nearly as interesting as my own.

A car with squeaking breaks pulled into a parking spot beside our apartment and I looked out the drawn living room drapes. "Maybe that's them."

"Come away from the window."

"But it might be them."

"Shush already."

I hurried to the kitchen and peeked out that window. "Nope, it's someone else."

"Get in here, young'un," Big Pam said, her voice stern. She pointed at the cushion on the sofa beside her. "Sit yourself right here."

When Dad finally arrived with Robin, I greeted her apprehensively. We hugged at the door and I saw that she was

fatigued, but she didn't seem bitter. That night when we went
to bed, Robin took the top bunk and I the lower.

"Robin?" I said.

"Yeah?" she replied

"Were you mad at me for leaving?"

"Why would I be mad? You did what you had to do, and
you're making the way for me and Steve."

"I feel lost," I said. "And awful."

Somewhere outside, a dog barked. Dad's dog, Trixie answered with a shrill yip.

"Is Mommy mad?" I said.

"She'll get over it," Robin said.

"Oh, that's just what I was afraid of." Tears welled up in my
eyes. "I didn't mean to hurt her." I sniffled. "Or you. Or Steven."

"Are you crying?"

"Uh-huh."

"Pam, don't cry, all right?"

"But I hurt you."

"Do you wanna come up here?"

I climbed the headboard to the top bunk. Robin opened
her blankets and I lay beside her. I tried stopping my tears, but
they kept coming. I had missed her so much and now that she
was here with me, I didn't want her to ever leave.

"Don't worry about what Mommy thinks, okay?" she said.
"It's her problem, not yours. You did the right thing."

"But, I left you and Steven."

"We'll be all right. Try to get some sleep."

I couldn't stop the inner deluge of worried thoughts.
"Robin," I said. "What if Steven's sad? You know, when you
leave Mommy to live here and he leaves her to live with Max.
He won't understand. He'll wonder where we are and maybe
he'll think we've abandoned him."

"It'll be better for him there. Don't worry, and please don't be sad. I have a feeling this is what we're supposed to do. I think God wants this for us. And who knows, maybe it'll help Mommy."

I liked the sound of that.

"Night," she said. "Sweet dreams." Robin reached for my hand under the blanket and squeezed it once. "I love you."

"I love you, too."

"I'm taking you to see your mother next weekend," Dad said. We had just returned Robin to Mother and Steven. "It's only fair. When you lived with her, you visited me a couple weekends every month and you need to do the same for her."

I longed to be near Mother, but I was also terrified. For a while, I stared out the window at the traffic going by in a blur and replayed the mental images of my exit from Mother's home. "Dad, I've been thinking about something. Mommy's gonna make my time with her miserable. She's mad. I know she is, and she hates me."

"She doesn't hate you. If you need to come home, give me a call and I'll come over and pick you up. Okay?"

The very next weekend, Dad parked outside a lone house on a quarter acre lot, and glanced down at a slip of paper in his lap that had an address scribbled on it. "I guess this is the place," he said with a measure of uncertainty.

It had been two weeks since I last saw Mother and Steven. "Mommy hates me," I said, "for moving in with you." A feeling of dread weighed on me. My heart pounded in my chest and my stomach quivered. "I guess I have to go inside."

"Take your time, honey," Dad said. "I'm in no hurry. We'll wait right here until you're ready."

"I don't think I'll ever be ready." I leaned over and kissed him goodbye.

It was late in the day. A cool breeze blew. The house wasn't more than a shack with brown boards nailed to the exterior walls for siding, and a dilapidated, shingle roof. White bed sheets hung in the two windows, facing the street. The fenceless grounds were bleak, without a single green or living thing in sight. Trash clung to the stiff, dead weeds between the cracks of a broken, concrete walkway. There were bubble gum wrappers, an old sales receipt, dirty tissues, a piece of white twine, and cigarette butts.

I knocked on the frame of a rickety screen door and it opened. "Pammie," Mother said, cheerfully. She wore what looked like a forced happy face. Her smile was so wide she revealed her full set of choppers. One of her canines, with a dab of red lipstick, protruded from the row of yellowing teeth. "We're glad you came," she said, letting me in.

The house belonged to Mother's latest boyfriend, Chet, a man she scarcely knew. A week or so after I moved in with Dad, the landlord of Mother's duplex served her a 72-hour eviction notice. She could have moved in with Uncle Bud and Aunt Marylou, but since they disapproved of her drinking, she moved in with Chet.

I wrapped my arms around Mother and she embraced me. Her breath reeked of vodka, and the lemony fragrance of her Jean Nate perfume lingered on her body. Booze odors always set off my internal alarms, cautioning me, telling me she was drunk and, therefore, her behavior would be unpredictable. My knees were weak and I wanted escape from this place.

A shirtless man with oily, black hair came down the hall and stopped near the range in the kitchen, just a few feet from us. "Hi," he said. He pointed his thumb at me, stained with black automotive grease. "You're Pam." Then he poked it into his chest. "And I'm Chet." He picked up an open can of beer from the counter and switched on the oven.

Mother moved away from me. "I bet you're hungry," she said. Her unblinking, staring, bloodshot eyes made me uncomfortable. "Your dad—" she put a hand to her hip and looked smug, "—got you a new outfit."

"Daddy and Big Pam took me shopping."

She rolled her eyes and raised one disapproving eyebrow. "Fannn-tastic!" she said. "I bet they did."

I had only been with Mother three minutes and already I felt wrong. Something about me was ugly. *It's what I said. I shouldn't have said I went shopping.* Robin, standing near the sofa, shook her head at me and shot me a concerned look.

Steven came running to me from another room. "Steven," I said, holding back the tears, lifting him into my arms, and hugging him. "I've missed you," I said, quietly. "I've really, really missed you."

Mother and Chet were away at the bar for most of the weekend, and my sister and I did things like we had before I moved in with Dad. Robin turned up the radio's volume and we danced in each other's arms. We stayed up late, talking, and laughing until our sides ached, and we played with Steven, kept him fed, and in dry diapers.

Summertime had arrived and after Robin spent two weeks with me at Dad's, I went with her to Mother and Chet's tiny house for several days. The first afternoon of my visit, Mother and Chet went out for what they said would be "a few drinks."

At dinnertime, Robin called from the kitchen. "Pam, come in here. There's something I know you'll want to see." She opened the freezer door. "Look," she said, with a hushed voice. It was stuffed full of several varieties of Popsicles. Her eyes widened and her eyebrows rose. "Guess where they came from."

"From Chet," I said.

"Yeah." She glanced behind us, as though someone might hear. "Guess where he got them from."

"The store."

Robin's shoulders dropped. "That's too obvious and that's not it." Her eyes sparkled. "Guess again."

"I don't know."

She pointed to the stash. "I think they're stolen goods," she said with an accusing tone.

My jaw dropped. "Really?"

Robin grinned. "Have one."

I took a Fudgesicle and began eating it. We went to the tiny living room with stained carpeting and worn out furniture. The house smelled old, but I didn't mind. The white bed sheets in the windows had yellowed and paint bubbled on one wall. Dark wood paneling covered another.

"Here's what happened," Robin said, licking her grape Popsicle. "Last Monday, he showed up with a truckload of all kinds of ice cream bars and Popsicles. He tells me to have all I want and then he leaves. I have no idea where he goes, but he's gone all the time. Later that same day, I turned on the radio to the news and I heard the news guy say someone held up the ice cream man's truck and stole all his merchandise. You know, Popsicles, Fudgesicles, ice cream bars, that kind of merchandise."

I gasped. Then, I giggled. "That's terrible," I said. "The poor ice cream man." I took another bite of my cold dessert.

"Chet gives me the creeps and he has a brother that comes over. Oh wait. He never has any money. So there's no way he could afford a truckload of popsicles and ice cream bars. I think he and his brother are both crooks. The good news is that now we have something to eat. Before these showed up," she held out her Popsicle to me, "we were out of food."

Big Pam used to supervise Robin and me at the apartment swimming pool, but that was before baby Keith arrived. His skin was fare and could burn, she had said. And since Dad worked days, she stayed indoors with the baby.

After my visit with Robin and Steven at Chet's place, one Sunday morning I headed outdoors. The air was motionless and hot. Many of our neighbors were at church and it was quieter than on any other day. I rode my bike around the complex and pedaled by the pool, stopped at the chain link fence surrounding it, and peered at a couple of men and a woman seated on lounge chairs in the shade near the pool's deepest end. A toddler floated in a blow-up ring in the shallow end, across the length of the pool from them.

"Hey," I said from the other side of the chain link fence, "are you gonna be here long enough for me to swim?"

One of the men laughed. "You can come swimming, if it's okay with your old man."

After I had Dad's permission, I returned in my bathing suit and dove off the side into the water, doing an underwater breaststroke across the length of the pool. I swam several laps. Each time I swam to the shallow side, I noted the toddler, contentedly floating in his ring.

I made another lap from one end of the pool to the other with my feet fluttering, arms stroking, and tendons flexing. Eighteen or twenty feet across from the baby's empty ring, I came up for air. *Where's the baby?* Thoughts whirred in my mind. *Maybe someone took him out of the water. I would've noticed someone else in the pool. Maybe his dad got in and out of the water before I saw him. The baby must be with his parents.*

The water was level with the bridge of my nose. I stood on my tippy toes, tilting my head back, and I shot a quick glance at where his mother and dad were sitting. They spoke excitedly with one another, laughing and gesturing with their hands. *The baby's not with them. Where is he?*

A strange feeling was in the pit of my stomach, like something awful had happened. I swam toward the ring, searching the water for the missing child. There were no sounds of distress. The water was practically motionless, except for the ripples created by my rapid movements. From about ten feet away, I spotted him under water, near his ring. My strokes and kicks increased until I came to the baby, reached under the water, and lifted him up out of it.

At first the eyelids of his pale face were closed. Then he sputtered, opened them, and coughed. He coughed some more as I carried him from the shallow side of the pool across the patio to where his parents chatted in the shade. Their child had been drowning, but they were too busy having a good time to notice.

"He was under the water," I said, handing him to his mother.

Later, I realized that everything, all the suffering I'd gone through, from the time we moved in with Nana and Poppy, the years of trauma, my terrific longing for Mother and her extreme neglect, led up to this moment and to saving my neighbor's baby.

If I didn't live with Dad, I wouldn't have been at the pool and the baby might have drowned. I sensed the influence of someone far greater than myself directing my steps and I had a tremendous, inexplicable anticipation—a cause of purpose. *Maybe there's a reason I was saved from the fires and maybe this has something to do with it.*

CHAPTER THIRTY-SEVEN

*M*other went to The Vagabond one afternoon and didn't return to the shack for three weeks. She left Robin, not knowing where she was, alone with Steven all that time. Finally, after several failed attempts reaching Mother at the bars, Dad spoke with her on the phone and arranged a weekend visit with Robin.

The Friday afternoon when I rode with Dad to pick up my sister was a hot day. She came to the car and got it. "Hi," she said. Her voice was low and sad. Dad reached across the front seat and patted her hand. "How you doing, honey?"

"I'm okay."

That's what she said whenever something was wrong. And this, combined with the sorrow in her voice, made me wonder what had happened.

"Just okay?" Dad said.

"I poured boiling spaghetti sauce on my leg a few weeks ago," she answered.

Several times, I had burned myself while cooking, and it had hurt. I couldn't imagine what boiling spaghetti sauce felt like, but I knew it couldn't be good. "You did?"

She nodded. "And guess what? Mommy wouldn't come home from the bar and take me to the hospital. Dave came by to see me and he was with me when it happened. It's a good thing he was there to help with Steven and—"

I interrupted her. "Our cousin Dave?"

"Uh-huh."

"That's neat that he came by to see you." I said and then I thought about her burn. "You needed a doctor? You had to have help?"

"Pam, it was *so* bad that Dave put wet towels in the freezer and every twenty minutes, he changed them and kept putting the frozen towels on my leg. He had to go home and I kept it up all night. Dave called Mommy at The Vagabond, but she wouldn't come home and then I called her. I told her the burns were very, very bad. I have no idea where Chet was for all that time." She sounded sad. "I called The Vagabond twice and told her, 'Mommy I burned my leg. I think a doctor needs to see it.' But she wouldn't come home. Three weeks later, she finally comes in the door, looks at my leg, and says it looks like I have blood poisoning. Then she took me to the doctor. Three weeks. She was gone three weeks." Robin shook her head and gazed out the window beside her.

I realized Mother still left my sister and brother alone, but I couldn't imagine why she didn't immediately respond to Robin's emergency. "Why didn't she come home?"

"For the same reason she leaves us without food or diapers. Pam, you know."

She had on shorts and a tank top. I leaned over the front seat and looked at her burns. Tender pink areas and dark, crusty patches of flesh covered a large area of her leg. I grimaced. "Does it hurt?"

"It did. That was the worst pain I've ever had. But it's tons better. The doctor said I have second and third degree burns."

Dad was a patient man with much self-control. I watched his face in the rear view mirror. His jaw tightened. He never got mad, but he was angry now. The vein in his neck pulsated. His gentle brown eyes had hardened like steel.

Chet's shack was forty minutes from our apartment. About halfway home, Dad pulled off the road and parked beside a cinder block building. A large black sign with gold, raised lettering over the door read, *Law Office of Christine Pierce.*

"What're we doing here?" I said.

"I have to run in and see my lawyer for a minute," Dad said. "Wait in the car."

Soon Dad returned. "Pammie and Robin, why don't you come inside and meet Mrs. Pierce."

We entered through a glass door into a waiting area. It wasn't anything fancy. Two chairs were against a wall with a large landscape painting. A small table, loaded with magazines, was across the narrow room. A tall counter separated the reception area from another with a desk, typewriter, phone, and file cabinets.

A woman in slacks and a short sleeved blouse walked around the desk and greeted us. "I'm Mrs. Pierce," she said.

Dad put his hand on Robin's shoulder. "These are my daughters, Robin and Pam."

Mrs. Pierce offered her hand to us and smiled warmly as we shook it. "Your Dad has told me lots about you and I've looked forward to the time when we would finally meet."

I had on shorts, a tube top that tied around my neck, and sandals. Robin's shorts and tank top were threadbare. She had on stained sneakers with thin soles. Her hair was neatly brushed into ponytails that fell below her shoulder blades.

Dad's attorney pointed toward her office, down a short hallway. "Why don't you come this way and we'll visit."

We went through the reception area to her office and sat on dark brown, upholstered chairs with large armrests.

Mrs. Pierce sat behind a long, wooden desk with files and loose papers piled on it. "Well, your dad brought you by to meet me because as soon as I can get your case on the docket, we'll be going to court."

Dad had already told us that he had hired an attorney, and we might have to see a judge about living with him permanently. He had said Mother might contest it and, when I said I didn't understand what he meant, he explained that this meant she would "put up a stink."

Mrs. Pierce looked over at Dad standing behind Robin and me. "Pam's already living with you. Since their mother has legal custody of her and her sister, you have no legal basis for keeping her." She smiled at Robin and me. "This is something we need to fix through the court. Do you wish to live with your dad and stepmom?"

The ringing of Mrs. Pierce's black phone gave us pause to consider her question. She picked up the receiver and listened. She immediately relaxed, warmly greeting the person on the other end of the line. I hated having to choose between Mother and Dad, and having to share secrets concerning life with Mother. My stomach trembled. It always did when I was terrified.

Dad had more rules than a centipede has legs, but I didn't mind too much. He told me to take out the trash, be home right after school, eat every last bit of food on my plate, always ask permission to go outside, take a bath each evening, and go to bed by nine, but I felt safe with him, and he made sure I knew I was loved. Yet, a part of me clung to a hope that Mother would get her life together and actively begin parenting us. As I thought of this, I remembered Robin's burn and that she had been alone with Steven for a long time. I now doubted we'd ever be a family again.

Mrs. Pierce hung up the phone and reclined in her leather chair. "Where were we?" She answered her question. "There's one way out of all this—the neglect, being exposed to danger, going without food, your mother's risky behavior. Your dad and stepmom are offering it to you." She stared thoughtfully at us.

"You asked us if we wanted to live with Dad," Robin said. "Yes, I do."

I would agree to go wherever Robin went and moved my head up-and-down at Mrs. Pierce. But my answer didn't mean I would give up on Mother. I believed people could change, had often prayed for Mother, and knew she could transform from a party girl into a parent. After everything that had happened, I still believed in her.

"Soon, we're all going to court," Mrs. Pierce said. "The judge might ask you some questions."

I chewed the inside of my lip and glanced at Robin. The corners of her eyes were moist.

Mrs. Pierce studied my face and then Robin's. "I know you girls will do fine," she said sweetly. "We shouldn't have to be in court for long and the judge won't ask questions you can't answer. He may want to know about the house fires, your living conditions, your mother's alcohol abuse, and where she is when she isn't home. He might ask about Steven. See, these are all questions you know the answers to."

On the way home, Dad talked with Robin and me about our role in helping the judge decide to let us live with him. He helped us understand that if we were called upon, we might have to go to the stand, and that we had to answer any questions. I decided if I had to rat on Mother, I would be mute. Dad had hired Mrs. Pierce, was paying her the big bucks, and she could handle it just fine.

Dad said the court might ask for witnesses. "Your Aunt Marylou and Uncle Bud might be subpoenaed."

"What's that?" I said.

Robin grinned proudly. "I know what that is. Dad, isn't it when the judge sends a letter to someone telling them they have to be in court and if they don't show up, the cops will arrest them?"

Dad said that was it, and I was proud of Robin for knowing so much. She knew what a baby needed to stay alive, how to get us out of the way of danger, and she even understood what Dad and Mrs. Pierce had been talking about. Court, judges, subpoenas—it was all over my head.

"We'll be ready for whatever happens in court," Dad said. "But getting this far has sure taken a long time. This all should've been behind us weeks ago. I thought getting an attorney would be faster than trying to convince someone from Child Protective Services to make a home visit."

"Mrs. Pierce is slow?" I said.

"Yeah," Dad said and chuckled. He shook his head. "Shoot, I hired Mrs. Pierce when you still lived at The Continental Gardens Apartment." His forehead was furrowed in deep thought. "I'm stumped. Those people at the state never followed through with what they said they'd do, and I don't know why. I called them three different times, and they told me someone would go by and check on you girls and Steve. Are you sure you didn't have a visit from them?"

Robin shrugged her shoulders. "Well, there was one time when we were living at Mission Avenue Apartments and we came home from The Green Parrot and there was a note taped to the door."

Dad looked briefly at her before returning his eyes to the traffic.

"Mommy went right then to the neighbors to get some food. We didn't have any. She brought it home and put it in the kitchen. Dad, maybe she was afraid they were on their way over. That's the only time I can think of."

"I hadn't heard about that. Well, I still don't think those people are doing their jobs," he said flatly then his voice rose a little. "I wish this whole darn thing would move along a heck of a lot faster, but it's out of my hands."

It was quiet in the car for several minutes as we continued on our way. "Dad," I said just before we were home, "why don't you talk to the judge for us? I don't want to do this." I thought of how much I loved my mother. "We'll hurt Mommy and I don't want to be without her and Steven. We might never see her again, not after she hears the terrible things that will be said about her."

CHAPTER THIRTY-EIGHT

*T*hree weeks later, we crossed town to the Sacramento Superior Court. Dad drove the four-lane freeway as Big Pam, Robin, and I sat in the car in somber silence. I stared out the window beside me, fighting back an urge to weep. "Pam," Robin said gently, "we'll be okay." She brushed her hand against my hair and I turned and looked at the compassion in her gaze. "Mommy and Steven will be all right, too. Really, they will." Her heart understood mine.

The courthouse blended into its monochromatic background. It and everything in the area seemed to be made of the same grey stuff. The grounds were concrete, as were the water fountain, benches, and twenty to thirty steps we'd have to climb to go inside the six-story building.

Dad, Big Pam, Robin, and I entered a massive foyer through the tall doors. We walked across the expansive room, past elevators and an information desk, and then we made our way to a waiting area. The building had a hollow feeling to it, like a mausoleum. Small sounds, the click of heels on the shiny terrazzo floors, and people speaking in low voices ricocheted off the huge walls and high-pitched ceiling. We sat in a row of seats and awaited Mrs. Pierce's arrival.

Every time someone in heels approached from around the corner or behind us, I turned around to see if it was Mother.

I knew she'd be there any second. How would she react to her daughters sitting with Dad and Big Pam? Would she think we loved them more than her? Would airing our dirty laundry in court break her heart? I wouldn't—I couldn't—answer the judge's questions about our suffering. If he wanted to know something, he'd have to ask Mrs. Pierce. It would be easier for everyone that way.

The feeling of dread in the pit of my stomach was far worse than what I experienced all eight times when I had entered a new school for the first time, and I wasn't in any hurry to see the judge. After fifteen minutes or so, Mrs. Pierce arrived, led us into the courtroom, and showed us where to sit.

An overhead air conditioner rattled as it blew cold air. A large clock on the neutral colored wall across from us had three hands, one showing the hour, another the minutes, and the third ticked away the seconds. A bailiff with a handgun in a hip holster stood near the door behind the judge's bench. He stared straight ahead, his stern face unflinching. The hands moved slower on this clock than on any other I'd watched. Time dripped by.

I wasn't cold, but it took every bit of self effort to keep my teeth from chattering. I pressed my lips together and sat as close to Robin as possible. Ten minutes passed. "Where's Mommy?"

"Beats me," Robin said.

"Geez, it's taking her forever to get here."

"Maybe she's not coming."

"Not coming?" I whispered. "Of course she's coming. Why wouldn't she?"

Robin shrugged her shoulders.

"All rise," the bailiff called. "The Honorable Judge Campbell presiding."

A man in a black robe with long, flowing sleeves entered. His outfit reminded me of the robes nuns wore, minus the white collar and habit. He sat at his bench. "You may be seated," he said.

When he mentioned our case, Mrs. Pierce stepped forward and explained to the court that Mother had not arrived.

"Mr. McKern," Judge Campbell said to Dad, "I have reviewed the file and I realize you're requesting full custody of your daughters on the basis of neglect and child endangerment." He shuffled through some papers, cleared his throat, and then sipped a small glass of water.

"Robin and Pam," Judge Campbell said. "I'd like to speak with you in my chambers." He stood. "Come this way." He waited for us near the door through which he'd entered. When we were right in front of him, his stern expression faded into a warm smile. "If you'd like," he said, "you may bring your dad and step mom."

We trailed behind Judge Campbell, his black robe spreading out like a sail as he walked, and entered his office. He pulled two leather chairs over to his shiny, oak desk. "Make yourselves comfortable," he said, then he turned to Dad. "I'm aware of the details of the case and I'd like to hear from your daughters. I'm interested in hearing their wishes. If you would," he said and motioned toward a door, "please step out into the hall. This'll just take a minute."

The tall and slender judge's thinning hair was beginning to grey. His voice was gentle, and crow's feet had formed at the corners of his light-filled eyes. "A law was passed that empowers children to assist the adults in their lives in making the types of decisions which are truly in their best interests," he said. "That law says children over the age of twelve can let the court know where they'd like to live and why." He leaned over his desk and continued smiling down at Robin and me. "How old are you?"

"Fourteen," Robin said.

"Twelve," I said.

"Perfect. I'll ask you a few questions." He took a pack of Good & Plenty from his desk drawer and offered Robin and me a couple of pieces. We thanked him and popped the pink and white, candy-coated licorice pieces in our mouths. "Has your dad or mom told you what you should say in court?"

"No," Robin said.

"Has *anyone* told you what you should say in court?"

"No," she said.

"Dad said we should call you *Your Honor,*" I said.

He chuckled. "Your dad's a wise man. He expressed serious concerns for the living conditions in your mother's home. There's a concern for your safety. He and others feel you would be better cared for in his home. Your mother's not here to testify on her own behalf and, so, I would like to hear from you. Are his concerns legitimate?"

For the past three weeks, since our visit at Mrs. Pierce's office, my heart had been conflicted. I fretted over the idea of having to face Mother in court, but I also hoped she'd walk in, promise to be a good mother, and insist we live with her. Tears stung my eyes. I sat up straight in the hard chair, trying to look like I wasn't scared out of my wits and very sad.

Robin folded her hands in her lap. She twirled her ankle and stared at it.

My insides quivered. I didn't want to be here. I hoped to never have to tell on Mother, and I didn't want to decide between her and Dad. *Where's Mommy?* If she'd just walk in the door, then Judge Campbell could base his decision on her words. *Maybe she's on her way. She could be stuck in traffic. Maybe she's lost somewhere in the courthouse. Anyone could get lost here.*

Through the partially open door, I heard someone's heels clicking across the terrazzo floor. I thought it could be Mother. The sound came closer to the office and I expected her to appear any second. Then it stopped.

Judge Campbell put his hands on the desk in front of him. He leaned forward. "Are there reasons why you should live with your mother?"

"No, Your Honor." Robin sounded confident.

"And you want to live with your dad and stepmom?"

"Yes."

"Pam, do you also want to live with your dad and stepmom?"

I nodded. "Yes."

"Have you ever been without food?"

Robin said that we had.

"Where?" he said.

"At home with Mommy," she said.

"You have a brother? Is he two years old?"

"He's almost three," Robin said.

"Has he gone without diapers?"

"Yes," Robin said.

"Has your mother left you for more than a day?"

Robin nodded.

"A week?"

She nodded again.

"Three weeks?"

"Yes."

He sighed before calling for Dad, Big Pam, and Mrs. Pierce to rejoin us in his chambers.

I watched Dad as he came into the office. His face looked grave. There were two more empty chairs in the room. He offered them to Big Pam and Mrs. Pierce.

"Mr. McKern, your daughters have expressed their wishes to live with you and your wife."

Dad's eyes filled with tears. He reached for Big Pam's hand and held it. Her eyes were also moist. "The court finds that the best placement for them is with you."

"Thank you," Dad said.

Judge Campbell smiled. "That's what we're here for." He scanned the document on his desk, put a couple fingers in his mouth to moisten them, flipped through several pages, and silently read. "I see here your attorney—" he glanced at Mrs. Pierce, sitting near the wall with her hands in her lap and her legs crossed, "has requested that the court assign a visitation schedule. Your request doesn't appear to include anything unusual or extraordinary. It's a typical arrangement. Mrs. Williams gets her daughters every other weekend, alternating holidays, and for two weeks each summer break." He glanced across his desk to Robin and me. "How does that sound?"

We both nodded.

"Says here that Robin and Pam have a brother, Steven." He glanced up at Dad. "Are you his father?"

"No, Your Honor."

"Well, the sibling attachment is strong and in some instances can be as binding as the parent-child bond. I'd imagine this is the situation with these siblings. Will their brother remain with Mrs. Williams?"

"No, Your Honor. Joy's aunt said they're arranging for Steven to go to his dad's."

"Is this being arranged through the court?"

"I believe without the court."

"Without?"

"Yes, your Honor, without."

Judge Campbell leaned back in his shiny, leather chair and stroked his chin. "To ensure their well being, visits between Mrs. Williams and all her children should be arranged on the same weekends. In other words, when Robin and Pam visit Mrs. Williams, someone should try and get baby brother there at the same time. Does anyone have any questions?"

"Your Honor." Dad let go of Big Pam's hand and leaned toward the judge. "When will this be official?"

"I'll sign it." He scribbled his name on the document and his pen made a scratching sound across the paper. "You have legal and physical custody as of now. I'll see that this is filed right away."

Everyone stood, and Judge Campbell showed us to the door. Before we left, Dad cupped his hand around the judge's and he smiled warmly. "Thank you," he said, pumping his hand up and down.

We exited the courthouse through the fancy glass doors and entered the warm afternoon sunshine. The anxiety of attending court, the great dread of testifying against Mother, and my mixed up emotions had nearly made me sick. "Mommy didn't come," I whispered to Robin beside me. Mother's absence sent a final chilling message and I wrapped my arms around myself. There wasn't room in her life for my siblings and me. My inner world was in a wrestling match. I had wanted Mother in court with us but, on the other hand, I was relieved she hadn't witnessed Robin and me speaking with the judge. I glanced back at the courthouse and thought how glad I was that it was all behind us.

At the bottom of the steps, Dad and Big Pam thanked Mrs. Pierce before hugging her good-bye. Lots of people milled around us, coming and going through those stately doors, with faces portraying personal crisis—their pain clearly worn on their eyes, lips, and shoulders, and I realized that my sister and I weren't the only ones who understood the meaning of horrible.

The nasty feelings that had been in my head and stomach slowly eased away until I felt weightless, as if a thousand fears were lifted from me, and I unwrapped my arms. Robin grinned at me, and I scrunched up my face playfully and smiled back at her.

"Guess what?" I said.

"You're hungry," she said, because I was always hungry.

"Yeah, but that's not it. Guess again."

"You're glad it's over."

I nodded. "But that's not the right guess either."

"Pam, tell me."

"We're finally together," I said and smiled the biggest smile possible.

Dad stepped between us, reached for my hand, wrapped an arm around Robin's shoulders, and pulled her close to himself. He bent over and kissed the top of her head. "I love you, honey," he said with his voice full of affection. Next, he leaned down and kissed the top of my head. "I love you, Little One."

EPILOGUE

The day of our court hearing, Robin moved in with us and Max took Steven to live with him. Later that month or maybe it was the next, Mother called to make arrangements for our first weekend together since court. Right away, I noticed that something about her had changed.

I had expected Mother to sound drunk, angry and bitter, but her voice was pleasant and it lacked all the typical signs of intoxication: the slur, long pauses, and sarcastic sting.

"I've gotten rid of Chet and I have an apartment in Rancho Cordova," she said. "Oh, and, Pammie, I have another surprise, but you'll have to wait until tomorrow to find out. I'll be by to pick you and your sister up at ten."

The next morning, I looked forward to Mother's arrival. Right at ten, a horn honked twice and I peeked out the window. Mother was behind the wheel of the richest looking vehicle anyone in our family had ever owned.

As soon as Robin and I were seated beside her, I blurted out, "You got a rich person's car. Where's the Impala?"

A tiny grimace appeared on her lips.

"Did you wreck it?"

"Girls, I have some sad news," she said, pulling away from the curb and driving down busy San Juan Avenue. She frowned and shook her head. "I was driving on the freeway when the Impala's engine caught fire."

Robin and I gasped.

"Luckily your Poppy was behind me. I saw all this smoke coming out from the hood. I pulled off the road and he was right there with a fire extinguisher." Her voice rose playfully. "Poppy to the rescue," she said and laughed. "Boy, am I glad he was there to put it out."

Mother had owned the Impala so long, since I was three, that it seemed like a part of our family, and I was crushed. "Mommy, it didn't get turned into a sheet of metal by a car smasher did it?"

She chuckled. "Geez, Pammie. No. The Impala will live on in another car. A man bought it to use for parts."

We all agreed that this was a better choice than total annihilation. Mother slid a cigarette between her lips and lit it with a butane lighter. "Ready for my good news?"

Robin and I nodded. "Uh-huh," we said.

A red light was ahead of us. Mother slowed and then stopped. She turned to my sister and me and beamed a big smile. "I got a job as a paralegal for a family law firm," she said, bursting at the seams with pride.

"You're a pair of what?" I said.

"Pammie, not a pair of anything, a paralegal," she answered. She was still smiling when she told us that she worked for Mr. Hugh, an attorney in Rancho Cordova. "I type, file, answer phones, and take notes during the initial consultation with his clients." She pulled away from the light and onto Fair Oaks Boulevard. "I also go to court with Mr. Hugh, but so far I've just been there to assist him with client files. This Lincoln Continental is his," she added. "He's letting me borrow it while I save enough money for a new car."

Mother didn't quit drinking, or going to the bars, or driving under the influence of alcohol. She began with beer in the morning and progressed to mixed drinks in the evening. As I later learned, she even kept a bottle of Vodka at the office. But, for the most part, her addiction didn't interfere with the quality of her work, and her weeks-long binge drinking and non-stop drunkenness, which attributed to our neglect, were behind her.

The changes in Mother continued. Two or three weekends each month, Robin and I reunited with Steven at her place. She'd take us to The Green Parrot on Saturday for two hours before returning us to her apartment and remaining there with us, and she never again let us starve.

In a surprising series of events, our situation had turned out as Robin had suggested that night when I was eleven and we lay on the top bunk. "I have a feeling this is what we're supposed to do," she had said. "I think God wants this for us. And who knows, maybe it'll help Mommy."

Robin and I were relieved of the responsibilities of struggling to care for ourselves and Steven—what a cause for celebration! Our lives used to be unstructured, but Dad and Big Pam kept us to a schedule. With machinelike regularity, we ate all our meals at set times. Dinner was followed by dishes, next came baths, and then bed. Most nights, Robin and I were under our covers by nine. One day a month, usually soon after Dad received his paycheck, we went to someplace fun, bowling, to the drive-in theater, or fishing at a nearby lake. Many happy memories were made at Dad and Big Pam's, but living with them wasn't without challenges.

Big Pam had a progressively worsening anxiety disorder and sometimes, when disciplining my sister and I, she used excessive or unusual punishments. Later, when I was in my mid-teens, she was diagnosed with a mental illness. There were days when she'd yell and scream at me and, at other times, she'd treat me with kindness and warmth. I never knew what to expect from her, and I learned to be very careful about what I said or did, as I tried to stay in her good graces.

When I was in my twenties, Big Pam had a very serious bout of depression. As a last resort, she sought help from God. She asked Jesus to come into her heart and take away the mental illness, and that one simple step transformed her life. She had fewer episodes of anxiety, she found life more enjoyable, and her demeanor toward Robin and I improved.

Robin and Steven were unable to join me at Mother's one weekend when I was sixteen. In the afternoon, we entered The Green Parrot and found it unusually quiet. We were the only customers.

"Edie," Mother said to the bartender waiting for our orders. "Would it be all right for Pammie to sit with me today?"

"As long as no one else comes in," she said, agreeing to Mother's request.

This was my first time sitting in the "adult only" area, and I felt like a grownup, seated with Mother, sipping a glass of 7-Up. Within the hour, Aunt Cindy came in and pulled up a barstool beside me. She told us that she had been driving by when she noticed Mother's car parked out front and decided to stop in and see us. Several minutes later, two of Aunt Cindy's male friends entered. The guy with red hair, Paul, told her that he spotted her green Maverick parked nearby and he wanted to speak with her about something.

"Well, since you all know each other," Edie said motioning at us with her hands. "I suppose it will be all right for Pammie to stay at the bar a little longer."

Aunt Cindy's other guy friend, Vern, sat on the empty seat beside me. As I later learned, he had just turned twenty-one, and he didn't go to bars, and he had made a silent vow to never date a girl who went to them.

Vern grinned at me. "How old are you?" He didn't ask why I was sitting at the bar, but I could see questions in his eyes.

"Sixteen," I said.

"You're just about the same age as my sister," he said and glanced around the barroom. After a couple minutes of silence, he asked about my interests.

Instead of telling him what I thought, that I hated being here, I told him about my love for animals and my special fondness for horses. When I left the Green Parrot later that afternoon, I had no idea that in four years I would see him again.

During my first year in college, while working in the field of my study as a sign language interpreter, Aunt Cindy called to speak with me. "Pammie, do you remember Vern?" she asked over the phone.

"Not really," I said, trying to recall why his name sounded a little familiar.

"You met him at The Parrot that day when he and Paul came in to see me. He was really nice, and you guys talked about horses."

"Oh, that Vern. Yeah, I remember him."

"I've seen him a couple times since then and he always asks about you. Well, today I saw him and Paul. And..."

"And what?" I said.

"He mentioned you again, so I suggested that we all go out for a bite to eat—Paul, Vern, you and me."

Later that evening, we met up at Round Table Pizza. Vern was tall with strawberry blond hair, and I thought he was handsome, intelligent, kind, and an interesting person.

Often, when visiting with people I barely knew, I had difficulty coming up with topics for conversation, but with Vern there wasn't any awkwardness. We dated for two years. Then one day, he proposed. July of 1986, we were married in an outdoor ceremony, and from our love, we had three children—Travis, Ryan and Sierra.

When our youngest child was two, Vern and I relocated our family north to Oregon. It was there that we began attending a non-denominational church. Before the move, I had no idea that there was pain in my heart associated with my childhood. Vern and I were happily married, and I loved being a wife and mother. There wasn't anything more I wanted than to care for my family.

The only signs of the former traumas were minor. For example, I was fearful of another house fire and a wailing siren still put me on edge, and, although I was not in any danger, sometimes I felt that I was, and I could not speak to a group without anxiety—my throat would practically constrict, and I'd feel lightheaded and weak.

My healing journey began years before the move to Oregon when Vern would take me in his arms and hold me. After we began attending the new church, my healing went to a new level. Several of the older church ladies began doing what my mother seldom did, if ever. They gave me motherly affection.

I also began meeting with my pastor for biblical counseling. During my weekly appointments, he showed me how to release emotional pain and he led me in steps to forgive those who had mistreated me. Forgiveness, I learned, is an important part of wholeness.

Around this same time, I met Rita. She was trained in techniques to help trauma victims find freedom from fear and terror. Rita and another woman, Edith, met with me in 1997 for a full day of prayer therapy. By the time we were done, I felt so light that I laughed with great joy.

The healing process didn't stop with hugs, Christian counseling, and prayer therapy. These all helped, but certain situations still triggered fear. This is because my childhood experiences had taught me that I wasn't safe, that I was unacceptable, that people couldn't be trusted. To get rid of the triggers, I filled my mind and heart with truth that I found in the Bible. Love, the Bible says, has no fear. So, the scriptures that I focused on were about God's love for us and our love for others.

Seeking wholeness is hard work, but the efforts are well worth it. In time, the triggers were removed and I entered into a new season, which included public speaking, organizing special events, and training volunteers to work with abused and neglected children.

At the end of 1997, while I was on the phone with Mother, we chatted for a few moments about the kids, chuckling as I described their antics. I worried about her. It was early in the day and I could tell by the sound of her voice that she was already drinking. Also, I was concerned with the changes in her physical appearance. She was no longer the gorgeous knockout with the hourglass figure. Ten years prior, Mother's skeletal structure began shrinking. Her skin shriveled. She lost her womanly shape and her outward beauty disappeared. At fifty-five, she weighed less than a hundred pounds and looked like a sickly eighty-year-old, but I couldn't detect any frailty in her voice.

She told me about her week, how she and Luke had gone to dinner with friends. "And dahling," she said in her Auntie Mame voice, "Luke rearranged the outdoor furniture on the veranda." Her veranda, a small patio through a sliding glass door, was a far cry from the luxurious one she had dreamed of during my childhood.

I filled her in on the past week's events. "The kids and I took lunch to Vern at his jobsite on Friday," I added. "Oh, and yesterday, we went to church."

"Church on Sunday? Surprise, surprise," she said, cackling.

"Yeah, I know." I smiled to myself. "Mother, I'm really enjoying it. Can I tell you what I learned from my pastor?"

"Darling, I only have a couple minutes before Luke gets home."

"Okay, I'll try and keep it short. My pastor said that unforgiveness keeps us imprisoned to pain but forgiveness sets us free."

Mother's ice tinkled in her glass.

"Mother?"

"I'm here."

"You know I forgave you for everything, don't you?"

"Yes, Pam."

"I'm just making sure you know it in your heart."

"I can't believe I did those things to you and your sister and brother," she said. Her voice was full of remorse. "I don't have any idea what was wrong with me."

"Mother," I said, "There's something else that I learned. When we hurt others, we may need to forgive ourselves." An uncomfortable silence followed. "Are you still there?"

"I'm sorry, darling. Yes, I'm right here. Well, you children turned out all right and I'm happy here with Luke, but I sure as heck regret the bad years." She sighed. "No one will ever know how much." Her voice brightened. "Well, what's done is done, and we ended up with the people we were meant for. Your dad has Big Pam. Max is happily married. And I got Luke."

Mother's words stung but they didn't surprise me. For years, I had suspected that her desire for Luke was the reason behind her neglect. He wasn't a kid kind of person. And, since she couldn't have him and us, she chose him.

After all these years, Mother still did and said things that were so hurtful that I wanted to throw up a wall of protection, a barrier to keep her at a distance, so that I would never be hurt by her again. But I loved her, and even if she wouldn't be a mama to me, I would be a daughter to her.

Through my experiences with my mother, I learned that people who make bad choices are not the sum total of their behaviors. I also learned to value the positive qualities in troubled people, to let go of emotional pain, and to accept the things I cannot change.

As a consequence of all that I had been through, I wanted to love Mother and others the Bible way, which meant I'd need to put a lot of scripture in my heart and then walk it out. To do this, I embraced love as a lifestyle and 1 Corinthians 13 became my motto—in particular these verses:

> *Love endures long and is patient and kind. Love does not insist on its own way, for it is not self-seeking. Love takes no account of the evil done to it. Love is ever ready to believe the best of every person, its hopes are fadeless under all circumstances, and it endures everything. Love never fails.*

Mother and I were still talking on the phone. "I just have one more thing to tell you. Do you have another minute?" I said.

"Luke's not home yet. Go ahead, but make it fast."

"I'd like your permission for something. When I speak to groups, sometimes I share parts of my testimony, but I've been uncomfortable talking about my childhood without your consent."

"Hmmm," she said, sounding deep in thought.

"It's not the easiest thing to do, but maybe it'll help those who are discouraged with their past and present circumstances." The other end of the line was silent, and I couldn't tell if she heard me. "Mother?"

"I'm here."

"You know, I'm convinced God's the reason we got through those years."

"Uh-huh."

I hadn't anticipated Mother's silence, and I thought she just needed a reason to grasp the value in this. "Something I've seen you do is move beyond your darkest hour. That's the definition of victory. Defeat is never trying again, but victory is falling down and getting back up. That's what I think you did. You were failing and the next thing I knew, you were driving a Lincoln Continental and working as a paralegal. Mother, do you realize how amazing that is?"

"You're right about that," she said smugly. "I got that job because of your Uncle Bud."

"What do you mean?"

"Uncle Bud told me to seek employment in the legal field and to leave Chet."

"Mother, that's great. How often did he encourage you like that?"

"Heck, it was so darned long ago, I don't know—once or twice."

"You moved forward on advice he gave you once or twice? There must've been something else going on in your heart." I wanted to understand what had motivated her to make such a drastic change. "Uncle Bud gave you advice one time or maybe two times, and you took it?" This seemed a little out of character for someone who had always resented being told what to do. "Was there no other reason? I mean, lots of people in crisis receive good advice, but never do anything with it. What was it that got you moving forward?"

Finally Mother answered. "Losing you girls and Steve. That was the worst time in my life. Oh, I can't even stand thinking about it. It was so awful."

"You know what else? You didn't let your past define who you are and neither have Robin, Steve, or I. Someone once said that the past is a stepping-stone to a better future. In other words, it's under our feet and we're moving up into the brighter day."

"You've got that right." There was a momentary pause. "Darling, Luke just got home. I'll talk to you next week."

"Mother, please think about it. I would really like to begin sharing my testimony more publicly."

Through the receiver, I heard Mother's Siamese cat meowing, the sliding glass door opening, and the musical tinkling of wind chimes from her patio. "Pammie, go ahead, if you think it will do some good. Darling, I have to go now."

"Mother, thank you. I love and miss you."

She blew kisses over the phone. "Uhm-mah. Love and miss you, too."

Amazingly, my sister and I beat the odds. Children with incarcerated parents are five times more likely than other children to commit crimes leading to their involvement in the criminal justice system. [1] Additionally, children with parents

1 CRB, California Research Bureau, Children of Incarcerated Parents by Charlene Wear Simmons Ph.D. Vol. 7, No. 2, March 2,000

addicted to alcohol are four times more likely than other children to misuse alcohol.[2]

Although, I wasn't aware of Dad's drinking until I was in my teens, he also had an addiction to the "cup," as did his brother and father. For the most part, Dad stuck to beer, drinking several cans of it every day. But unlike Mother, his addiction didn't impair his ability to be a parent and it didn't make him mean or bitter.

Robin married her high school sweetheart, and they became the parents to four children. She and her family relocated from Sacramento to a foothill community. Soon after their move, Robin began serving in a nondenominational church. Overtime, the senior pastor gave her more responsibility. Then one day, he appointed her as his associate pastor. Robin is a Bible teacher with special gifts in counseling women with broken hearts and helping them find the healing they need.

Steven also escaped the tragedy of generational alcohol abuse and that whole lifestyle. He has a compassionate heart and, in his profession, helps underprivileged people with their medical insurance claims. He's also an artist with showings in downtown Sacramento.

Mother's dream never materialized of having an Auntie Mame house, though she still spoke of it. Instead, she married The Vagabond's bartender, Luke. She died in 2010 at the age of sixty-eight, a few weeks after I began writing this memoir, of liver disease and other complications associated with alcohol abuse.

---

2   American Academy of Child & Adolescent Psychiatry, No. 17, Updated Dec. 2011, www.acap.org

I've often contemplated my childhood, and in particular that voice, the one that kept me from dying during the last and most horrific house fire. The question of who spoke to me was resolved in my heart years ago, but another question of why has been a mystery that I am only now beginning to uncover.

Robin, Steven and Pamela
Barkley Square Apartments

Pamela age four and Robin age six
Sporting new hair cuts

Joy and Keith's
wedding day.

This
was before Joy
became a blond

LETTER FROM ROBIN

February 4, 2010—a full 40 years after the fires, I stood with my precious thirty-something-year-old brother, Steven, as well as our pastor and close friend, Rick, and other family members, and blew a final goodbye kiss to Mother, who I imagined was now, after stepping out of her tired body, hovering somewhere above us. Soon after, I was left alone with her body and wondered at the freedom I was feeling—not the kind of running-wild-in-an-open-meadow kind of freedom, but the kind of liberty that comes from realizing I was no longer bound by this woman. I was free of all unforgiveness; any debt I felt she owed me was wiped away. More than that, though, I was at liberty to freely grieve the loss of my mother.

Sitting alone in that hospital room with only staff discreetly entering and leaving, I pondered the past and, quietly but firmly, resolved that I would tell the truth of my childhood, even if that truth carried some ugliness, but I would not disrespect nor dishonor this woman who carried me in her womb. And, I will tell my story only when and where I believe it will benefit others. Eight very short months later while out on a drive, without any warning whatsoever, I suffered a massive stroke which nearly took my life.

During my long weeks of recovery and rehabilitation, I continued to grieve Mother's departure: How I longed to feel her hand on my forehead or hear her soft, encouraging voice. What an ironic set of circumstances I was now experiencing. I purposely gave very little thought to the responsibilities I carried in childhood as I watched over my younger sister and brother. But now, here I was receiving that same kind of care from Pamela, who offered me that longed-for comfort all the while I was in the hospital.

We both were, of course, influenced by our Auntie Mame/ Marilyn Monroe/Barbra Streisand wannabe mother and, I believe, are better for it. What a life we had with her! As I continue to recover, I find much comfort in the idea that while her physical presence may be gone, she continues to positively impact my life by the good memories upon which I choose to think.

My great hope and prayer is that my four children will find comfort in each other and that I may leave them, when my time comes, with many wonderful memories that will ultimately strengthen them in their moments of pain and trials.

Pamela's sister
Robin L.M. Davis

DISCUSSION QUESTIONS

1. What is the significance of the memoir's title, *JoyRide*?

2. Joy has her own agenda and her own way of parenting. How would you describe her at the stage in her life when she consults Pamela and Robin about whom she should marry?

3. By chapter 33, we feel Pamela's desire for her mother. What does every child need for healthy physical, spiritual, mental and emotional development? Which of these needs does Joy provide? How does the deficit affect each of her children differently?

4. Nana had an important role in Pamela and Robin's early childhood. How did Nana's negative behaviors affect Pamela's view of strangers? How did you react when she locked Pamela in the closet? What were Nana's positive contributions to Pamela and Robin?

5. How did Pamela describe Poppy? How does her view of him influence her perception of all father figures?

6. Contrast the life Pamela had with Mother with the life that she had with Aunt Marylou and Uncle Bud. What childhood values did Pamela learn from her aunt and uncle?

7. Where did Mother go on "vacation"? As a reader, how were you impacted by her actual whereabouts?

8. Small children see their parents as incapable of making mistakes, and it is typical for small children to blame themselves when they are abused. When a parent harms a child, it's imperative that the child knows that the parent's actions caused the harm. Otherwise, it affects the child's emotional health. Pamela confronted her mother about her role in the house fires. What was your reaction to this?

9. How does having a baby in the home affect Pamela and Robin?

10. What is the importance of faith in Pamela's life?

11. What are the strongest themes throughout the story?

12. Pamela helped to avert tragedy at the swimming pool when she was eleven. What was the symbolism in this account?

13. What are Pamela's strengths? What are Robin's strengths? How did their experiences contribute to their strengths?

14. What benefit does *JoyRide* offer people who have suffered trauma or abuse?

15. Do you feel that Pamela's childhood experiences contributed something positive to her life? Was there a time in your life when a challenge or painful situation benefited you? Please explain your answers.

QUESTIONS AND ANSWERS WITH THE AUTHOR

Q: Why do you think you were able to overcome so much?

A: Bitterness is a major contributor to emotional instability. The counsel that Dad gave me about forgiveness stayed with me, and I had a real life example, in my mother, of what happens when we stuff pain and hold onto un-forgiveness. I realized Dad was right. If I wanted to be well, I would not hold onto grudges. There were other things of equal importance—love, faith, and hope. The love between my siblings and I, especially that of my sister, eased the pain. My faith in God sustained me and I am so grateful to Him. And I had hope. Hope is not wishing for something. It is a confident expectation of a good outcome. Even while my life was turned upside down, I believed my situation would improve.

Q: In *JoyRide* you mentioned a relationship with Jesus beginning when you were seven. What else can you tell us about your faith?

A: I love this question because the power of knowing that Jesus saved me from the final house fire is what really kept me striving towards something better. I'm not a legalistic, religious zealot, but I am committed to living the great commandment to love God with all my life and others as myself. It's a goal of mine to grow in my ability to love, and to walk it out through serving and helping others.

Q: Tell us about your current relationship with Robin and Steven.

A: Children who grow up together have a shared history that makes their relationship unique. My sister and I know each other in an emotionally intimate way that stems from what we experienced in childhood and later as adults.

Our roles temporarily reversed when she had the stroke. For my entire life—that's more than forty years, I drew strength from my sister, often turning to her for consolation and advice. She has four children and me (laughter). I'm her little sister and she's supposed to look after me, right?

During the months following the stroke, there was much Robin couldn't do. Slowly, she's regained what was lost, and this has enabled her to resume many of her usual activities—singing in the choir, teaching Sunday school and, once again, she's the encouraging, supportive voice with which I grew up.

After Steven became an adult, we began spending less and less time together. This sometimes happens when there's a wide age gap between siblings, like there is with Steven and me. Even though we don't often see each other, the bond between us remains strong. Both of my brothers are special people in my life.

Q: This book makes your readers want to know the rest of the story! Do you plan on writing a sequel?

A: I've been asked this same question several times. There was much more I wanted to tell readers, but I didn't want *JoyRide* becoming a five-hundred page book, so I stopped at a major transition point.

Q. If there's a sequel, can you give us a glimpse at what we might find in it?

A: After I moved in with Dad, the next seven years had some happy times, but it was also an extremely difficult season in my life. Living with someone having a mental illness is not what I had expected, and it certainly presented an entirely new level of challenges. I would like to connect with readers who have been touched by someone who suffers with mental illness.

As I reflect upon my childhood, I remember how fearful I used to be. You couldn't have paid me to stand before a crowd of people. There was no way you could've convinced me to speak publicly. But, I have been so transformed that now I'll fight you for the microphone—I love public speaking. Helping others "move the mountains" in their lives gives me tremendous joy.

If I write a sequel, I would like to share the details of my personal healing journey with readers, but ending there would be a disservice. This story doesn't stop with the restoration of my heart; that was such an important piece of a much bigger picture. Healing was pivotal to what happened next—it prepared me for the call upon my life to share the profound, yet simple knowledge that I've gained through my experiences and to pray for people with chronic physical conditions.

I love hearing stories that encourage me or put me in awe. To date, there have been hundreds of wonderful testimonies from people who attended events where I spoke. The most remarkable miracle involves a woman named Trudy Rink. She was healed of Parkinson's Disease, Fibromyalgia, and Aplastic Anemia. This is medically verifiable. Her testimony can be watched on my Youtube channel. On it, Trudy talks about her amazing journey from death's door to wholeness. She's such a beautiful encouragement to all of us that with God nothing is impossible. It's these types of testimonies that I hope to include in a book someday, maybe as a closing chapter in my sequel.

Q. Is there a life principle that you want readers to hang onto?

A. Have faith in God. Don't give up on troubled people and don't give up on yourself. Pursue pure love.

SHARE THE LOVE

Please help us spread *JoyRide's* message of triumph and hope.

1. Your purchase contributes toward a fund for disadvantaged youth and incarcerated persons. To learn more, visit www.joyridebook.com.

2. Your feedback on Amazon can place *JoyRide* at the top of booklists. This will help others to find it. Please locate *JoyRide–Life, Death and Forgiveness* on Amazon and leave a short review. If you're already registered with Amazon, this will take two minutes. If you haven't registered, registering is quick and easy.

3. Leave feedback on GoodReads.com

4. You are invited to see the author's childhood photos at www.joyridebook.com.

5. We can all do something to make a difference in someone's life. Please consider suggesting this book to a friend, colleague, book club, support group, Bible study, or youth group.

6. Is a copy of *JoyRide* in your public library? If not, please consider donating a copy or suggesting that the librarian add *JoyRide* to the book collection. Ask your friends and family in other counties to do the same.

7. Encourage your local independent bookstore to carry this book.

8. Ask your local newspaper or radio program to review *JoyRide*.

9. Host a book-signing event.

10. The electronic version of *JoyRide* is available for e-book readers through Amazon and other e-book retailers.

11. Additional paperback copies may be purchased from GoldenTree Press, from the JoyRidebook.com website, and from bookstores.

12. A special edition, hardbound copy of *JoyRide* will be available after October 2013 from GoldenTree Press and Amazon.com.

13. E-book versions can be loaned for up to fourteen days by Amazon and Apple customers.

14. Other than Amazon's and Apple's book loaning, free e-book versions are not available for distribution. If you have received a free e-book copy, please honor the author's work by purchasing it from Amazon or another e-book retailer.

15 A limited number of free hard copies are available for disadvantaged youth and incarcerated persons living in the United States. Write to GoldenTree Press. One book per address or group. Requests must include name and phone number.

ACKNOWLEDGMENTS

The path to *JoyRide's* completion was not without heartache. My journey of writing began a few months before my mother Joy passed out of this life. Eight months later, my sister Robin suffered a massive stroke. I grieved for my mother as if she had been the best parent on the planet, which I find remarkable, and I ministered to my sister as though her life were my own; this gives me pause for thought. There is tremendous potential in all people to love selflessly and to hope without fail.

I am grateful for the journey and for friends, family, and associates along the way who were a vital part of *JoyRide's* completion. I regret that I cannot acknowledge each person and their contribution in this limited space. Thank you for standing with me, reviewing my memoir, contributing endorsements, and for your assistance with the technical aspects of writing and publication.

A special thanks to my editors Ann Kempner Fisher, Dawn Kinzer, and to special friends who proofread the edited version—Joann Dickson and Roxanne Swim. Steve Fryer designed the cover and Lee Pierce designed *JoyRide's* interior. This book could not have materialized without the masterful work of these talented individuals.

My pastor assured me that my story mattered and would touch hearts. Donna, thank you for motivating me to persevere and for your beautiful optimism. Your words of encouragement helped me slay the enemies of creativity.

I am blessed to have a network of friends whose prayers and love-filled words are of greater value than gold. Thank you Lakeview Ministries family and Advancing the Kingdom friends and supporters.

Aunt Marylou, thank you for rescuing Robin, Steven and me. Dad, I know that your shoulder is always there when I need it. How do I express my gratitude for what you did? If you hadn't intervened, Robin and I would've had an entirely different outcome.

JoyRide wouldn't be the story it is without my sister, Robin—that's a no-brainer. In addition to her role in my life, she contributed several memories of our childhood that are included in the book. Robin and I spent hours on the phone, exchanging remembrances and dreaming about the book tours and speaking engagements we'd get to go on together. Robin, I love you more than words can tell. Thank you for always being there for Steven and me. We wouldn't have made it without you.

My daughter Sierra, a gifted writer, helped unstick me when I got stuck on particular paragraphs. Sierra, thanks for your critiques, vocabulary suggestions, and for typing the question and answer pages. You are my sunshine.

Vern, my husband of over twenty-five years, was hand-picked for me. The circumstances through which we met confirm the Scripture in which God says, "I will take your curse and turn it to a blessing." The Green Parrot was a thorn in my heel, which became a blessing because it was there that I met Vern—what an amazing turn of events! I'm immeasurably grateful to you, sweetheart. Thank you for your encouraging words and for working hard so that I could write. You are a remarkable companion, partner, father, and friend.

I conclude my acknowledgments by saying thank you to the One who delivered me from the final house fire and who has been with me through the years. Thank you Lord for loving me beyond reason.

We invite you to continue the conversation about JoyRide *at our website:*

JoyRideBook.com

- Learn how others were impacted by JoyRide

- Share how you feel about the book

- Communicate with the author

- Read Pamela's blog

- Purchase additional copies of JoyRide

- Find the latest author updates

For information about having the author speak to your group or at your special event, please contact GoldenTree Press, Info@joyridebook.com

GoldenTree Press
P.O. Box 728
Lakeview, Oregon 97630
Info@joyridebook.com

(541) 219-2674